HUMANISM IN WITTENBERG
1485 – 1517

BIBLIOTHECA

HUMANISTICA & REFORMATORICA

VOLUME XI

ISBN 90 6004 333 2

The Castle Church
from the Wittenberger Heiligtumsbuch
by Lucas Cranach the Elder 1509

HUMANISM IN WITTENBERG
1485 - 1517

by

MARIA GROSSMANN

NIEUWKOOP
B. DE GRAAF
1975

TABLE OF CONTENTS

ABBREVIATIONS

ARG	Archiv für Reformationsgeschichte
ASG	Archiv für Sächsische Geschichte
CB	*see* ZB
CR	Corpus Reformatorum
HZ	Historische Zeitschrift
MGDESG	Mitteilungen der Gesellschaft für deutsche Erziehungs- und Schulgeschichte
NASG	Neues Archiv für Sächsische Geschichte
NMGHAF	Neue Mitteilungen aus dem Gebiet historisch-antiquarischer Forschungen
RK	Repertorium für Kunstwissenschaft
WA	Luther, Martin. Werke. Weimar, 1883ff
WAB	Luther, Martin. Briefwechsel. Weimar 1930ff
WATR	Luther, Martin. Tischreden. Weimar, 1912ff
ZB	Zentralblatt für Bibliothekswesen
ZK	Zeitschrift für Kirchengeschichte

INTRODUCTION

The course of humanism in Germany was decisively altered by the impact of the Reformation. In spite of all the research that has been devoted to the German Reformation, scholars have neglected the humanistic movement which preceded it, particularly in the East and the North. An attempt to delineate and evaluate the early humanistic forces in Wittenberg promises to be especially rewarding because that town, more than any other, is identified with the origin of the Reformation. Such an investigation of humanism should contribute to an understanding of northern humanism in general, and should be particularly interesting because it deals with one of the major elements in the cultural atmosphere in that part of Germany where Martin Luther lived and studied. This study attempts therefore to analyze the humanistic endeavors in all spheres of Wittenberg's cultural and intellectual life in the years from 1486 to 1517.

There have been many analyses of the terms 'Renaissance' and 'Humanism', and of the differences and relationships between the Italian Renaissance and Italian Humanism, the Northern Renaissance and German Humanism.[1] All of these movements have some of the following elements in common: the revival and rediscovery of pagan and Christian antiquity, a reaction against the Catholic Church and its practices and abuses, scholasticism, mysticism, and the rediscovery of the Bible in its original languages. Let us then assume that a new concept had begun to emerge in the latter part of the fifteenth century, not suddenly but slowly and was at its height in Germany at the beginning of the sixteenth century. As the religious elements of humanism gained momentum, the movement was an important element in paving the way for the reception of the Reformation.

Humanism was transformed and transmuted when it crossed the Alps to the North. Different political, economic, social, and cultural elements in both geo-

---

1 Some of the fundamental studies of German humanism are: G. Ritter, 'Die geschichtliche Bedeutung des deutschen Humanismus', *HZ*, 127 (1922–1923), 393–453; P. Joachimsen, 'Der Humanismus und die Entwicklung des deutschen Geistes', *Deutsche Vierteljahrsschrift für Literaturwissenschaft und Geistesgeschichte*, 8 (1930), 419–480; P. Joachimsen, 'Renaissance, Humanismus und Reformation', *Zeitwende*, 1 (1925), 402–425; Heinz Otto Burger, *Renaissance, Humanismus, Reformation* (Bad Homburg, Berlin, 1969: Frankfurter Beiträge zur Germanistik, 7); James E. Engel, *Renaissance, Humanismus, Reformation* (Bern, 1969: Handbuch der deutschen Literaturgeschichte, II. Abteilung, Bibliographien, vol. IV); H. Hermelink, *Die religiösen Reformbestrebungen des deutschen Humanismus* (Tübingen, 1907); Werner Kaegi, 'Nationale und universale Denkformen im deutschen Humanismus des 16. Jahrhunderts', *Die Erziehung*, 10 (1935), 145–159; Werner Näf, 'Aus der Forschung zur Geschichte des deutschen Humanismus', *Schweizer Beiträge zur allgemeinen Geschichte*, 2 (1944), 211–226; Richard Newald, *Probleme und Gestalten des deutschen Humanismus. Studien* (Berlin, 1963); Lewis W. Spitz, *The Religious Renaissance of the German Humanists* (Cambridge, Mass., 1963); Helmar Junghans, 'Der Einfluss des Humanismus auf Luthers Entwicklung bis 1518', *Luther-Jahrbuch*, 37 (1970), 37–101.

graphical areas account for much of that change: differences in traditions and in religious backgrounds. Italian humanism, which was probably the strongest influence on northern humanism had been transmitted chiefly by students and wandering poets who had spent some time in Italy. But the peculiarities of the North were significant when Italian humanism confronted the northern traditions. There is no need to be apologetic about German humanism as compared with Italian humanism or with the Reformation; it was a movement of its own, with its own peculiarities and contributions, and it deserves to be studied more than it has been.

Humanism in the eastern part of Germany has not received much attention in recent times; Gustav Bauch concerned himself with the subject in the 1890's and 1900's, but unfortunately his many excellent studies of individual towns like Wittenberg, Leipzig, Ingolstadt and Erfurt, of little-known personalities, and on the introduction of the Greek and Hebrew languages in northern Germany have never been drawn together into a comprehensive work.[2] His investigations were all based on consultation of the archives and on a thorough knowledge of the period. Scholars interested in any aspect of northern humanism are greatly indebted to him for gathering the material on which all further work must draw.

Since Bauch's time only a few important studies have been published. The first volume of the *Festschrift* of the Martin-Luther-Universität Halle-Wittenberg contains many contributions which discuss various aspects of the university in its early years.[3] *450 Jahre Reformation* likewise contains several essays connected with the early years of the university.[4] In addition, Ernest Schwiebert has published several articles on the subject of Wittenberg during our period, and recent works by Lewis W. Spitz and by Helmar Junghans have added much insight on the subject of German humanism.[5] Valuable source material has been published by Erich Kleineidam, who has also done excellent work on Erfurt, especially its university.[6]

2 *Die Anfänge des Humanismus in Ingolstadt* (Munich, 1901: Historische Bibliothek, 13); 'Die Anfänge des Studiums der griechischen Sprache und Litteratur in Norddeutschland', *MGDESG*, 6 (1896), 47–98, 163–193; 'Beiträge zur Litteraturgeschichte des schlesischen Humanismus', *Zeitschrift des Vereins für Geschichte und Alterthum Schlesiens*, 26 (1893), 213–248; 30 (1896), 123–164; *Geschichte des Leipziger Frühhumanismus* (Leipzig, 1899: *CB*, Beiheft 22); 'Dr. Johann von Kitzscher. Ein meissnischer Edelmann der Renaissance', *NASG*, 20 (1899), 286–321; *Die Universität Erfurt im Zeitalter des Frühhumanismus* (Breslau, 1904); 'Wittenberg und die Scholastik', *NASG*, 18 (1897), 285–339. For other works see the bibliography.
3 *450 Jahre Martin-Luther-Universität Halle-Wittenberg* (3 vols., Halle-Wittenberg, 1945–1952).
4 *450 Jahre Reformation*; ed. Leo Stern and Max Steinmetz. (Berlin, 1967).
5 Ernest G. Schwiebert, 'New groups and ideas at the University of Wittenberg', *ARG*, 49 (1958), 60–79; 'The Reformation and theological education at Wittenberg', *The Springfielder*, 28, no. 3 (Autumn 1964), 9–43; 'The Theses and Wittenberg', In: *Luther for an Ecumenical Age*, Essays in commemoration of the 450th anniversary of the Reformation, ed. Carl S. Meyer (St. Louis, 1967), 120–143; Spitz, *Religious Renaissance*; Junghans, 'Der Einfluss des Humanismus auf Luthers Entwicklung', 37–101.
6 Erich Kleineidam, 'Die Universität Erfurt in den Jahren 1501–1505', *Reformata Reformanda*, Festgabe für Hubert Jedin, ed. E. Iserloh and Konrad Repgen (2 vols., Munich, 1965: Reformationsgeschichtliche Studien und Texte, Supplementband 1), I, 142–195; and *Universitas Studii Erffordensis*: Überblick über die Geschichte der Universität Erfurt im Mittelalter, 1392–1521 (2 vols., Leipzig, 1964, 1969: Erfurter Theologische Studien, 14, 22).

Why, then, whenever German humanism is studied, is the emphasis on the western and southern parts of Germany, with hardly any reference to the East? One obvious reason is that humanism in western and southern Germany was much more important: these areas had a longer cultural tradition and were in closer contact with the cultural centers of Europe during the Middle Ages. But why has there been so little attention paid to the territory in which the Reformation had its beginnings, where it was strongest in its early development, and whence it spread to all corners of the earth. Studies on the background of the Reformation are usually incidental to Luther research and concern themselves only with the religious aspects. But other aspects of this background must be studied, since the religious life of the times did not occur in a vacuum, but was the product, at least to some extent, of its cultural environment. Schubert reasoned that Luther's early development was totally independent of humanism and that the Reformation took place without any reference to it.[7] Luther's concerns were certainly primarily religious, or even exclusively so, but these concerns derived from his early life experiences, which — in addition to those frequently emphasized, like the *Devotio Moderna* and the Augustinian Order — included humanism, especially during his years at Erfurt. Even the making of a *homo religiosus* like Luther occurred in the context of this world.

Let us then turn to humanism at Wittenberg. Bauch's article on Wittenberg and Scholasticism bears directly on the subject.[8] Although he observes certain evidences of humanism throughout the work, he treats them only in connection with the university proper.[9] Like Bauch, Friedensburg concerned himself almost exclusively with the organization of the university, with scholastic controversies and the curriculum.[10] He did, however, see how important the early influence of humanism was and gave it the emphasis it deserves.

The ambitions and artistic tastes of Elector Frederick the Wise of Saxony were largely responsible for the fact that Wittenberg's cultural life rose to such heights in pre-Reformation days. Unfortunately, there is no scholarly biography of this Elector who shaped the policy and intellectual life of Wittenberg during these years. Those studies which deal with him, — and they are few and slender — are chiefly concerned with the religious attitudes of his later years. They raise such questions as whether Frederick protected Luther as a just and honest territorial master or because he was actually in sympathy with Luther's religious views; these, once more, are problems tangential to Luther research. But the Elector's later views, whatever one interprets them to be, were rooted in his earlier education, training and experiences.

The history of Saxony from 1485 (the date of the Leipzig partition) to 1517 is the history of the territory within whose boundaries the Reformation had its

---

7 Hans von Schubert, 'Reformation und Humanismus', *Luther-Jahrbuch*, 8 (1926), 1–26.
8 G. Bauch, 'Wittenberg und die Scholastik', *NASG*, 18 (1897), 285–339.
9 O. Schwarzer, 'Gustav Bauch. Ein Lebensbild', *Zeitschrift des Vereins für Geschichte Schlesiens*, 59 (1925), 180–187, made a list of Bauch's publications. He included at the end a list of manuscripts then in the Breslau City Library. Among them he mentions 'Wittenberg Humanismus I. 1502–1505. 1902'. According to recent information none of these manuscripts are there and none are recorded in the catalog of manuscripts of the library at Wroclaw (Breslau).
10 W. Friedensburg, *Geschichte der Universität Wittenberg* (Halle, 1917).

beginning. The problems of administration of Frederick the Wise, like the cultural scene at Wittenberg, changed completely when the religious issues came to the foreground and determined all subsequent actions. An investigation of the cultural climate in Saxony, and particularly in Wittenberg, before 1517 may therefore help to explain the early and swift success of Luther in his own state and the state's transition to a Protestant principality. By attempting to bring to light all signs and expressions of humanistic activity in all branches of cultural life, scholarly and artistic, this study should also contribute to an understanding of some questions arising from the problems of northern humanism.

CHAPTER I

HISTORICAL SURVEY OF SAXONY BEFORE 1486

When Frederick the Wise became ruler of Saxony in 1486, the territory that he was to rule for thirty-nine years consisted of Electoral Saxony, the larger part of Thuringia and some smaller territories. These were the lands allotted in the Leipzig partition of 1485 to the Ernestine line of the house of Wettin, whereas northern Thuringia and Meissen, the third component of the territorial unit that had been called Saxony since the fifteenth century, went to the younger Wettin line, the Albertines. From the start of Frederick's rule Wittenberg was the cultural center of Electoral Saxony. Some knowledge of the rather obscure and intricate political, social and intellectual past of Saxony is indispensable to our understanding of the cultural developments that took place in Wittenberg in the years 1486–1517.[1]

I

The history of Meissen, the most prominent part of Saxony, can be traced back into the tenth century.[2] Meissen did not become an important part of the Empire until the end of the eleventh century when it passed into the hands of Henry of Eilenburg, the first margrave of the Wettin line whose ancestral castle was near Halle on the Saale river. Conrad the Great, the real founder of the Wettin *Hausmacht* in the twelfth century, unified the territory.[3] When Conrad died in 1157, his territory was divided among his sons, leaving Meissen a loose conglomeration of smaller parts. Henry of Meissen unified these various parts again in the thirteenth century and the landgraviate of Thuringia was added to this territory.

Thuringia had become an independent principality by the middle of the twelfth century. Its rulers, who had only recently received the title of landgrave, took an active part in the affairs of the Empire. When Pope Innocent IV had Frederick II deposed at the Council of Lyons in 1245, the papal faction of the German princes elected as anti-King Henry Raspe, the landgrave of Thuringia.[4] But he died in

---

1 Most of the sources for early Saxon history are printed in: Jo. Burchardus Menckenius, *Scriptores rerum Germanicarum, praecipue Saxonicarum . . .* (3 vols., Leipzig, 1718–1730; vol. II quoted as Mencken); *Geschichtsquellen der Provinz Sachsen*, ed. Historische Commission der Provinz Sachsen (Halle, 1870ff.); Ch. Schöttgen and G.Ch. Kreysig, *Diplomatische und curieuse Nachlese der Historie von Ober-Sachsen und angrentzenden Ländern . . .* (3 vols., Dresden, 1730–1733); and J.Ch. Adelung, *Directorium d.i. chronologisches Verzeichnis der Quellen der süd-sächsischen Geschichte . . .* (Meissen, 1802).
2 Mencken, pp. 313ff, 811ff.
3 W. Hoppe, 'Markgraf Konrad von Meissen, der Reichsfürst und der Gründer des Wettinischen Staates', *NASG*, 40 (1919), pp. 1–53.
4 Mencken, pp. 324ff, 1735ff. R. Malsch, *Heinrich Raspe, Landgraf von Thüringen und deutscher König* (Halle, 1911: Forschungen zur thüringisch-sächsischen Geschichte, 1).

1247, and the line became extinct. From this date on the fate of Thuringia, which never regained its independence, was tied to that of Meissen and later Saxony.

Following the death of Henry Raspe, Henry of Meissen, a close relative of the Thuringian line, claimed the rights to the territory of Thuringia. After a long-drawn-out war of succession, he was finally able to consolidate Meissen and Thuringia in the 1260's.

By the thirteenth century the Wettin lands had become the most important territory in central Germany. In the South were the Przemyslids, Habsburgs and Luxemburgs, in the North the Ascanians and Hohenzollern. In peace and war communications between eastern and western Europe had to go through Wettin territories. The house of Wettin at the height of its power, even reached after the imperial crown. When Conradin, the last male heir of the Hohenstaufen, died in 1268, the Ghibellines in Italy started a movement to make Friedrich der Freidige of Meissen, son of the daughter of Frederick II, a rival candidate for the imperial crown against the contender, Charles of Anjou.[5] But Pope Gregory X, who did not want to see another member of the Hohenstaufen family on the imperial throne, thwarted the ambitions of the Ghibellines and Thuringians — with the result that relations between the house of Wettin and the papacy became very strained.

The medieval curse of territorial divisions afflicted the Wettin lands, and wars of successions, private wars and general unrest continued throughout the fourteenth century.[6] Many side lines were created and became extinct, wars of succession sprang up, yet the dream of a unified territory was never abandoned.

The partition of Chemnitz of 1382[7] finally achieved a definitive division of the Wettin territories. Three parts were created: Meissen, Thuringia and the territory between them, the Osterland. After its ruler's death in 1407, the Osterland was divided between Frederick the Valiant of Meissen and Frederick of Thuringia. Meissen had been awarded the principality of Saxony, one of the seven electorates of the Empire, in the course of the Hussite wars on its borders. It was the more important of the two Wettin territories which existed peacefully side by side until they were reunited when in 1440 the Thuringian line became extinct.[8]

Electoral Saxony[9] can be traced back to the year 1180 when Henry the Lion, after his conflict with Frederick Barbarossa, was deprived of all his possessions, the Duchy of Saxony with its title being awarded to Bernhard of Ascania, the son of Albert the Bear of Brandenburg. Bernhard died in 1211 and was succeeded by his younger son Albert I, who raised the cultural and political level of Electoral

5 O. Dobenecker, 'Ein Kaisertraum des Hauses Wettin', in: *Festschrift Armin Tille zum 60. Geburtstag* (Weimar, 1930), pp. 7–38.

6 Mencken, pp. 328ff, 1774ff.

7 *Ibid.*, p. 334; Cf. also Johann Gottlob Horn, *Lebens- und Heldengeschichte. . . . Friedrichs des Streitbaren* (Leipzig, 1733), p. 658; and H. Beschorner, 'Die Chemnitzer Teilung der Wettinischen Lande von 1382', *NASG*, 54 (1933), 135–142.

8 For the time after 1400 we have another good source in addition to the ones quoted in note 1, p. 1 of this chapter. J.S. Müller, *Des Chur- und Fürstlichen Hauses Sachsen, Ernestin- und Albertinischer Linien Annales von Anno 1400 bis 1700* (Weimar, 1701): quoted as Müller, *Annales*).

9 In addition to the sources already mentioned, cf. Carl Gretschel, *Geschichte des sächsischen Volkes und Staates* (3 vols., Leipzig, 1843–1853); and K.W. Boettiger, *Geschichte des Kurstaates und Königreichs Sachsen* (2 vols., Hamburg, 1830–1831).

Saxony and made Wittenberg the capital. His two sons, Albert II and John, were the founders of two Saxon lines: Sachsen-Wittenberg, which retained the electoral vote, and Sachsen-Lauenburg, whose subsequent claims were all unsuccessful.[10] Charles IV, in the Golden Bull of 1356, explicity designated the Wittenberg line as possessor of the electoral vote and of the territory.

When the Wittenberg-Ascanian line of Saxon electors became extinct in 1422, Electoral Saxony was already a powerful state. Emperor Sigismund, who considered it his privilege to award this fief to whomever he chose, set aside any rights or claims of the Sachsen-Lauenburg line or of Elector Frederick I of Brandenburg and in 1423 awarded the electorate of Saxony to Frederick the Valiant of Meissen who was accepted into the electoral college in the following year. The Wettins had in fact no claim to the electorate but Emperor Sigismund was anxious for an opportunity to reward Frederick the Valiant for his help in the Hussite wars.[11] Sigismund had thus created on the banks of the Middle-Elbe a powerful state on which he could rely as a bulwark against the Hussites. The union of electoral Saxony with Meissen and Thuringia proved to be a decisive event in Germany for many years to come. After the Thuringian line of the Wettin house became extinct (1440),[12] the two territories were once more united under Frederick II and his younger brother Wilhelm. After five years of joint rule, they decided to divide their territories,[13] thereby precipitating many disputes and negotiations which culminated in the unfortunate *Bruderkrieg*. When the war came to an end in 1451, the division was decisively established. Thuringia was again ruled separately until 1482 when for the last time it was reunited with the electoral Saxon line.

Elector Frederick II of Saxony died in 1464 after a very beneficent reign. In a will he made as early as 1447, his stated wish was that Saxony not be divided again.[14] When he revised his testament in 1459, he excluded future divisions of Saxon territories altogether and stipulated that the oldest son Ernst, who would inherit the electorate, should rule all territories in his and his brother's name.[15] Emperor Frederick III invested Ernst and his brother Albrecht with the territories in 1465 and the future founders of the two Saxon lines reigned together peacefully for some years. When their uncle William died childless in 1482, Thuringia reverted to the brothers. Differences arose between them, as Ernst pressed for dividing their territories and the old Wettin tradition was reenacted in the Leipzig partition of 1485. Never again was Saxony to be united — significant for the future of Germany as well as for Saxony itself.

---

10 F. Sachse, 'Der Streit um die sächsische Kurwürde bis zur Entscheidung durch Kaiser Karl IV', *ASG*, 5 (1867), 203–229.
11 Mencken, p. 1817; Müller, *Annales*, pp. 11ff; J.J. Müller, *Des heil. röm. Reichs . . . Reichstagtheatrum . . . unter Keyser Friedrichs V . . . Regierung . . .* (2 vols., Jena, 1713), I, V. Vorstellung, chap. xiii. Also J.J. Müller, *Des heil. röm. Reichs . . . Reichstagstheatrum . . . unter Keyser Maximilian I . . . Regierung . . .* (2 vols., Jena, 1718–1719), II. Vorst., chap. lviii, where the document is given. These volumes will be cited as *RTTh*.
12 Müller, *Annales*, pp. 21; Mencken, p. 1823.
13 Müller, *Annales*, p. 23; M. Naumann, 'Die Wettinische Landesteilung von 1445', *NASG*, 60 (1939), 171–213.
14 F. Hänsch, *Die Wettinische Hauptteilung von 1485 und die aus ihr folgenden Streitigkeiten bis 1491* (Leipzig, 1909), pp. 6ff.
15 Müller, *Annales*, p. 33.

This course of action contrasts with the policy adopted in the last part of the fifteenth century by other German princes, who had finally broken with the tradition. The Hohenzollern in their *Dispositio Achillea* of 1473, Württemberg in 1492, and Bavaria in 1506 were among those who recognized the importance of primogeniture and unity of the land.

According to old Saxon custom, the older brother was to make the division — the younger to choose which territory he desired. The electorate naturally remained with Ernst as the older brother. The division of the territories — some to the Ernestine line, some to the Albertines, some remaining in common possession — was an artificial one.[16] Presumably it was designed to avoid future differences: if some of their lands were intermixed, they would work together for their common interests. This assumption proved to be wrong and many quarrels arose which were not settled even temporarily until the *Oschatzer Schied* of 1491, and not definitely until 1536.

Albrecht had chosen the more valuable territory, Meissen, to the disappointment of Ernst. Therefore when his son Frederick inherited the electorate of Saxony in 1486, it was attached for the first time in the history of the Saxon lands, to Thuringia and not to Meissen. Between the acquisition of the electoral vote in 1423 and the Leipzig partition of 1485, electoral Saxony had been held by the same line that held Meissen, while Thuringia was of secondary importance. This territorial realignment may explain in part why the cultural picture of electoral Saxony changed so radically under the rule of Frederick the Wise. Attached to a politically rather 'backward' territory, the electoral lands had to prove themselves worthy of their national importance.

<h1 style="text-align:center">II</h1>

The social and economic life in the Saxon territories had undergone considerable change in the fifteenth century. By the end of the century Saxony's institutions and cultural achievements could be compared with those in western and southern Germany. When the most powerful movement of the early sixteenth century was emerging, Saxony proved politically strong enough to nurture the base of the Reformation and to provide the necessary cultural climate.

During the fifteenth century, when the imperial government was weak and the attempts of the princes to strengthen their power had met the resistance of the estates, Saxony had consolidated its own territorial power — as had most other German principalities. Thus, during the Hussite wars Frederick the Valiant had to rely on the estates to provide him with funds, with the result that in 1423–1424 he conceded to his knights and cities the right to advise him in territorial affairs.

The first territorial diet in Meissen was called by Frederick II and his brother Wilhelm in 1438.[17] Representatives of counts, freeholders, and knights of the towns of Meissen and electoral Saxony were called to consider financial matters and asked to allow the levying of more taxes. The estates consented on condition

16 *Ibid.*, pp. 49–51.
17 Cf. Herbert Helbig, *Der wettinische Ständestaat;* Untersuchungen zur Geschichte des Ständewesens und der landständischen Verfassung in Mitteldeutschland bis 1485 (Münster, 1955) p. 148.

that if new taxes were to be imposed in the future, they could convene on their own initiative to consider matters. It became the pattern of later territorial diets: the estates were willing to make financial concessions in return for rights and privileges that seemed desirable to them. The ruler was willing to meet their demands, knowing full well that he could circumvent the rights of the estates if he chose to do so.

Other territorial diets followed. In 1466 the estates demanded that the elector concede them the right to be heard in case he decided in the future on war and peace. This right was later reconfirmed by Ernst and Albrecht.

In Thuringia Wilhelm called the estates together in Weissensee in 1446 and discussed with them financial matters and also a territorial code of laws — the first in the Saxon lands.[18] In Meissen the sovereign was much stronger than in neighboring Thuringia where the lower aristocracy and the knights had upheld their own privileges. Thus it was not until 1482 that a general territorial legislation was proclaimed in Meissen, establishing rules for coinage, wages, luxuries in food, drink and dress, brewing and inns and artisan shops.

During the negotiations for the partition of 1445, the estates had taken a very active part in contrast to the negotiations of 1485 when they showed no interest in the proceedings and were not even asked for advice; they were only informed of the results.[19] By the end of the century they had gained what was their chief interest, the right to approve taxes. In 1458 and 1466 they had assured themselves of their right to be consulted in case of war, but it was of no real political consequence since the Wettins did not keep their promise and the estates did not even care. They were consulted in coinage affairs and in the territorial legislation of 1482, but, conservative in their opinions, they showed interest in general policy. Thus their political importance slowly diminished until by 1485 their existence was acknowledged but no longer counted as a political force. Burkhardt, who made a thorough study of the territorial diets in electoral Saxony from 1487 to 1532, came to the conclusion that by the end of the fifteenth century the Elector had established his power so strongly that he no longer needed to take into consideration the estates' views on foreign matters.[20]

Although no unified law system existed for the Saxon territories as a whole, the proceedings of the courts were regularized. Especially in Thuringia Wilhelm pressed for the establishment of peace courts that would prevent or reduce the local feuds of contesting factions. In Meissen, where there was less occasion for such conflicts, it was not till the Diet of Worms in 1495 that Frederick the Wise, in concert with other princes of the empire, officially established his peace of the land for all of electoral Saxony. But during the reign of Ernst and Albrecht the princely courts in the several parts of Meissen had already been strengthened and a supreme court established for the whole land. After the partition of 1485 there were courts in Dresden, Weimar, Eckartsberga and in Leipzig,[21] where in the 1490's it became a supreme court for settling common affairs for the Albertine

18 Müller, *Annales*, p. 25.
19 Hänsch, pp. 71ff.
20 C.A.H. Burkhardt, ed. *Ernestinische Landtagsakten*, I. Die Landtage von 1487–1532 (Jena, 1902: Thüringische Geschichtsquellen, N.S. V), p. iii.
21 *Ibid.*, p. li.

and Ernestine lands. Further judicial reforms were made at the beginning of the sixteenth century under Frederick, Albrecht and Georg.

In the sphere of monetary reform the first steps were made by Frederick II and Duke Wilhelm,[22] who issued a coinage regulation in 1444. They established a detailed order of fixed payments, set the value of money within the land and the value of Saxon money in exchange for foreign money, and regulated the relation of gold and silver. The document states that the rulers had drawn up these detailed regulations in response to complaints that everybody was trying to exploit his neighbors. The same careful attention was given to a new mint and to the elaborate reorganization of the princely fiscal system with many officials headed by a marshal and chancellor.[23]

Changes in the social and economic fabric of Saxon territories made necessary these administrative measures which in their turn accelerated the process.[24] A small bourgeoisie arose through commerce, and the artisan became an important part of society. The silver and ore discoveries in the Erzgebirge led to the founding of mining towns like Annaberg and Schneeberg, and the mining of the metals became a source of wealth for all of Saxony. At the time of the partition of 1485 the Schneeberg with the Neustädtel and the use of its mines remained common possession of the two Saxon lines and thus often became the source of arguments between them. Throughout the territories, the cities became stronger — especially the three most important ones, Dresden, Leipzig and Erfurt, the latter acknowledging Saxony's protectorate even while clinging to its own independence.

III

Intellectual life in fifteenth-century Saxony was almost medieval in character. The Italian Renaissance that found an enthusiastic reception in some parts of southern and western Germany toward the latter part of the century, found little response in Saxony until the beginning of the next century. The only noteworthy intellectual endeavors in fifteenth-century Saxony are some chronicles that transmit information about Saxony's earlier time. An awakening of local patriotism, pride and interest in the past, typical of the Renaissance and of humanism, stimulated these first historical writtings.

The four most important chronicles are: *Annales Vetero Cellenses*,[25] the first attempt at a Meissen-Saxon history; Johannes Rothe's *Chronicon Thuringiae*,[26] in which the author continually attempts to connect Thuringian history with world

22 J. Falke, 'Beitrag zur sächsischen Münzgeschichte, 1444–1461', *Mittheilungen des königlich-sächsichen Vereins für Erforschung und Erhaltung vaterländischer Geschichts- und Kunstdenkmäler*, 16 (1866), 77–106; *ibid.*, 17 (1867), 78–103 (for the period 1461–1470); and *ibid.*, 18 (1868), 93–119 (for the period 1474–1486).
23 R. Goldfriedrich, *Die Geschäftsbücher der kursächsischen Kanzlei im 15. Jahrhundert* (Leipzig, 1930); J. Falke, 'Bete, Zise und Ungeld im Kurfürstenthum Sachsen bis zur Theilung von 1485', *Mittheilungen des königlich-sächsischen Vereins für Erforschung und Erhaltung vaterländischer Geschichts- und Kunstdenkmäler*, 19 (1869), 31–59; and 'Die Finanzwirtschaft im Kurfürstenthum Sachsen um das Jahr 1470', *ibid.*, 20 (1870), 78–106.
24 Gretschel, pp. 304ff.
25 Mencken, pp. 378ff.
26 *Ibid.*, pp. 1634ff.

history; the *Chronik* of Hartung Cammermeister,[27] the best source of the time for the years 1375–1467; and the *Memoriale* of Konrad Stolle.[28] There are lesser ones which are included in the compilations of Mencken. As works of literature they are negligible; their interest lies in the historical information that they preserve.

In this connection the *Onomasticon* of the Dominican monk Johann Lindner ought to be mentioned, although it was concluded as late as 1530 when its author was eighty years old.[29] The work is a dictionary, glossary and gazetteer, divided in its several parts into 'famous men of Saxony', 'geography of Saxony's neighbouring states', 'famous men connected with Saxon history', 'Saxon geography'. In his opinions Lindner reflects the anti-humanistic orientation of his order, especially in his censoring Frederick the Wise for having founded the University of Wittenberg, whence so many unchristian and pagan errors and doctrines were promulgated throughout Germany.[30]

Little effort was made to provide education for the people. The art of writing and reading was often unknown, even in upper circles. Duke Wilhelm of Thuringia for instance had to inform the Council of Frankfurt in 1405 that he had never been to school and therefore had never learned to read or write.[31] The schools of the cathedrals and convents limited themselves to preparing men for the priesthood and neglected any popular and secular education. The emerging bourgeoisie, through their own governments, established 'public schools', often in bitter conflict with the ecclesiastical schools. The Nikolai school of Leipzig is well known; other schools were founded at Freiberg, Chemnitz, Dresden and Gotha. The famous school at Schneeberg was founded in the middle of the fifteenth century and as a result of the growing mining industry, schools were also founded at Marienberg and Annaberg. At Zwickau Martin Römer, a wealthy and public-spirited citizen, provided for a school building in 1479 and also provided money for the operation of the school. At the end of the fifteenth century the Zwickau institution was so well known that students were enrolled not only from Saxony but from all over Germany.[32]

In the fifteenth century two universities were located in the Wettin territories: in Erfurt and in Leipzig. Erfurt, considered the capital of Thuringia in spite of its dependence on the Archbishop of Mainz, had good schools in the fourteenth

27 *Die Chronik Hartung Cammermeisters*, ed. R. Reiche (Halle, 1896; Geschichtsquellen der Provinz Sachsen, 35).
28 *Memoriale thüringisch-erfurtische Chronik von Konrad Stolle*, ed. R. Thiel (Halle, 1900: Geschichtsquellen der Provinz Sachsen, 39).
29 Mencken, pp. 1447ff. Cf. also K.E.H. Müller, 'Das Onomasticum mundi generale des Dominikanermönches Johannes Lindner zu Pirna und seine Quellen', *NASG*, 24 (1903), 217–247.
30 '... durch weliche Hoschule so vilfeldige, unchristliche und heydnissche unart und yrtumer in landen und steten, beuorh in dewczser Nacion sein awfgesprut ...' (Mencken, p. 1471)
31 '... als wist, daz wir ny zu keiner schule gegangen habin daz wir leider wider schriben noch lesen koenn ...' Cf. Konrad Sturmhoefel, *Illustrierte Geschichte der Sächsischen Lande und ihrer Herrscher*, (2 vols., Leipzig, 1897–1909), I, 2, p. 981.
32 F. Herzog, *Chronik der Kreisstadt Zwickau* (2 vols., Zwickau, 1839–1845), II, 140ff.

century and was therefore well prepared for the establishment of a university.[33] From its beginnings in 1392 the University of Erfurt became a representative of the *via moderna*, the teachings of Nominalism or Occamism. By the middle of the fifteenth century it was one of the best known universities, with many students, and by the end of that century early northern humanism had penetrated its walls.[34] The university was organized according to faculties – art, law, medicine, theology. The circle of humanists there maintained close relations with the humanists in Wittenberg who were later to model their university along the same lines. The same pattern obtained also at Tübingen.

In 1409[35] when the German students at the University of Prague had become dissatisfied with their treatment by Bohemian colleagues, Frederick the Valiant and his brother Wilhelm invited them to Leipzig to found a new university. It was organized into nationalities on the pattern of Paris and Prague: Meissen, Saxon, Bavarian and Polish. Leipzig was not very receptive to early humanism and when Peter Luder of Erfurt came to Leipzig in 1462 to teach poetry and rhetoric, he could not remain because his ideas were too advanced for his colleagues.[36] Even as late as 1502 several people, hoping for a more progressive and humanistically-oriented atmosphere, left Leipzig for Wittenberg where Frederick the Wise had recently founded a university.

In the field of art Saxony was backward. The unsettled conditions in the Wettin territories all through the fourteenth century were highly unfavorable to artistic creation. Not until the fifteenth century, under late Gothic influence, were some important churches, *Hallenkirchen*, constructed, with side naves the same length as the middle nave. During the Hussite wars many churches were destroyed or burnt down and a program of rebuilding was started in the second half of the fifteenth century. It was then that the Freiberg cathedral and the Kunigundenkirche in Rochlitz were built – and the Marienkirche in Zwickau. All these churches show the influence of Meister Arnold of Westphalia and his student Konrad Pflüger.

Among the secular buildings of prominence, the city halls at Freiberg and Zwickau are the best known. Most impressive was the Albrechtsburg in Meissen, which was built during the reign of Ernst and Albrecht under the direction of Arnold of Westphalia. After the partition of 1485 Albrecht chose Dresden as his residence and lost interest in the Albrechtsburg which was not finished in all its beauty until many years later. The building industry, like stonecutting, weaving and other industries, was highly organized and mostly dependent on western German shops, especially the famous one at Strassburg.

Towards the end of the century great architectural projects were started by Albrecht and Frederick the Wise, both of whom favored large and representative buildings.

In painting, the influence of the Bohemian school that had prevailed in the first

33 *Acten der Erfurter Universitaet*, ed. J.C. Hermann Weissenborn (3 vols., Halle, 1881–1899: Geschichtsquellen der Provinz Sachsen 8), I, xiv.
34 Bauch, *Erfurt*, pp. 11ff *et passim*.
35 *Urkundenbuch der Universität Leipzig von 1409 bis 1555*. Ed. Bruno Stübel (Leipzig, 1879. Cod. Dipl. Sax. Reg., II, 11) pp. 1–6.
36 Cf. Ludwig Geiger, *Renaissance und Humanismus in Italien und Deutschland.* (Berlin, 1882), pp. 327ff.

part of the century gave way to the schools of Cologne and Flanders. Little Renaissance influence can be seen except for attempts to simplify the late Gothic style.

Printing presses were established in Erfurt and Leipzig by the end of the fifteenth century in response to the need of the universities, where books were in great demand and equally scarce. In Erfurt the presses of Wolfgang Schenck, Hans Knapp, Henricus Sartorius and Nikolaus Marschalk were rapidly turning out books. In Leipzig, later to become Germany's greatest printing city, Kunz Kachelofen began printing, probably in the late 1480's, and his son-in-law Melchior Lotter, who printed Luther's famous Bible translation, continued the printing tradition of the family. The presses of Martin Landsberg, Wolfgang Stöckel and Jakob Thanner were also active in Leipzig.

Intellectually, then, Saxony was just beginning to wake up towards the latter part of the fifteenth century. Certain preparatory steps were taken, such as the founding of town schools, some reforms at the two universities and the printing presses, which made the reception of new ideas possible. However, if new humanistic tendencies were to develop freely and to shape effectively the cultural life of Saxony, they would have to find the full support and approval of its rulers. In Frederick the Wise Saxony found a prince who took the initiative in introducing humanistic learning and Renaissance art.

CHAPTER II

FREDERICK THE WISE: THE MAN AND THE POLICY

When his father died on August 26, 1486, Frederick the Wise became the sole ruler of electoral Saxony. The remaining parts of Ernestine Saxony were ruled jointly by the two brothers, Frederick and Johann, for a period of nearly forty years. But it was Frederick who emerged as the leader and *Kulturpolitiker* in the period 1486–1517.

I

Almost the only source for a study of Frederick the Wise is Spalatin's *Friedrichs des Weisen Leben und Zeitgeschichte*.[1] This eulogy by Frederick's most trusted friend, adviser and secretary has been used by many historians almost indiscriminately, by others with certain reservations.[2] An examination of this work, in the light of Spalatin's own position at the court of Frederick and of later influences on him by Frederick's successors, will help us to assess this valuable document.

Spalatin was born in 1484 in Spalt, not far from Nürnberg. His real name was Georg Burckhardt, and not until 1503, when he received his M.A. in Wittenberg, did he begin to use the humanist name Georgius Spalatinus.[3] At the age of thirteen he moved to Nürnberg and there attended the famous St. Sebaldus school where he perfected his knowledge of Latin. In 1498 he matriculated at the University of Erfurt.[4] His teachers were Hennig Göde, Jodocus Trutfetter and Nikolaus Marschalk, who in particular was to have a decisive influence on Spalatin's later life. Spalatin learned Greek from him and became one of the men in Marschalk's circle around whom the humanistic efforts in Erfurt centered. Spalatin received his B.A. after only one year and contributed a glossary to the *Laus Musarum*,[5] the

1 C.G. Neudecker and L. Preller, eds., *Georg Spalatins historischer Nachlass und Briefe* (vol. I: *Friedrichs des Weisen Leben und Zeitgeschichte*, Jena, 1851; no more volumes published; quoted as 'Spalatin').
2 Irmgard Höss, *Georg Spalatin, 1484–1545*; ein Leben in der Zeit des Humanismus und der Reformation (Weimar, 1956). This excellent work filled the need for a modern biography of Spalatin. All the source materials, published and unpublished, have been carefully examined, especially the *Ernestinisches Gesamtarchiv* in Weimar and the *Landesarchiv* in Altenburg.
3 *Ibid.*, p. 14.
4 *Akten der Erfurter Universität*, II, 204.
5 *Laus musarum ex Hesiodi Ascraei Theogonia* . . . Erfurt, 1501. Cf. Georg Wolfgang Panzer, *Annales typographici ab artis inventae origine ad anno* [*MDXXXVI*] . . . (11 vols.; Nürnberg, 1793–1803) VI, 494. Robert Proctor, *An Index of German Books, 1501–1520 in the British Museum.* 2nd ed. (London, 1954), 11230; G. Bauch, 'Wolfgang Schenk und Nikolaus

first work printed on Marschalk's own press in Erfurt. When Marschalk went to the new university at Wittenberg in 1502, Spalatin followed and matriculated there, receiving his M.A. in 1503.[6] In 1505 he was back in Erfurt and became, next to Urbanus, Mutian's closest friend and student. Many letters went between Spalatin in Erfurt and Mutian in Gotha as can be seen from Mutian's correspondence of these years. Mutian, who had been a student of Alexander Hegius at Deventer while Erasmus was there, and who had been to Italy in the 1490's, was the center of a humanistic circle in Gotha, where his house was always open to students of poetry, literature and philosophy. Through Mutian's efforts, Spalatin, who was forced to earn a living, went in 1505 to the monastery of Georgenthal, where he became a teacher of the young monks and was in general charge of education and of the library. These quiet years were beneficial to Spalatin since he had time to perfect his knowledge of Greek; in this period he also started to study the Bible, having purchased in 1507 a Vulgate edition which he kept all his life.[7] The experience in the monastery, his contacts with Aldus Manutius and his passion for book collecting proved useful to Spalatin when Frederick the Wise appointed him librarian at Wittenberg in 1512.

In 1508 Frederick, apparently concerned with providing a humanistic education for his successor, asked Mutian to recommend an appropriate teacher for his nephew, Johann Friedrich.[8] The leader of the humanist circle at Gotha suggested that Spalatin be engaged. Not long after the tutor arrived at Torgau, the Elector recognized his abilities far beyond those required and employed him as translator, as collector of historical material and as advisor at large. The court painter Lucas Cranach painted the portait of the young tutor only a year after his arrival – a further indication of how rapidly Spalatin had found favor and prestige with the Elector.[9]

Spalatin never left the service of Frederick: he became the educator of Frederick's nephews, the dukes Otto and Ernst of Braunschweig and Lunenburg, and also of Sebastian of Jessen, one of Frederick's illegitimate sons. The most important role Spalatin played in the history of the Reformation was as intermediary between Martin Luther, whose cause he ardently championed, and his own cautious prince.

Up to the year of Frederick's death (1525) more than nine hundred letters were exchanged between Spalatin and Luther. In the capacity of advisor and historian, Spalatin kept the elector informed of affairs concerning the university. During

Marschalk', *CB*, 12 (1895), 368; Hans Volz, 'Bibliographie der im 16. Jahrhundert erschienenen Schriften Georg Spalatins', *Zeitschrift für Bibliothekswesen und Bibliographie* 5 (1958), no. 1; Martin von Hase, *Bibliographie der Erfurter Drucke von 1501–1550*, 3. erweiterte Auflage. (Nieuwkoop, 1968), no. 90.

6 *Album Academiae Vitebergensis*, ed. Carl Eduard Foerstemann (3 vols., Leipzig, 1894 –1906), p. 5.

7 Georg Spalatin, *Spalatiniana*, ed. Georg Berbig (Leipzig, 1908: Quellen und Darstellungen aus der Geschichte des Reformationsjahrhunderts, V), p. 17.

8 Mutian, *Der Briefwechsel des Conradus Mutianus*, ed. K. Gillert (Halle, 1890: Geschichtsquellen der Provinz Sachsen, 18), no. 105.

9 For a discussion of the identification of Cranach's portrait of Spalatin, cf. H. Sander, 'Zur Identifizierung zweier Bildnisse von Lucas Cranach d. Ae,' *Repertorium für Kunstwissenschaft*, 4 (1950), 35–48.

Frederick's last days he was constantly with him and even records that Frederick's last words were addressed to him.[10] After the elector's death Spalatin left the court for Altenburg, where he became pastor of the local church. He often returned on special assignments to the official service of the Saxon electors but did not leave peaceful Altenburg and his scholarly studies for any length of time. He was entrusted with many church visitations; he played a part in the Schmalkaldic negotiations; and he took an active interest in the reform movement until his death in 1545.

Spalatin wrote several historical works, using historical documents and data which he had collected. In addition, he left his own autobiography as a record of his own time and the role he played in it.[11] His writings, which have been used extensively,[12] have in some instances been questioned as to their exactness and impartiality. Yet, even Catholic historians, who recognized in him a staunch supporter of Luther, did not doubt his honesty as a historian.[13] It was only natural that he maintained his devotion to the house of Saxony and its electors, as for instance, in his work on the origin of the Saxon dukes in which he repudiated the claims of Duke Heinrich von Braunschweig.[14]

The attitude of complete devotion is also apparent in his life of Frederick the Wise. Frederick was the person he esteemed above everyone and with whom he could find no fault. Spalatin started the work shortly after Frederick's death, continuing with it for as much as twenty years;[15] internal evidence suggests that Spalatin died before putting the finishing touches to it; in 1539 he was still writing the description of Frederick's journey to the Holy Land.[16] The work developed slowly under the influence of Frederick's successors who were ardent Protestants — among them the Elector Johann Friedrich,[17] who made revisions designed to eradicate any traces of Roman Catholicism from the life of Frederick and to prove that his uncle's sympathies were always with Luther. Spalatin, who was himself not so convinced, expressed his opinion of Frederick's attitude toward the Reformation more cautiously and without reference to Frederick's waverings and doubts in religious matters.[18] His aim in writing the life of Frederick was to express his love and devotion to the elector; Johann Friedrich's concern was to prove Frederick a thorough Protestant.

Spalatin's *Friedrichs des Weisen Leben und Zeitgeschichte* is divided into two

10 Spalatin, p. 67.
11 For a bibliography of Spalatin's published works see Hans Volz, 'Bibliographie der im 16. Jahrhundert erschienenen Schriften Georg Spalatins', *Zeitschrift für Bibliothekswesen und Bibliographie*, 5 (1958), 83—119.
12 Especially by Hortleder and Seckendorf; Hortleder even copied large parts of Spalatin's works by hand. Several passages have been published in the works of Struve, Cyprian, Mencken and others, but only parts — and often not correct.
13 Cf. A. Seelheim, *Georg Spalatin als sächsischer Historiograph* ... (Halle, 1876: Hallesche Abhandlungen zur neueren Geschichte, 5) pp. 39—40.
14 *Chronica und Herkomen der Churfürsten und Fürsten des löblichen Haus zu Sachsen, gegen Herzog Heinrichs zu Braunschweig, welcher sich den Jüngern nennet, herkomen, ...* (Wittenberg, 1541).
15 Spalatin, p. 129.
16 *Ibid.*, p. 89.
17 *Ibid.*, pp. 31, 39, 113, 145.
18 *Ibid.*, p. 30.

parts: the first recounts the personal life of Frederick, and the second is a chronicle of the years 1463 to 1525. This division leads to many repetitions. The chronological part cannot be altogether trusted; many errors in dating occur, and the additions of Johann Friedrich distort the picture severely. Of greater importance are the documents that are found in the appendices to both parts. Among these are a diary of Frederick's journey to the Holy Land, written by one of the fellow travelers, and an incomplete diary of the trip to the Netherlands in 1494 by a native of Weimar who accompanied Frederick. The documents of general historical significance are Maximilian's proposition at the Diet of Constanz in 1507, and papers and letters from Charles V, Henry VIII and Francis I to Frederick the Wise; and also Charles V's *Decretum Electionis*.

The first part of Spalatin's account is subdivided into many short passages dealing with Frederick's birth, education, imperial activities; wisdom, fear of God, daily proverbs, patience and magnanimity; his love of scholarship and architecture, his treatment of the poor and his own staff, his leisure time — all described in almost childlike fashion and filled with many uplifting examples, culminating in a beautiful account of the last two days of Frederick's life. Here Spalatin gives word for word what Frederick said, to whom he said it and how he finally took communion in both forms before his death. The work concludes with a description of the funeral of Frederick and quotes the inscriptions by Melanchthon on the elector's gravestone.

Spalatin considers Frederick's most outstanding virtue to have been his love for peace; the Emperor Maximilian likewise admired the Elector for never having gone to war against anybody.[19] He did not go to war against Erfurt or Hessen and he managed not to get involved in any of the imperial wars of his time.[20] Spalatin was aware that Frederick had been severely criticized and compared with Q. Fabius Cunctator because he was slow to make decisions. In defense of Frederick his biographer points out that Fabius Cunctator's delaying tactics saved the Roman Empire, as was already the judgement of Ennius and Virgil.[21] Thus in Spalatin's eyes Frederick's caution became a virtue. When Frederick was urged to make war on Erfurt with the argument that it would not take more than five men to take the city by force, he replied that even the death of one man he would consider too much.[22] Content with the territories he ruled, Frederick never wanted to add to his lands.[23] This attitude of self-restraint, epitomized in Frederick's famous motto: *tantum quantum possum*,[24] together with a certain awareness of the vanity of human endeavors, seems to be characteristic of Frederick. It also finds expression in many of his sayings.[25]

Frederick's love for peace also won Luther's praise: as early as 1516, in his

19 *Ibid.*, p. 25.
20 *Ibid.*, pp. 24–25.
21 *Ibid.*, p. 26.
22 Cf. P. Kirn, *Friedrich der Weise und die Kirche* (Leipzig, 1926: Beiträge zur Kulturgeschichte des Mittelalters und der Renaissance, 30), p. 13: 'Es wäre an einem zu viel'.
23 Spalatin, p. 53.
24 Müller, *Annales*, p. 78.
25 Spalatin, p. 63.

lectures on the *Epistle to the Romans*,[26] and again in 1526 in his *Ob Kriegsleute auch in seligem Stande sein können.* [27]

Of the elector's generosity, his kindness towards other people in all walks of life Spalatin makes frequent mention. Upon his death many people bore him testimonies of praise; among them the funeral sermons of Luther and Melanchthon which overflow with love and respect for their late ruler.[28]

Although Spalatin and the other friends of the elector certainly tended to idealize him, all other contemporary accounts and characterizations confirm the fact that Frederick enjoyed the admiration and love of those who knew him well. Even allowing for the customary exaggeration in the eulogies of the elector, the fact remains that he was known to all his contemporaries as kind, intelligent, honest, peace-loving and unselfishly concerned with the good of his people as well as of the empire.

II

Frederick the Wise received the education and training customary for a prince of his time. He was born in 1463 in Torgau, which was to be his favorite residence in later years, but it was in Grimma, with his three brothers, that he was educated by private tutors.[29] The only one whose name we know was Magister Ulrich Kemmerlin, later deacon at Aschaffenburg, whom Frederick often remembered with kind thoughts, for he had apparently made a strong impression on the young prince.[30] Frederick learned Latin well, but not enough to speak it fluently. In 1520 at Cologne Frederick questioned Erasmus, in the presence of Spalatin, on his opinion on Luther. The elector understood Erasmus, who spoke in Latin, but asked Spalatin to answer for him in Latin.[31] Of the classical authors he recalled in later times he had studied mostly Terence and Cato whose sayings were similar to German proverbs.[32]

Frederick also understood some French,[33] but no Italian. In 1494 he needed an interpreter to converse with the Italian wife of Maximilian, Queen Bianca.[34] Among his princely contemporaries there were many who knew more languages. Maximilian is reputed to have known seven languages; Joachim of Brandenburg

26 Cf. *WA* 56, 448, 25–29.
27 *Ibid.*, 19, 646, 17–28.
28 *Ibid.*, 17, part 1, nos. 30, 31, 32. Cf. also *WAB*, 3, no. 868. Cf. also *CR*, 11, 90–98.
29 Spalatin says expressly 'Thumstuben' (p. 22) and not 'Turmschule' or 'Domschule'. Cf. C.G. Lorenz, *Die Stadt Grimma im Königreich Sachsen* (Leipzig, 1865), p. 513, where the author says that there was at that time no cathedral school in Grimma. Cf. also M.M. Tutzschmann, *Friedrich der Weise, Kurfürst von Sachsen*; ein Lebensbild aus dem Zeitalter der Reformation, nach den Quellen für all Stände dargestellt. (Grimma, 1848), p. 10.
30 Spalatin, pp. 22, 46.
31 *Ibid.*, 22. Cf. also Spalatin, *Annales Reformationis*, oder Jahrbücher von der Reformation Lutheri. Aus dessen Autographo ans Licht gestellt von Ernst Salomon Cyprian. In: Wilhelm Ernst Tentzel, *Historischer Bericht vom Anfang und ersten Fortgang der Reformation Lutheri* (Leipzig, 1718), p. 28. Cf. also *Deutsche Reichstagsakte, Jüngere Reihe*, 1, 567 (April 18, 1519).
32 Spalatin, p. 22.
33 *Ibid.*, p. 22.
34 *Ibid.*, p. 225.

had learned Latin, French and Italian; Georg of Ducal Saxony was said to have a knowledge of Latin superior to Frederick's; and Albrecht of Bavaria had the reputation of knowing Latin better than any of his fellow princes.[35] By contrast, neither Frederick's father Ernest nor his uncles Albrecht and Wilhelm knew any Latin at all.

Like all princes at that time, Frederick was trained in physical exercise; he was a good hunter, a skilled target-shooter and in racing and other competitive games he was equal to many. He participated in tournaments and even joined emperor Maximilian in 1510 at the Diet of Augsburg in jousting.[36] In later years his health did not allow him to participate in tournaments but his interest remained keen. He also enjoyed more bourgeois entertainments like archery at Zwickau in 1489 and at the Diet of Augsburg, where Maximilian and other princes joined in.[37]

Extensive travels shaped much of the young prince's thinking and he later recalled these early experiences with much pleasure. He went to the court of the elector of Mainz, Diether von Isenburg, to broaden his education and to improve his knowledge of French.[38] The time he spent at the urbane court of Maximilian provided an excellent opportunity to polish the manners of the young man and to acquaint him with some of the first achievements of the arts of his generation.[39] Probably the most educational experience, although somewhat later in his career, was Frederick's journey to the Holy Land in 1493,[40] though little was left of the zeal of the crusaders. It was proper for a Christian prince to have seen the Holy Sepulchre and the many commemorative places, shrines, and landmarks on the route. Frederick's uncle Albrecht of Ducal Saxony had made the trip in 1476, and his uncle Duke Wilhelm of Thuringia in 1461 had distinguished himself by spending more money on this journey than any of his fellow German princes.[41] Many persons who later distinguished themselves accompanied the elector; among these were Duke Christoph of Bavaria, Degenhard Pfeffinger, Hans Hundt, Leopold von Hermannsgrün, Martin Polich von Mellerstadt and Lucas Cranach. From a fellow traveler's account of the expedition, in an appendix to Spalatin's life of Frederick, we learn many interesting details. The pilgrims went by way of Vienna where Frederick took leave of the emperor Maximilian, who died before Frederick's return. The journey continued to Venice, where Frederick made his first acquaintance with some of the great works of the Italian Renaissance. Then the party sailed down the Adriatic Sea by way of Candia; there Frederick took sick but quickly recovered following treatment by his personal physician Martin Polich von Mellerstadt. The voyage proceeded to Rhodes and Cyprus, and finally Frederick and his entourage landed at Jaffa. In Jerusalem Frederick was made a Knight of the Holy Sepulchre by Heinrich of Schaumburg, who was of his party.

35 Cf. Kirn, *Friedrich der Weise*, p. 9.
36 Spalatin, pp. 32, 149.
37 Kirn, *Friedrich der Weise*, p. 7.
38 Spalatin, p. 22.
39 *Ibid.*, p. 24.
40 *Ibid.*, pp. 26 and 76ff., where the account of one of his fellow travelers is given. Cf. also R. Röhricht, *Deutsche Pilgerreisen nach dem Heiligen Lande* (new ed., Innsbruck, 1900), pp. 172ff.; 'Hans Hundts Rechnungsbuch', ed. R. Röhricht and H. Meisner, in *NASG*, 4 (1883), 37–100; Müller, *Annales*, p. 55.
41 Röhricht, *Deutsche Pilgerreisen*, pp. 7, 127ff., 142ff.

After three days in the Holy Land they started their return voyage. The elector went *incognito* all the time because the Saracens were constantly trying to spot important individuals from whom they asked large sums of money. In Rhodes Duke Christoph of Bavaria died and Leopold von Hermannsgrün had to be left behind because of illness but he later returned home safely. Frederick landed again in Venice, where he was received royally, and arrived in Torgau in September 1493. There he erected a replica of the Chapel of the Holy Sepulchre of Jerusalem to which he gave some of the relics collected on the journey.[42] Most of these, however, he gave to his beloved castle church in Wittenberg.[43] Lucas Cranach later painted for the elector a panel showing all the cities and towns they had visited on their pilgrimage; it was installed in the castle church in Wittenberg, but was unfortunately destroyed in the eighteenth century during the siege of Wittenberg in the Seven Years' War.[44]

A detailed first-hand account of Frederick's trip to the Netherlands in 1494 is provided by the diary of one of his subjects from Weimar.[45] The occasion for the journey was the celebration of the transfer of the rule of the province from Emperor Maximilian to his son Philip. Having traveled from Torgau to Weimar and Frankfurt and then by boat down the Rhine to Cologne, Frederick met the Emperor and his brilliant entourage near the city of Maastricht. For the first time Frederick saw the prosperous and culturally advanced Netherlands, the cities of Louvain, Mecheln and Antwerp. The days were filled with tournaments, banquets, entertainments by local actors and jesters, and dances,[46] and Frederick shared the luxurious and opulent bourgeois life of the Dutch communities, which he must have found very different from that on the banks of the Elbe. The travels Frederick undertook in his later years were mainly in the interest of his rule: beginning with the Diet of Worms in 1495, to the end of his life, he attended almost every diet of the empire.

For a picture of Frederick's personal character we have to lean strongly on Spalatin, who described him as a shy man. This trait, perhaps derived from his Wittelsbach ancestry,[47] is also confirmed by an episode of which Frederick wrote to his brother in 1521. Having pretended that he neither saw nor heard a large group of people who wanted to present a serenade to him, he excused himself as follows: 'Ich besthe gancz ubel, ich entschlage mich aller gesellschaft allsso auss zcu warthen'.[48] This shyness may also help to explain why he remained unmarried. Staupitz once went to the Netherlands to consider a bride for Frederick

42 Mencken, p. 570; Spalatin, p. 28.
43 Cf. J. Köstlin, *Friedrich der Weise und die Schlosskirche zu Wittenberg* (Wittenberg, 1892), pp. 14ff.
44 Christian Schuchardt, *Lucas Cranach des Älteren Leben und Werke* (3 vols., Leipzig, 1851–1871), I, p. 112.
45 Spalatin, pp. 221ff; cf. K. v. Reitzenstein, 'Unvollständiges Tagebuch auf der Reise Kurfürst Friedrichs des Weisen von Sachsen in die Niederlande zum Römischen König Maximilian I, 1494', *Zeitschrift des Vereins für Thüringische Geschichte*. 4 (1861), pp. 127–137.
46 Spalatin, p. 227.
47 *Ibid.*, p. 48.
48 C.E. Foerstemann, ed., *Neues Urkundenbuch zur Geschichte der evangelischen Kirchenreformation* (Hamburg, 1842), no. 13.

but advised against the marriage because he considered the pair unsuited to each other.[49] However, it is well known that Frederick had three, possibly four, children, whose mother was Anna Weller of Molsdorf. Everybody knew about his two sons, Sebastian and Fritz, who were always with him at his court; and there must have been rumors of a marriage between him and Anna. When his brother Ernst, Archbishop of Magdeburg, referred to Frederick's plans to marry a commoner, Frederick's response was: 'sein Gnad sei nicht befunden der torhayt dass [ir] zurgemessen solt werden, dass sie ere und standes vorgessen würde'.[50]

Since Frederick lacked an official family, he was the more attentive to the family of his brother Johann, whom he considered his best friend. He treated his nephew, the future Elector Johann Friedrich, like his own son, and any differences within the family circle were distasteful to him.

No more can the manners and customs at the elector's court be compared to the lavish and refined style of life of a Lorenzo de' Medici or Philip of Burgundy than the life of the citizens of Torgau, Altenburg or Wittenberg could to that of the proud merchants of Florence or Brugge. But even in electoral Saxony the traditionally-minded territorial diets felt the need for new ordinances and regulations restraining any display of luxury and defining the proper attire for each estate. According to one of Luther's forceful tabletalks, although the elector supported this policy, he was thwarted in implementing it by his cousin Georg who benefited from the budding trade in luxury items at the Leipzig Fairs.[51] It was there that the cloth for the electoral wardrobe was purchased annually, and members of the electoral court had their clothes made by the court tailors.[52] At the wedding of Duke Johann and the Mecklenburg princess Sophie in 1500, every Saxon was dressed in red.[53] And even from the Diet of Worms in 1495 Frederick commented to his brother Johann about the clothes of the Bavarian princes.[54] It was customary to have initials embroidered on the clothes of people attending the court, and Frederick chose for his the letters CCSN, which stood for *Crux Christi Salus Nostra* and VDMIA which stood for *Verbum Dei Manet in Aeternum.*[55]

Such was Frederick's fondness for music that he maintained at court an orchestra, under the direction of Conrad von Ruppisch, which accompanied him even to the imperial diets.[56] He also kept a court fool to amuse him.[57] During his

49 *WATR*, IV, no. 4455.
50 Cf. Kirn, *Friedrich der Weise*, p. 16.
51 *WATR*, III, no. 3782.
52 R. Bruck, *Friedrich der Weise als Förderer der Kunst* (Strassburg, 1903: Studien zur deutschen Kunstgeschichte, 45), pp. 133ff.
53 Cf. C.A.H. Burkhardt, 'Die Vermählung des Herzogs Johann von Sachsen, 1. bis 5. März, 1500', *NASG*, 15 (1894), 288ff.
54 Cf. Kirn, *Friedrich der Weise*, p. 10.
55 Müller, *Annales*, p. 78; Mencken, p. 614; these sayings are an interesting sidelight of rulers at the time. Philip of Hessen in 1543 wrote to Elector Johann Friedrich: 'Wenn E.L., Herzog Moritz und wir so evangelisch wären, wie wir das auf den Aermeln führen, so würden wir um solch geringer Sachen willen miteinander nich so sehr zanken'. *WATR*. IV, no. 455ff.; Kirn, *Friedrich der Weise*, p. 11.
56 Spalatin, p. 53; Nikolaus Müller, *Die Wittenberger Bewegung 1521 und 1522*. Die Vorgänge in und um Wittenberg während Luthers Wartburgaufenthalt (Zweite Auflage. Leipzig, 1911) pp. 395–403; *Die Musik in Geschichte und Gegenwart*, XI, cols. 11–25, where the literature is given.
57 *Neues Urkundenbuch*, ed. Foerstemann, no. 24.

life five are mentioned by name, one of whom Frederick took along on his journey to the Holy Land, at least as far as Venice. At the Diet of Worms he received a letter from his fool Fritz, who made several remarks about Luther and the Cardinals which amused Frederick. And in his last will he asked his brother Johann to take his fool Albrecht into his own house and treat him well.

Frederick's health, which was poor even in his early life, worsened after 1519. At imperial diets he had to be carried, since he was unable to walk. During the Diet of Worms he could not leave his residence for weeks.[58] If indeed he was offered the imperial crown in 1519, as Kalkoff assumes[59] contrary to the views of many other historians, the consensus is that the foremost reason for his refusal was his bad health — not *morbus diplomaticus* as the nuntius Aleander once claimed.[60] He suffered most from 'Stein', which was confirmed by the autopsy made after his death. He suffered for many years and we are told that he took his ills with patience and as a fate against which he did not rebel. Frederick died on May 5, 1525, at his beloved castle at Lochau.

III

Frederick's imperial policy shows him a staunch defender of the rights of the electors. A loyal supporter of the house of Habsburg, he was willing to give to the emperor what was his due. But at the many diets he attended (Spalatin says there were about thirty[61]) he remained a strong champion of the Electoral party. He was chiefly interested in imperial reforms and he found himself early in his reign in close agreement with the Archbishop of Mainz, Berthold von Henneberg, the leader of the reform party. Frederick did not want to strengthen imperial power to further the unity of the empire; he desired rather to increase the authority of the electors as the highest estate in the empire and to supervise and check imperial policy. In order not to dismiss this position as a merely selfish approach by an elector, one has to keep in mind the continuously wavering policies of Maximilian. The electoral scheme for imperial reform, intended to enforce peace and to consolidate taxation and jurisdiction, was, however, to terminate all hopes for a strong unified empire — at that time still a lofty concept in the people's mind. Thus to disperse the central authority among the various territories meant the destruction of the one force strong enough 'to awaken the nations of Europe to a consciousness of their own existence and importance . . .'[62] While in France, England, Spain, Poland and Hungary the kings found ways and means to establish a centralized power, in Germany developments took the opposite direction. Maximilian's predecessor, Frederick III, had not even visited the empire for many

---

58 *Ibid.*, nos. 20, 25, 26, 29.
59 P. Kalkoff, *Die Kaiserwahl Friedrichs IV und Karls V (am 27. u. 28. Juni, 1519)* (Weimar, 1925). Cf. also Spalatin, pp. 41, 162; Müller, *Annales*, p. 72.
60 P. Kalkoff, *Die Depeschen des Nuntius Aleander vom Wormser Reichstag, 1521* (2nd ed., Halle, 1897), p. 226.
61 Spalatin, p. 39.
62 Leopold von Ranke, *History of the Reformation in Germany,* transl. from the last edition of the German by Sarah Austin (Philadelphia, 1844), p. 88.

years; the 'power which, according to the received idea, ruled the world, had become an object of contemptuous pity',[63]

At the Diet of Nürnberg in 1487, when Frederick III invested Frederick and Johann with their territories,[64] the restoration of the public peace was the most pressing issue and many pronouncements were made on this subject. But it was evident that as long as Frederick was emperor no serious attempt at a reform of the empire was possible and that no tangible progress would be made at the many diets which were held, but no serious actions taken.

After Frederick III's death in 1493, Maximilian became emperor and opened his first Diet at Worms in 1495, where Frederick the Wise was again invested with his lands.[65] The constitutional history of the Diet of Worms is well documented.[66] The estates met the demands of Maximilian for military help against the French with a comprehensive plan for a constitution for the empire. Maximilian reluctantly gave his consent since he could not otherwise get help against Charles VIII of France, but he made the concessions with the firm intent to repudiate them as soon as he could.

To elector Frederick it seemed that a reform movement could emanate only from the territories and their rulers. This implied that the princes would set themselves against the two powers which, traditionally, had ruled the empire: Emperor and Pope. This policy was at a later date to draw the two powers closer together against the most threatening force within the empire, the party of the reformed religion. But for the time under consideration the issues were not yet so well drawn and the emperor was still bartering with the princes for the needed assistance in his military expeditions in Italy and the Netherlands. When the princes withheld aid for the wars which they feared would benefit chiefly Habsburg dynastic interests, the emperor patiently called another diet and tried to persuade the estates to support an imperial policy which he considered would serve the common good. Frederick the Wise often went home from these diets with best intentions — or at least pretended that he did — to collect money or to recruit men for the imperial wars. But actually these efforts were negligible and we find Frederick occupied primarily with internal Saxon affairs and busy putting his own house in order. This is not to say that Frederick did not try conscientiously to work for peace and for the improvement of conditions in the empire, but he was foremost a territorial prince, concerned with the well-being of his lands and its people.

Frederick was called upon for many important imperial duties in the following years. According to the Golden Bull of 1356 the elector of Saxony was imperial vicar of the eastern half of the empire whenever the emperor was absent or during an interregnum;[67] Frederick had to fulfill this function many times while Maximilian was absent on his imperial wars. Also, Maximilian knew how skillful a

---

63 *Ibid.*, p. 90.
64 Müller, *Annales*, p. 52.
65 Spalatin, p. 128; Müller, *Annales*, p. 57.
66 The whole first volume of Müller's *RTTh unter Max.* is taken up with recounting the events of the Diet of Worms.
67 Cf. K. Zeumer, *Die Goldene Bulle Kaiser Karls IV.* (Weimar, 1908: Quellen und Studien zur Verfassungsgeschichte des deutschen Reiches im Mittelalter und Neuzeit, 2).

negotiator Frederick was and used him in this capacity many times. When the imperial council was established at the Diet of Augsburg in 1500, Frederick became its president.

One provision of the Diet of Augsburg, affecting Saxony directly, was the first attempt to divide the empire into districts (*Kreise*) in order to help maintain the public peace and simplify administrative procedures. The name Upper Saxony (*Obersachsen*) emerged for the first time, and what had usually been referred to as Saxony became Lower Saxony (*Niedersachsen*). In the upper Saxon district were included electoral Saxony with the other Wettin lands, Brandenburg, Pomerania and some other smaller territories.

Berthold von Henneberg, the major leader of the reform party in the empire, died in 1504, and thereafter Maximilian's fortunes rose for a time: the estates were more willing to compromise than before. But when Maximilian's wars in Italy were unsuccessful, the estates changed their minds. As Frederick disassociated himself more and more from Maximilian's imperial and dynastic policies, the tension between them increased until in 1512 at the Diet of Cologne Frederick was the leader of the opposition. To understand why Frederick became more hostile to imperial policy, one has to consider Maximilian's changed attitude towards the house of Wettin as a consequence of Saxony's newly gained strength in several directions. The bishopric of Magdeburg had been in the hands of Frederick's brother Ernst since 1476; Frederick's sister Margarethe was duchess of Lüneburg; his other sister Christina was Queen of Denmark; his cousin was Grand Master of the Teutonic Order. In 1510, after the death of Landgraf Wilhelm of Hesse, Frederick became guardian of young Philip of Hesse, at the request of the Hessian estates; and the political leaders there were friends of Frederick.[68] Thus since Wettin's influence extended far and wide, Maximilian was unwilling to take any action that would further add to the strength of Saxony. Therefore in the controversy over the succession in the principalities of Jülich and Berg, Maximilian ignored the rights of Saxony as claimed at several diets.[69]

At the beginning of his reign Frederick had been willing to take part in imperial affairs, to work towards the establishment of order and peace, and to devote much time and energy in serving the emperor. However, many frustrating experiences taught him that the time was not yet ripe for establishing a real constitution for the empire and he saw that the emperor was trying to undermine the measures pronounced by the diets. Also Maximilian's wars in Italy were repulsive to Frederick, and for all these reasons, he gradually withdrew his support. Finally, when we consider the state of the elector's health, one can easily understand his shift of interests from the national to the domestic scene. It was not until the time of Luther's controversy with Pope and Emperor that Frederick again took an active part in imperial affairs, and then in the interest of one of his own citizens.

---

68 Spalatin, p. 148; Cf. H. Glagau, *Eine Vorkämpferin landesherrlicher Macht, Anna von Hessen, die Mutter Philipps des Grossmütigen, 1485–1525.* (Marburg, 1899).
69 Müller, *Annales*, p. 66.

30

Electoral Saxony tried to maintain peaceful relations with neighboring territories and in his thirty-nine years of rule Frederick succeeded in avoiding all military clashes with his neighbors. The critical situations which arose in relation to Albertine Saxony and the city of Erfurt, however, almost involved him in crucial confrontations.

The relationship between the two Saxonies was amicable in the early years of Frederick's reign, but gradually deteriorated.[70] The greatest source of disagreement was the partition of 1485, following which so many issues remained undecided. Several territories were under common jurisdiction[71] and this led immediately to differences which were temporarily settled at the *Oschatzer Schied* in 1491.[72] Frederick's difficulties with Albrecht never seemed great enough to arouse much animosity. Furthermore it seemed quite possible that the electoral line of Saxony would become extinct and Ernestine Saxony would revert to the Albertines. Frederick was not married; Johann married just before Albrecht's death in 1500 and the future elector Johann Friedrich was not born till 1503. When Georg succeeded Albrecht in ducal Saxony in 1500, the tensions between the two Saxonies mounted. Duke Georg, different as he was from Frederick, had one thing in common with the elector: an unbending stubbornness in standing up for what he considered his rights. The two main sources of trouble were the use of the mines at Annaberg and Schneeberg, which had remained under common administration, and the use of the highways that connected Poland and Silesia with Meissen, electoral Saxony and Thuringia.[73] When Duke Georg restricted the use of both the mines and the highways, the Ernestines insisted on the suspension of the restrictive measures in order to negotiate on an equal basis, but Georg refused to negotiate.[74] By 1508 events seemed to come to a head and Duke Georg mobilized part of his army to reaffirm what he considered to be his rights to the mines and the roads. The Ernestines informed the emperor about Georg's threatening war and Maximilian issued a mandate on February 29, 1508, forbidding any military action against electoral Saxony and ordering both parties to settle their differences peacefully. Formal peace was thus established, but with no better understanding between the two Wettin lines. These tensions in the economic sphere had become so deep that differences in the political field followed. Georg had always been a strong supporter of the house of Habsburg and its dynastic policies, and Frederick was a proponent of the electoral reform party. In religious matters also sharp differences existed: ducal Saxony, which remained Roman Catholic much longer than electoral Saxony, actually intrigued against Luther and electoral Saxony.

70 Cf. W. Goerlitz, ed., *Staat und Stände unter den Herzögen Albrecht und Georg, 1485–1539* (Leipzig, 1928: Sächsische Landtagsakte, I). and Burkhardt, *Ernestinische Landtagsakte*, I.
71 Müller, *Annales*, p. 51.
72 Hänsch, *Die wettinische Hauptteilung*, pp. 120ff; Müller, *Annales*, p. 54; H. Virck, 'Die Ernestiner und Herzog Georg von 1500 bis 1508', *NASG*, 30 (1909), 1–75.
73 J. Falke, 'Zur Geschichte der hohen Landstrasse in Sachsen', *ASG*, 7 (1869), 113ff.
74 Burkhardt, *Ernestinische Landstagsakte*, nos. 100, 101.

The other major domestic concern of Frederick was Saxony's relations with Erfurt and therefore indirectly with the Archbishop of Mainz, who had always claimed territorial rights over the town.[75]

According to the double loyalty Mainz was the *Landesherr* of Erfurt while Saxony was the *Schirmherr* — a confused legal situation which led to many frictions. Frederick's brother Albrecht had been Archbishop of Mainz from 1480 until 1484. Saxony made every effort to have another Wettin duke appointed as his successor but was unable to block the appointment of Berthold von Henneberg. Although Frederick remained on friendly terms with him, he became involved in a long struggle over Erfurt with the next archbishop, Uriel von Gemmingen, who ruled the archdiocese from 1508 to 1514.

The situation came to a head in 1509 in 'das tolle Jahr zu Erfurt',[76] when the town was in complete upheaval because of a financial and social crisis; people were executed and lynched; the university and with it its valuable library was almost completely destroyed. Negotiations between Mainz and Saxony and Erfurt were carried on until 1516. Then, through the mediation of Henning Göde, the famous legal counselor who had found refuge with Frederick the Wise, a treaty between Erfurt and Saxony was signed, by which the old order was reestablished and amnesty was announced for everybody. Erfurt was now allied with Saxony against the Archbishop of Mainz (in a battle that continued into the seventeenth century when Mainz finally won against Saxony). Frederick was greatly angered by the whole Erfurt affair; Maximilian had counteracted him at every point of the struggle, Duke Georg of Saxony had shown a complete lack of good will, and he himself had lost a large sum of money. It again confirms Frederick's peace-loving nature that nowhere is there evidence that he was willing to use force to achieve his objectives.

Ecclesiastical conditions in Saxony were as confused as they were in every other German territory toward the end of the Middle Ages. The electoral line shared with Albertine Saxony the protectorate over the archbishopric of Meissen, while Naumburg was solely an Ernestine proctectorate, as was Merseburg an Albertine protectorate. Other dioceses possessed rights in ecclesiastical seats located in Ernestine Saxony; these were Mainz, Halberstadt, Magdeburg, Brandenburg, Bamberg, and Würzburg. Among the many other extra-territorial ecclesiastical bodies also situated in the elector's territory were over one hundred establishments by monastic orders, who owed allegiance and obedience to their authorities outside of Saxony. Thus the functioning of the ecclesiastical judiciary was complicated and it took many years and court actions on many levels to settle cases. Any attempt to bring order out of such chaos had to come from the territorial ruler. The Wettin princes chose two ways: they tried to bring the smaller and

75 Much has been written about Erfurt, its place in the empire and its relations to Mainz and Saxony. Most original sources have been published and used by many scholars. For a good bibliography of earlier works, cf. Walther Schultze, *Die Geschichtsquellen der Provinz Sachsen im Mittelalter und in der Reformationszeit* (Halle, 1893); for later literature cf. F. Benary, *Zur Geschichte der Stadt und der Universität Erfurt am Ausgang des Mittelalters*, ed. A. Overmann (Gotha, 1919).
76 C.A.H. Burkhardt, 'Das tolle Jahr zu Erfurt und seine Folgen, 1509–1523', *ASG*, 12 (1874), 337–426.

weaker bishoprics in their territories directly under their own rule, while filling the larger bishoprics with members of their own families as they had in Mainz, Halberstadt and Magdeburg.[77]

During the negotiations of the Leipzig partition the estates were simply kept informed about events but were no longer asked to give advice in making decisions. Under Frederick the Wise's rule this rule of the estates did not change much. Frederick treated them very politely, but whenever he thought they might refuse his requests, he just decided not to call them. When weighty decisions had to be made, Frederick and his brother Johann consulted together as to whether it was advisable to call a territorial diet or at least a representative or executive committee of a diet. This attitude is understandable in the light of his experiences at imperial diets, where he had observed the futility of many negotiations and the unwieldiness of a large body of deliberators.

Diets were frequently called to discuss the emperor's continuous requests for support in money and men. After the Diet of Worms when the 'Common Penny' was levied, Frederick and Johann wrote letters to the estates exhorting them to do their duty and collect the money for the empire.[78] Frederick himself found all kinds of excuses for not calling a diet. Many more letters had to be written to remind the estates of their duties; the estates resented this and some refused help altogether. In 1497 Frederick noted that the estates of Albertine Saxony had been much better at collecting the money than the Ernestines,[79] in part, perhaps, reflecting the lack of enthusiasm on the part of their ruler.

When he needed the help of the estates in his own territorial interests, Frederick acted differently. In 1514, during his feud with Erfurt, he called them together and, in return for their help, promised to intervene with emperor Maximilian in the matter of the 'Common Penny'. Often he called local diets, restricted to individual parts of his territory, in order to avoid a situation in which the estates in one part of his land would work against those of other parts. Thus the diets were actually at the mercy of the princes. When the latter wanted to call them, they had to assemble; what the princes wanted discussed the estates had to discuss. The basis for territorial legislation was a code of laws issued under Duke Wilhelm of Thuringia in 1446, with additions in 1452; in 1482 Elector Ernst and Duke Albrecht continued this tradition.[80] Several special laws were enacted in both territories between 1482 and 1502 but no general legislation was enacted; it was not until the time of Johann Friedrich that a new code of laws was finally established.

Judiciary matters were of a complex nature, mostly because of the many different kinds of courts under ducal, ecclesiastical and town authority. The nobility claimed to be subject in their territory only to the sovereign; the lower strata of society also attempted to escape from local justice and carry their trials to the ducal court. In 1493 a common supreme court for the two Saxonies was estab-

77 R. Zieschang, *Die Anfänge eines landesherrlichen Kirchenregiments in Sachsen am Ausgange des Mittelalters* (Leipzig, 1909).
78 Müller, *RTTh. unter Max.*, I, II. Vorst., chap. xxxxii.
79 Burckhardt, *Ernestinische Landtagsaakte*, p. 60.
80 W. Goerlitz, *Staat und Stände*, pp. 193ff.

lished,[81] located sometimes in Leipzig and sometimes in Altenburg, with members appointed from both Saxonies. In addition, there were ducal courts in Weimar and Coburg, and later in Wittenberg. Many complaints were made against the system of justice, some of the estates even demanding the abolition of the supreme court. This Elector Frederick rejected, since he wanted an independent judicial system. In fact, during his lifetime no major revisions or reforms were made in this area.

Although trade and banking were not as highly developed as in southern and western Germany, the economic life of both Saxonies was largely dependent on mining and the mints. Both Wettin lines shared the mines, the silver of which was mostly used for minting. In view of this common ownership and the general interlocking of economic affairs, the two Saxonies needed a unified monetary policy. A major goal was to keep foreign money out of their territories because it was mostly inferior to the Saxon currency. Yet in spite of regulations with respect to exchange, devaluation and curbs on minting, many monetary problems remained unsolved.

The wealth of the silver, copper, iron and even gold mines of the Schneeberg and Annaberg largely determined the output of local industry. Pottery was also extensively manufactured throughout the state, chiefly in Waldenburg, Zeitz, Penig and Schmiedeberg. Frederick was interested in the development of the linen industry that had a good start in Chemnitz and Zwickau. He imported weavers from the Netherlands and new weaving industries sprang up in Gotha, Zwickau, Grimma and Arnstadt. The finished material found an excellent market at the Leipzig Fairs each year.

All manufacturing and industry was subject to regulations and taxation, but no systematic trade policy had as yet developed. The many local customs barriers and, especially, the bad conditions of the roads made trade still very hazardous. Like other territorial rulers the Saxon princes took refuge in protective tariffs to shield their industry against the competitive influx of goods from other territories.

The major benefactors if not the initiators of the growth of trade and industry were, of course, the burghers of the cities. In the larger towns, like Naumburg, Zwickau, Altenburg, Gotha and Eisenach a self-conscious bourgeoisie developed which sought better education and was ready to receive new ideas. Frederick protected these cities with all their rights since he realized their value to his land.

From the above description one might conclude that the treasury of Electoral Saxony must have been full. Yet, the contrary is true: Frederick was continually in financial difficulties, and there was never enough money to pay for current expenses; new taxes had to be imposed and new sources of revenue had continuously to be explored. The cost of living had become higher than ever; the simplicity of courtly life in Saxony had come to an end; and a new style of life, more akin to renaissance court life, was introduced.

Frederick's real concern was with those enterprises that were directed toward elevating the cultural life of Saxony and he did not hesitate to spend lavishly and generously for that purpose. Frederick relentlessly devoted time, money and energy to the projects really dear to him, such as the University at Wittenberg, the collecting of books, the many castles and churches — some of which he had built

81 *Ibid.*, p. 184.

and adorned by the foremost artists of his time. He shied away from no costs and labors when he saw an opportunity to attract able and interesting men who would assist him in his many cultural interests — historiographic, educational, aesthetic and religious. And the center of these cultural activities became the elector's capital: Wittenberg.

CHAPTER III

THE BEGINNINGS OF HUMANISM AND THE
FOUNDING OF THE UNIVERSITY OF WITTENBERG

Any account of humanistic activities in Wittenberg must center upon Frederick's highly significant contribution to its scholarly and cultural life: the founding of a university in 1502.

Little is known of Wittenberg in the early Middle Ages; indeed, it seems probable that the town itself did not emerge until the twelfth century.[1] It was founded on the German frontier – far from the Mediterranean world and the more cultured parts of west and south Germany where centuries of tradition prevailed. Even Luther felt that Wittenberg was still *in termino civilitatis*; had it been founded a little more to the East, it would have been *in mediam barbariam.*[2]

It was in the second part of the twelfth century that Albrecht the Bear destroyed the Wend population (the Sorbs) that had settled in the Middle Elbe region, thus eradicating most Slavic elements from this territory. Eager to repopulate it, he called on Rhenish and Flemish colonists, who came to start a new life in this region. One of their settlements was Wittenberg, which was built as a frontier town and bulwark against the Slavs. Most likely it was also the new Flemish immigrants who gave the town its name: the Low-German form of *Weissenburg* or *Weissenberg*, the *weiss* deriving from the white sand of the Elbe River and the *berg* or *burg* from the hills of the town. In trying to explain the transformation of the modest hills to mountains, Schwiebert writes: ' . . . to the Flemisch settlers, recalling the flat lands of their native home, this sandy hill seemed like an actual mountain.[3]

Various Greek, Latin and hybrid translations and transformations for the name 'Wittenberg' appear in numerous texts.[4] Wittenberg became *Albiburgium* in Petrus of Ravenna's *Clypeus doctoris Petri Rauennati contra doctorem Caium impugnantem suum consilium*; or *Albioris*, as in the verse of the same author on the

---

1 Cf. A. M. Meyner, *Geschichte der Stadt Wittenberg* (Dessau, 1845), pp. 5ff, where all the possible hypotheses as to the origin of Wittenberg are given; G. Stier, *Wittenberg im Mittelalter;* Übersicht der Geschichte der Stadt von ihrem Ursprung bis zum Tode Friedrichs des Weisen (Wittenberg, 1855).

2 *WATR*, II, no. 2800b; *WATR*, III, no. 3433.

3 Ernest G. Schwiebert, *Luther and his times;* the Reformation from a new perspective (St. Louis, Mo., 1950). Other attempts to explain the origins of the name go back to the Saxon duke Wittekind, and an allegorical interpretation of the Reformation era refers to the 'Mountain of Wisdom', p.199. das von diesem Wissenberg die recht weissheyt in all welt solte ausgestrewet werden." Cf. J. Mathesius, *Ausgewählte Werke*, ed. G. Loesche, (Prague, 1906: Bibliothek deutscher Schriftsteller aus Böhmen, 6), II, 405, 411; cf. also J. C. A. Grohmann, *Annalen der Universität Wittenberg* (2 vols., Meissen, 1801), I, 10.

4 C. G. Brandis, *Beiträge aus der Universitätsbibliothek zu Jena . . .* (Jena, 1917: Zeitschrift des Vereins für Thüringische Geschichte und Altertumskunde, Neue Folge, Beiheft 8), pp. 24–26.

title-page of his *Compendium Iuriscanonici*.[5] The same version of the name is used in the book by Tartaretus that Wolfgang Stöckel printed in 1504. Other instances of Latinizing the name Wittenberg occur in Georgius Sibutus' *Silvula in Albiorim illustratam*, Meinhardi's *Dialogus* and the *Album Academiae Vitebergensis*, and Chilian Reuter's dedication for his edition of Aristotle's *De Anima* reads 'Amplissimis viris dominis Albiorensis studii Reformatoribus' and is dated 'In Albiori Anno 1509'.

The purely Greek name *Leucorium* is less frequent. Tileman Conradi used the Greek version in his *Teratologia* and in his translation of the pseudo-Homeric *Batrachomyomachia*. Brandis mentions the interesting fact that in a prologue to a performance of Plautus' *Captivi* in 1553 in Torgau, Paul Eber, the poet of the prologue, makes the sisters Argelia and Leucoris the representatives of Torgau and Wittenberg and the father *Albis pater*.[6]

The most awkward version of the name of Wittenberg was invented by the so-called poet Henricus Aquilonipolensis. In his *Sophologia* he called Wittenberg *Albiberospolitana*, somewhat loosely referring to Albis (Elbe) and polis (town).

Of the various names used by the humanists for Wittenberg, none became standard; probably the most used was *Albioris* and its derivatives. *Leucopolis*, though occasionally used, remained an exception, as the 'polis' version found fewer admirers than the form in which the second part of the name, the 'berg' was retained. This association led even to such phantasies as the title-drawing to the *Wittenberg Heiligtumsbuch*, which shows Elector Frederick and Duke Johann against a background of mountains, supposedly sketching Wittenberg's surroundings. The fullest attempt to give a humanist connotation to the name of Wittenberg was made by Georgius Sibutus in his *Silvula in Albiorim illustratam* when he wrote: 'Albiorim dicunt, nomen quod fertur ab amne ... Mons illic candens, illic et cernitur Albis, qui gemino nitidos perstringit flumine muros. Dictus abui tot tractu perlabitur Albis, Illic pons forti perdurat plurimus arcu'.[7]

The town of Wittenberg is first mentioned in a document of 1180.[8] In 1181 Bernhard of Ascania, a son of Albrecht the Bear, took up residence in Wittenberg, where he founded the castle and its church. A century later Albrecht II granted town privileges to Wittenberg, whereby it became a self-governing community with a mayor and council. These privileges extended to Wittenberg the right of navigation, free of customs duties, on the Elbe. These and other legal and financial privileges account for much of the town's later prosperity. As the town grew in size, a system of fortifications was developed around its dwellings by means of a wall with three gates: the Elbtor, the Schlosstor and the Elstertor.

Wittenberg gained in importance when it became the permanent residence of the electors of Saxony. Albrecht I founded the Franciscan convent there in 1328 and in 1353 Rudolf I founded the *Allerheiligenstift*.[9] In 1364 the establishment of the

5 T. Muther, *Aus dem Universitäts- und Gelehrtenleben im Zeitalter der Reformation* (Erlangen, 1866), p. 379.
6 Brandis, *Beiträge*, p. 26.
7 *Ibid.*
8 Cf. Friedensburg, *Geschichte*, p. 4.
9 F. Israel, *Das Wittenberger Universitätsarchiv, seine Geschichte und seine Bestände* (Halle, 1913: Forschungen zur Thüringisch-Sächsischen Geschichte, 4), pp. 28–30.

monastic house of the Augustinian Hermits at the Elstertor is recorded, at that time a very modest and unassuming institution.

When the line of the Ascanian electors died out in 1422 and the Margrave of Meissen, Frederick the Valiant, was invested with the electorate, the town of Wittenberg declined again in importance. The Wettin electors resided mostly in Altenburg or Weimar, the towns of their ancestral lands. However, Wittenberg was still the largest town in electoral Saxony and when Frederick the Wise became elector in 1486, he again made it the center of his domain.

I

Wittenberg did not play a significant role in the intellectual life of Germany before the foundation of its university. Yet by the end of the fifteenth century we detect in the Elbe region intellectual activities that were stimulated by the very same humanists who later participated in establishing the University of Wittenberg, members of two literary sodalities.[10] The *Sodalitas Polychiana*, named after its most important member, Martin Polich von Mellerstadt, probably had its seat at Leipzig, where Mellerstadt was then teaching. He later assisted Frederick the Wise with the founding of the university in Wittenberg. Of the other society, the *Sodalitas Leucopolitana* we know only that it is mentioned together with the *sodalitates Rhenana* and *Danubiana* in Mellerstadt's *Laconismos*.[11] He refers also to Matthäus Lupinus, who then lived in Leipzig and was the teacher of Johann Cuspinian, as a member of the *Leucopolitana*, and to Bohuslaus Lobkowitz von Hassenstein, the famous Bohemian humanist and friend of Mellerstadt, as its president.[12] As to the date when the *Leucopolitana* flourished, one can at least conclude that it must have been previous to the writing of Mellerstadt's *Laconismos* early in 1502. Brandis is of the opinion that, like other sodalities of the time, it was named after a geographical location – the region of electoral Saxony – rather than a specific town; that the sodality was named for, but not limited to the capital city of Wittenberg where the resident prince was sympathetic towards humanism. Celtis once conceived of seven sodalities and included in his list the sodality *Albinus Luneburgensis*. Since *Albis* certainly refers to the river Elbe and *Luneburgensis* is obviously a latinization of Luneburg, Brandis is probably correct in assuming that this sodality is identical with the *Leucopolitana*.[13] There were at least two literary societies in existence at that time in the Elbe region.

Fortunately it is possible to follow the career of at least one nobleman who belonged to the *Leucopolitana* and was one of the earliest advisors and friends of Frederick the Wise. How many scholars and gentlemen like 'Heinrich von Bünau zu Teuchern mit den Stelzen'[14] there were at this time in Saxony we do not know; to speak of him as a representative of a group would be rash. Yet there is no

---

10 Cf. Brandis' essay 'Sodalitas Polychiana und Sodalitas Leucopolitana', in his *Beiträge*, pp. 12–24.
11 Cf. Bauch, *Leipziger Frühhumanismus*, p. 114.
12 *Ibid.*, p. 137.
13 Cf. Spitz, *Religious Renaissance*, p. 58; Brandis, *Beiträge*, p. 23.
14 Spalatin, p. 34.

reason to feel that he was unique in his humanistic interests, which he pursued with great ardor and certainly with the approbation of his prince.

Heinrich von Bünau, a native of Saxony, studied in Erfurt in 1476, moved on to Leipzig University where he received his B.A. in 1480 and then studied law; later on he also matriculated at Ingolstadt. After Bünau finished his studies, Frederick made him his secretary and advisor. He went with Frederick to the Holy Land[15] and was among Frederick's advisors at the Diet of Worms. It was there that he suffered an accident while horseback riding which made Bünau a cripple for life.[16] While he was recuperating in Worms, he came in contact with the Rhenish humanists, especially Conrad Celtis and Johann von Dalberg, Bishop of Worms and chancellor of the Palatinate. He used this enforced leisure to pursue his studies and literary interests; when Celtis invited Bünau to become a member of the *Sodalitas literaria Rhenana*[17] that he started in Heidelberg, in 1495, Bünau declined with regret; his accident prevented his joining their humanistic circle. He did however ask Celtis for a Greek grammar and seriously undertook the study of Greek.[18] When Bünau was well enough to travel, he joined the members of the sodality in a visit to Sponheim where the famous abbot Trithemius had assembled a magnificent library.[19] A close friendship developed between the abbot and Bünau, and in 1496 Trithemius dedicated to Bünau his edition of Jason Alpheus Ursinus' *Melpomenecon.* Under the influence of the Rhenish sodality Bünau also became interested in astronomy and mathematics and acquired a cosmographical globe which he took to Saxony.

Upon his return there he resumed his active service for the elector and accompanied him to the Diet of Freiburg in 1498. He used the occasion for a short trip to Basel where he visited Sebastian Brant who dedicated to him his treatise *De Anticipatione Horologii Basiliensium.* In the following years Bünau was again active at the Diets of Cologne and Worms on behalf of the Saxon elector. In 1501 he went with Frederick to the Diet of Nürnberg, active as his representative after the elector's return home. In this capacity he signed the imperial recess. He was joined in Nürnberg by Celtis, Johann von Dalberg and other members of the *Sodalitas literaria*; it was at this meeting that they published the famous work of Hrosvitha which they dedicated to Frederick the Wise.[20]

We know little of Bünau during his last years. In 1505 Petrus of Ravenna added to his *Sermones Extraordinarii* several dedications, one of them to Heinrich von Bünau, whom he praises as Frederick's most illustrious counselor but intimates that he was in bad health. Vincentius of Ravenna, son of Petrus, praised Bünau in a speech dedicated to Frederick the Wise, in which he called him the most important member of Frederick's entourage, better educated and more erudite than anybody he knew. Bünau probably died in 1506; Trithemius in 1507 referred to

15 *Ibid.*, 90.
16 Cf. G. Bauch, "Der sächsische Rat und Humanist Heinrich von Bünau, Herr in Teuchern', *NASG*, 26 (1905), 41–62.
17 *Der Briefwechsel des Konrad Celtis*, ed. Hans Rupprich (Munich, 1934: Veröffentlichungen der Kommission zur Erforschung der Geschichte der Reformation und Gegenreformation, Humanistenbriefe, III), p. 164.
18 Celtis, *Briefwechsel*, p. 181.
19 Johannes Trithemius, *Opera historica* (2 vols., Frankfurt, 1601), II, 408.
20 "sub priuilegio sodalitatis Celticae".

the 'doctissimus orator' of the Saxon elector[21] and asked Frederick to return some books to him that Bünau had borrowed.[22] Bünau's intellectual endeavors had brought him in contact with the great centers of humanism in Germany where he was welcomed as nobleman and as diplomat.

Although information concerning members and activities of these literary societies is scant, their very existence and composition is evidence that there was in the Elbe region a community of humanists to prepare the ground for further humanistic studies and enterprises.

Many explanations for the establishment of the University of Wittenberg at this particular time have been ventured, but all agree that an important factor was Frederick the Wise's desire to provide for his land an institution of learning that would enhance the cultural life of Wittenberg and the Saxon electorate.

After the Leipzig partition electoral Saxony was without a university, since Leipzig with its university was apportioned to the Albertine Line. As early as 1493 Frederick the Wise was apparently considering the plan for a university in his lands. In a will drawn up at Torgau before embarking on his journey to the Holy Land, he established six scholarships for poor students, to be used at Erfurt or Leipzig, until a university should be established in his own lands.[23] Thus he anticipated by two years Maximilian's recommendation that each elector should have a university in his territory.[24] Since all other electorates had their universities, this could only apply to electoral Saxony and Brandenburg and in fact both these territories established universities within their realms a few years later: Saxony in 1502 and Brandenburg in 1506. Whether or not Maximilian actually ever expressed this wish, his contemporaries considered it plausible that he might have done so — thereby implying that they associated the furthering of arts and sciences with the dignity and obligations of an electorate.

Choice of a site for the new university fell on Wittenberg, the capital of electoral Saxony and by far its largest town. At that time most of the German universities were situated in the south-western part of the country — Mainz, Cologne, Heidelberg, Tübingen, Freiburg, Basel, Ingolstadt and Vienna. In the north, by contrast, there were only two universities: Rostock and Greifswald. Between these and the universities at Erfurt and Leipzig, in the central part of Germany, stretched a wide territory devoid of any institution of higher learning. This vacuum was now, in the beginning of the sixteenth century, filled by the founding of two new universities, one in Wittenberg and the other in Frankfurt a.d. Oder.

Since this new center of learning would form a vital part of the cultural life of Wittenberg, a thorough examination of the new humanistic spirit at work there during the years of the founding of the university is central to an assessment of the influence of the new movement — its nature and its scope.[25]

21 Trithemius, *Opera historica*, II, 559.
22 *Ibid.*, 518.
23 Grohmann, *Annalen*, I, 4, 63.
24 Müller, *RTTh. unter Max.*, vol. I, II, Vorst. chap. xxxxv; Grohmann, *Annalen*, I, 6.
25 In addition to Friedensburg's excellent *Geschichte*, see also the first volume of the *Festschrift* of the Martin-Luther-Universität Halle-Wittenberg, devoted exclusively to the history of the University of Wittenberg; the essays offer much valuable material and interesting interpretations: *450 Jahre Martin-Luther-Universität Halle-Wittenberg*, I: Wittenberg, 1501–1817 (Halle, 1952).

40

The German universities had been created by territorial rulers, in contrast to the Italian universities founded by the emperor. By custom only a papal *privilegium* made the act valid; imperial approval was granted afterwards. Thus the ecclesiastical character of the universities was assumed and not even the emperor objected. Frederick the Wise, however, although a devout son of the church, did not first approach the Pope, but asked the Emperor for permission to establish a university in his territory. Maximilian responded favorably and sent a charter letter, dated July 6, 1502.[26] Only after the opening of the university did Frederick ask the ecclesiastical authorities for approval which was granted in due course.[27] The procedure chosen by Frederick for founding the university was thus no longer the traditional medieval one, resting on the concept of a universal Christian Empire of the German nation. It rested rather on a new view of the territorial state, seen as an independent entity not yet in conflict with the church authorities but developing a new will and strength of its own, and destined to destroy the idea of a unity represented by church and emperor. Frederick's action, though certainly not consciously based on these presuppositions, just as certainly reflects a new attitude of territorial rulers already anticipating the waning of the empire.

Wittenberg thus became the first German university founded without the permission of ecclesiastical authorities and hence without recourse to the traditional benefices. In the early years Frederick therefore had to find most of the funds for the university in his own treasury. It was not till 1507, when the Pope granted special privileges, that the income from All Saints Church could be used for the purpose of the university. This obviously had important implications for the future relationship with ecclesiastical authority. In addition, the chancellors of the medieval universities had been the representatives of the ecclesiastical authorities; most were the bishops or archbishops in whose territories the universities were located; the Bishop of Merseburg for Leipzig, the Bishop of Lebus for Frankfurt a.d. Oder, the Archbishop of Mainz for Erfurt, to mention a few. In Wittenberg, however, the chancellor was a minor ecclesiastical officer, Goswin of Orsoy, *praeceptor* of the Antonines, at Lichtenberg. He never gained much influence, most of his duties in the period 1502–1513 being taken over by Martin Polich von Mellerstadt, the vice-chancellor, who became one of the most influential men in the university. As ecclesiastical authorities progressively lost their absolute power over the universities, the territorial rulers, whether consciously or not, were asserting their new-found rights.

The foundation document confirms the establishment of an institution of higher learning in Wittenberg with all the rights and privileges accorded to the older universities of the empire. It entitled the new establishment to provide for the

26 Cf. *Urkundenbuch der Universität Wittenberg*, ed. W. Friendensburg, I, 1502–1611 (Magdeburg, 1926: Geschichtsquellen der Provinz Sachsen und des Freistaates Anhalt, Neue Reihe, 3), 1–3. Israel, *Wittenberger Universitätsarchiv*, pp. 96–99; A. Blaschka, "Der Stiftsbrief Maximilians I und das Patent Friedrichs des Weisen zur 'Gründung der Wittenberger Universität" In: *450 Jahre Martin-Luther-Universität*, pp. 72–80, where a facsimile of the document is given.
27 Ecclesiastical approval was sought and received in 1503 by Cardinal Raymund, Bishop of Gurk, apostolic legate for Germany; the Pope gave his approval in 1507. Friedensburg, *Urkundenbuch*, no. 4. Israel, *Wittenberger Universitätsarchiv*, no. 3 (Anhang II).

study of the *scientiae, bonae artes* and *studia liberalia*; included in the stated privileges of the university is the right to teach sacred theology. The right of the secular authority to grant permission for the teaching of theology was later discussed by Petrus of Ravenna, one of the first personalities with humanistic inclinations who came to the new university. In his oration of 1503 *De potestate pontificis* he asserted that the emperor is empowered to establish universities and to extend to them the right to teach theology and canon law without ecclesiastical approval. Petrus' pronouncements, made at the university a few months after its opening, certainly touched a vital issue for the university community and re-enforced Frederick's procedure in having founded his university without papal sanction.

On August 24, 1502, Frederick, together with his co-regent brother Johann, issued from Weimar a letter of invitation to the formal opening of the University of Wittenberg for October 18, 1502.[28] The letter was written in German, which was unusual for its time. The first official statement also announces that at the new university, besides the traditional subjects, *humaniora* will be taught.[29]

On the appointed date the University of Wittenberg was formally opened with great celebration. In the electoral castle Hermann von dem Busche, the 'poet', welcomed the people to the university. After mass at the church, formal exercises were begun and the rector, chancellor and deans were elected.

It has often been argued[30] that the University of Wittenberg was not different from other universities of that age; that its constitution, its statutes, its actual government were conservative and that no new ideas were incorporated; and that it was not until Luther's and Melanchthon's times that changes occurred. The documents pertaining to the foundation of the university and its statutes as published by Friedensburg, support the verdict that its forms and structure were patterned after its predecessors. Yet those who have observed only the traditional late medieval patterns up to the year 1517 have overlooked the fact that at Wittenberg there was from the beginning no hostility toward humanism. At most universities teachers of the *humaniora* could be found, employed for the most part only privately or temporarily, and only slowly being accepted on a permanent basis. But in the new university at Wittenberg, where the *humaniora* played an important role from the beginning, the teachers too gained recognition early.[31]

Among the major figures in the early life of the university were Martin Polich von Mellerstadt, its first rector, and Johann von Staupitz, the first dean of the faculty of theology. Mellerstadt, a native of Mellrichstadt in Lower Franconia, came to the University of Leipzig in 1470, receiving his B.A. in 1472 and his M.A. in 1475–76. He lectured there on Aristotle's *Organon* in strictly Thomistic

---

28 Friedensburg, *Urkundenbuch*, no. 2; Israel, *Wittenberger Universitätsarchiv*, no. 2 (Anhang II).
29. '. . . poeterei und andern künsten'.
30 Cf. K. Aland, 'Die theologische Fakultät Wittenberg und ihre Stellung im Gesamtzusammenhang der Leucorea während des 16. Jahrhunderts', in: *450 Jahre Martin-Luther-Universität*, pp. 162ff.
31 Cf. Herbert Schöffler, *Wirkungen der Reformation*; religionssoziologische Folgerungen für England und Deutschland, (Frankfurt, 1960), pp. 121ff., where he points out that one of the reasons for the acceptance of humanism in Wittenberg was that Wittenberg was without medieval tradition and had a very young faculty which was receptive to the new ideas.

fashion, yet he also devoted much time to the study of medicine and astronomy. In 1482 his reputation in the field of medicine secured him the position of personal physician to Frederick the Wise. In 1493 Mellerstadt accompanied the elector to the Holy Land, and from then on never left Frederick's service.

According to a legendary story which arose in the sixteenth century, the new universities of Wittenberg and Frankfurt a.d. Oder were founded as a result of the quarrel at Leipzig between Frederick's physician and Simon Pistoris, the physician of Johann Cicero of Brandenburg, concerning the *malum francum* or *morbus gallicus* as syphilis was called.[32]

Mellerstadt, while studying astronomy, had also taken an interest in astrology. In the 1490's he came in close contact with some early humanists, with Conrad Celtis and Bohuslaw von Hassenstein, and was a member of their sodalities. He had gradually freed himself of the concepts of astrology and came to the conclusion that the diseases of man cannot find their explanations in the stars.[33] The *Libellus de Epidimia* of the Italian humanist physician Nicolo Leoniceno,[34] who preferred the Greek and Roman physicians to those of the Arabs, impressed Mellerstadt greatly, and he publicly lectured on this work. This brought upon him the wrath of the conservative professor Simon Pistoris, who lectured against Leoniceno and attacked Mellerstadt in a treatise.[35] Thus began the first part of a feud that lasted for three years (1498–1501) and was waged with great animosity on both sides. Mellerstadt, as the representative of reason against astrology and superstition, finally defeated his opponent. However, the faculty at Leipzig was unwilling to accept Mellerstadt's scientific proposition and stood firmly with the defeated contestant, while both men continued to publish their violent reactions to each other's writings.

There now arose a new controversy on the relative positions of poetry and theology — which shows even more strongly how humanistic issues began to occupy scholars and theologians. In this instance Mellerstadt suspected his former colleague and friend Konrad Wimpina, professor of theology at Leipzig, of having written some of Pistoris' arguments in the earlier controversy and of having led the opposition. The new uproar began with two pamphlets by Wimpina in which he attacked humanism in all its manifestations, and especially a certain humanist who claimed the superiority of the art of poetry over sacred theology. Mellerstadt, convinced that the accusations were directed against himself,[36] answered with a violent treatise, the *Laconismos*. He contended that he never thought of putting poetry over and above sacred theology and that such accusations served only one purpose: to discourage humanistic studies altogether.[37] Mellerstadt had a violent

---

32 Bauch, *Leipziger Frühhumanismus, passim.*
33 The materials for these controversies have been collected by C. H. Fuchs, *Die ältesten Schriftsteller über die Lustseuche in Deutschland von 1495 bis 1510.* (Göttingen, 1843). Concerning this particular controversy between Simon Pistoris and Martin Mellerstadt, cf. pp. 27–288.
34 Concerning Leoniceno cf. *Enciclopedia Italiana,* XX, 912.
35 Cf. Fuchs, *Schriftsteller über Lustseuche,* 127.
36 It seems certain that Wimpina actually attacked Sigismund Buchwald, (or Fagilicus), a young Leipzig humanist. Cf. Friedensburg, *Geschichte,* p. 11; and G. Bauch in *NASG* 18 (1897), 293.
37 Bauch, *Leipziger Frühhumanismus,* p. 115.

temper (Scheurl once called him *delirus senex* and *tyranni litterarii*)[38] and made use of common and coarse language without inhibition; his method of argumentation, abstruse and arbitrary, relied on misinterpreted Aristotelian categories; he included some classical references and made use of quotations from Picus de la Mirandola. Answers and counter-answers in this literary feud continued after Mellerstadt moved to Wittenberg, where he became the university's first rector. Both the university and the elector stood firmly behind him; the degree of doctor of theology was awarded to him in 1503, an honor which shortly before had been bestowed upon Wimpina in Leipzig. When Wimpina went so far as to attack the University of Wittenberg, Frederick felt offended by this foremost representative of Leipzig. Both Saxonies were becoming tired of a fight which only damaged the prestige of their respective universities, and negotiations to end it were initiated in 1504. Archbishop Ernst of Magdeburg, Staupitz and Goswin of Orsoy, the chancellor of Wittenberg, who were acting as mediators, asked both Mellerstadt and Wimpina to discontinue their writings.

In his controversies at Leipzig Mellerstadt had represented the forward-looking forces. His point of view is typical for this age as he tried to combine scholasticism, which already was on the defensive, and humanism, which was on the rise. Mellerstadt was acquainted with the classical authors, as can be seen from his writings, and he himself wrote Latin poetry. In his way of thinking and methods of argumentation he shows himself far removed from the early humanists. But when the University of Wittenberg was founded in 1502 he seemed to champion the new forces, eager for more knowledge in all spheres of life and willing to bring more representatives of the new learning to Wittenberg.

During the early years of the university, Johann von Staupitz was in large measure responsible for its organization and served as first dean of the faculty of theology. Though Staupitz was not a humanist and hardly interested in humanism's program, no other person in these first years of the university did more to create an atmosphere in which free expression of individual beliefs and ideas, however controversial, became possible. Staupitz was a member of an old Saxon noble family. Almost nothing is known about his youth and early schooling; the first definitive information we have about him is that in 1497 he joined the Augustinian convent in Tübingen to study theology at the university there and that he received his doctorate of theology in 1500. Staupitz was then transferred to Munich where he became prior of the Augustinian convent. From there Frederick the Wise called him to the university, and entrusted him with its formal organization. It is therefore natural that the statutes of Wittenberg University repeat almost word for word those of Tübingen. Staupitz brought many scholars from Tübingen to Wittenberg; among them Sigismund Epp, the first dean of the faculty of arts, Wolfgang Stähelin, the first dean of the law faculty and the jurists Ambrosius Volland and Hieronymus Schurff. Staupitz' teaching career at Wittenberg was short. In 1503 he became Vicar-General of the Augustinian Hermits in Germany, interrupting his teaching on several occasions to undertake journeys in the interest of his order. He managed a longer stay in Wittenberg between the

---

38 C. Scheurl, *Briefbuch*, ed. F. v. Soden and J. K. F. Knaake (2 vols., Potsdam, 1867–1872), I, no. 48.

years 1508 and 1511, when he resigned his teaching position and went to Southern Germany. During his general vicariat the connections between his order and the university were maintained, with more than one hundred Augustinians being matriculated and seventeen becoming members of the teaching staff at Wittenberg,

When we examine the first known work by Staupitz, the *Decisio questionis de audientia misse in parochiali ecclesia dominicis et festivis diebus*, we find that he uses the language of scholasticism and quotes extensively from Scotus, Bonaventura, Biel and other scholastic writers. New, however, are his evaluation of human merit, which he makes solely dependent on God's grace, and his concept of the Christian conscience; he emphasizes the right of choice but does not yet draw the conclusion that soon led others to the new evangelical idea of Christian freedom. Like the later reformers, Staupitz was already deeply influenced by the mystical writings of Suso, Tauler and Ruisbroeck. He defended contemplation against speculation, he believed in silence and waiting and in complete union with, and in, God. His giving up oneself completely to the divine is not meant metaphysically but ethically as the complete giving of oneself to the *Logos*.

Staupitz was not a conservative, Thomistic theologian who wrote expository treatises on Aristotelian philosophy and fought the battles of the scholastics over Scotism, Thomism and Nominalism. His concerns were more for this world and, like the mystic, he found his motivation in inwardly directed religion. Christianity for him was a way of life; this may have been not the least of the reasons why Luther was so much drawn to him. Even when Staupitz later turned away from the reform movement, Luther attempted to convince his friend that their theological views were so similar that they should not stand apart. But Staupitz, who originally had brought Luther to the University of Wittenberg and had made him his successor in his theological chair in 1511, was too much of a quietistic theologian to accept the excesses and violence of the Lutheran movement. He did not have the zeal of a reformer and he disliked the outbursts of individual self-righteousness and unrestrained factionalism. He did not care for the outward signs either of the Catholic church or of Lutheranism, he felt that the Christian lot was the *imitatio Christi*. In his later years Staupitz was suspected by the Catholic church of heresy; his works were burned and put on the Index from which they were not removed until the nineteenth century.

Like Staupitz, Frederick the Wise remained to the end of his life within the old forms of worship; his religion was not an outward religion, but an inner, intuitive belief and trust in God. It may be that the similar attitudes towards religious issues which Frederick the Wise and Staupitz shared, may well have strengthened their bond of sympathy and made it possible for them to work together congenially for several years.

In summary, then, the University of Wittenberg, organized along the old conservative lines, did not differ radically from other institutions in Germany. Frederick the Wise certainly did not intend his new center of learning to become a rallying-point for men opposed to the scholastic and religious traditions. Yet, for all the traditional structure, a number of signs point towards the dawn of a new era. Frederick, in founding the university without ecclesiastical approval, depended only on secular authority. In the foundation document the *humaniora* are listed as a subject to be taught at the new university. Frederick's main advisor in university matters, Martin Polich von Mellerstadt, who had left Leipzig in protest against the dominating adherents of scholasticism, favored the new learning. And Staupitz, the most influential man in the religious field, was not a spokesman for the old medieval tradition, but was concerned with the reform of the church and favored modes of piety that allowed for individual liberty in religious matters.

II

When Mellerstadt moved from Leipzig to the newly established University of Wittenberg, he brought with him his good friend Hermann von dem Busche.[39] This humanist, the first lecturer in the humanities at Wittenberg, was appointed to give the inaugural address in the presence of the city council at the opening celebrations.[40] Busche was born in 1468 in Westphalia, had started his studies early, first at Deventer with Alexander Hegius and then at Heidelberg with Rudolf Agricola and Rudolf von Langen.[41] When Agricola died, Busche, upon Langen's advice, went to Italy in 1486 and spent the following five years there. He learned excellent Latin and developed great enthusiasm for the country. He published two books of epigrams, dedicated to Hegius, in which he speaks of Italy and of the new learning and thanks his teacher for all he had taught him.[42] On his return to Germany he became the first itinerant teacher of humanism and travelled all over northern and western Germany. In 1501 he went to Rostock and got involved in a literary controversy with Tilman Heuerling, who disliked the new learning and its spokesmen.[43] Busche was forced to leave and went to Leipzig, arriving there in the middle of the Mellerstadt-Pistoris-Wimpina controversy. He sided with Mellerstadt and published an open letter which actually ran into a short essay on the new learning,[44] praising Mellerstadt's *Laconismos* for its views on the relation of poetry to theology.[45]

39 No modern study on Busche has been written. The first study of Busche is by Hermann Hammelmann, *De vita, studiis, itineribus, scriptis et laboribus Hermanni Buschii . . .* 1583; published in Hermann Hammelmanns *Geschichtliche Werke*, ed. Heinrich Detmer (3 vols., Münster, 1908–1940; vols. 1 and 2: Veröffentlichungen der Historischen Kommission der Provinz Westfalen; vol. 3: Veröffentlichungen der Historischen Kommission des Provinzial-instituts für Westfälische Landes- und Volkskunde), vol. 1, Heft 2, 35–112. H. J. Liessem published his *De Hermanni Buschii vita et scriptis commentatio historica* in 1866 and his *Hermann von dem Busche, sein Leben und seine Schriften* in 1884, which unfortunately carries Busche's life only to his Cologne time. Liessem also compiled a careful bibliography of the works of Busche: *Bibliographisches Verzeichnis der Schriften Hermanns von dem Busche* (Cologne, 1887–1889, 1905–1908: Programm des Kaiser Wilhelm-Gymnasiums in Köln). For an appreciation of Busche from the literary point of view, cf. the excellent exposition in Georg Ellinger, *Geschichte der neulateinischen Literatur Deutschlands im sechzehnten Jahrhundert* (3 vols., Berlin, 1929-1933), I (*Italien und der deutsche Humanismus in der neulateinischen Lyrik*), 421-427.
40 Cf. *Album*, p. 2; and *Liber Decanorum Facultatis Theologicae Academiae Vitebergensis*, ed. C. A. Foerstemann (Leipzig, 1838), p. 2.
41 Cf. *Allgemeine Deutsche Biographie*, XVII, 659 ff.
42 Cf. Liessem, *Hermann von dem Busche*, p. 2.
43 *Ibid.*, p. 10.
44 Cf. Bauch, *Leipziger Frühhumanismus*, pp. 132ff.
45 *Ibid.*

For Busche the lectureship at Wittenberg was only a fleeting experience in his eventful life, for he remained only a few months. For Wittenberg it was significant that one of the foremost German humanists had given the opening lecture at the university and thus had told the world that this new place of learning would be a friend of the humanists. To his announcement of lectures on Ovid Busche added a *Praelectio*[46] in praise of the new movement in literature and poetry. He maintained, only the combined study of the seven disciplines with the new *humaniora* can lift man beyond his immediate circumstances and establish a well balanced human being worthy of being called man in the true sense. He urged the students to study rhetoric, history and philosophy because he believed that only men trained in these disciplines could be the true educators of the new generation; he reminded them of the Greek pedagogues who saw in the study of philosophy the only true education.

After these words of encouragement Busche moved on to Leipzig where, as in Wittenberg, he became the first professor of the *humaniora*; he stayed for three years, still keeping up his contact with Wittenberg colleagues and friends. Though he had had differences with Mellerstadt himself, he kept up his friendship with his son Wolfgang Polich and with Vincentius of Ravenna, the son of Petrus.[47] At this time he was also in touch with the Erfurt circle of Mutian including Eobanus Hessus, Euricius Cordus and Jakob Montanus.[48] He now studied philosophy with renewed vigor and, under the direct impact of Mutian's Christian philosophy, published selected works of Diogenes Laertius.[49] But in 1507 Busche left Leipzig and Saxony for his native Westphalia. His departure was later deplored as Johannes Rhagius Aesticampianus recalled in 1511, just before he himself had to leave Leipzig owing to the persisting hostility towards humanism.

At the very opening of the university Nikolaus Marschalk, another humanist, joined the faculty of the liberal arts.[50] A native of Thuringia, Marschalk was born around 1470; when he matriculated at the University of Erfurt in 1491, he had already earned his B.A. from the University of Louvain.[51] After receiving his M.A. from Erfurt in 1496, he continued to study law there. During these early years at Erfurt Marschalk benefited from the presence of Mutian. Marschalk soon began to lecture on the *humaniora*, probably also on law and became the first to promote Greek studies at Erfurt. Together with Wolfgang Schenck he printed several books which were to be the foundation for future humanistic studies at Erfurt. Among these was Martianus Felix Capella's *De Arte Grammatica* (1500) which started the open battle between the Erfurt humanists on the one side, the scholas-

---

46 Liessem, *Bibliographisches Verzeichnis*, no. 20.
47 For the correspondence between these friends, cf. Liessem, *Hermann van dem Busche*, pp. 11ff.
48 The influence of these contacts and experiences on Busche's works has been pointed out by Hamelmann, *Geschichtliche Werke* I, part 1, 62. Cf. Liessem, *Hermann von dem Busche*, p. 25.
49 Liessem, *Bibliographisches Verzeichnis*, no. 25.
50 The only life of Marschalk is by Christian Schoettgen, *Commentatio de vita N. Marschalci Thurii* (Rostock, 1752). Otherwise his contributions to the intellectual life of Erfurt, Wittenberg and Rostock have always been connected with his printing activities, which will be discussed, as far as they relate to Wittenberg, in chapter VI below.
51 Cf. Bauch, 'Die Anfänge des Studiums', p. 49.

tics on the other – as represented by the *Doctrinale* of Alexander de Villa Dei, the grammar which had dominated scholastic teachings since the beginning of the thirteenth century. In 1501 Marschalk printed two books which are considered the first Greek primers in Germany: his *Orthographia* of Latin and Greek, and in the same year his *Grammatica Exegetica* came from his press.[52] In contrast to the casuistic speculation of scholastic grammarians, Marschalk used concrete examples from classical texts to demonstrate syntax and orthography and the arts of narrative prose-writing, letter-writing and poetry. These smaller works were followed by an extensive anthology, *The Enchiridion Poetarum Clarissimorum* (1502), divided into four parts and including excerpts from Homer, Pindar, Hesiod, Caesar and Cicero and other Latin and Greek authors. While teaching at Erfurt, Marschalk gathered around him a group of young men on whom he made a lasting impression: among these were Spalatin and Trebelius, who would play an important role at Wittenberg; Johann Lang who was one of the first to teach Greek there, and later became the reformer of Erfurt; and Crotus Rubeanus and Carlstadt. Of all of Marschalk's students, only Carlstadt did not join the humanist camp in later years.

In the fall of 1502 Marschalk left Erfurt for Wittenberg to be one of the first to matriculate at the new university as 'Nicolaus Marscalcus Thurius arcium magister et utriusque iuris baccalaureus erfordiensis.'[53] He brought with him from Erfurt his press, and the first work he printed in Wittenberg was the first commencement speech which he himself delivered in 1503.[54] Marschalk taught *humaniora* at Wittenberg and at the same time studied law, receiving his degree of doctor of law in 1504. In the following year he left Wittenberg on account of disagreements with the more conservative members of the faculty. After some traveling he went to Rostock where he continued the pioneer work in humanistic studies he had started in Erfurt and Wittenberg. It was undoubtedly due to Marschalk's efforts that interest in Greek language and literature was fostered at Wittenberg from the very beginning, and that some study of Greek persisted in the years preceding the arrival of Melanchthon in 1518.

Marschalk's co-worker and pupil Hermann Trebelius, who had come from Erfurt with him, tried to continue his work.[55] Not only did Trebelius take over the printing press, but he also tried to continue the tutoring in Greek. He encouraged the growing interest in poetry among the students and himself contributed many dedicatory poems to the work of others, as was customary among humanists. Trebelius left Wittenberg in 1506 for his native Eisenach and from there went to the newly established university at Frankfurt a. d. Oder, where he likewise taught Greek and published poetry.

After Marschalk's time at Wittenberg, the study and teaching of Greek was carried on without interruption by Trebelius, Carlstadt, Tileman Conradi, Johann Lang, Johannes Rhagius Aesticampianus and finally Melanchthon. The

---

52 Cf. Panzer, *Annales*, VI, 494, no. 4; Proctor, *Index*, no. 11216. and Proctor, *Index*, no. 11229. Cf. O. Kluge, 'Die griechischen Studien in Renaissance und Humanismus', *Zeitschrift für Geschichte der Erziehung und des Unterrichts*, 24 (1934), p. 18.
53 *Album*, p. 1.
54 Panzer, *Annales*, IX, 65, 1; Proctor, *Index*, 11826.
55 Cf. *Album*, p. 4: 'Hermannus Trebelius de eysennach'.

interest at first was chiefly in classical Greek but later extended to the study of the *koine* as the basis for future biblical humanism.

Under the influence of its neighbor university in Erfurt, and especially of Marschalk's efforts, Wittenberg came at a relatively early date to include the study of Greek in its curriculum. In a letter written not later than 1508 Mutian reports that the canons at Gotha considered that he and his friends, Spalatin and Urbanus, were not pious men, since they were poets and spoke Greek.[56] Poetry, the Greek language and impiety — all were one to the pious colleagues of the great humanist. Greek was unknown to them, and therefore suspected and hated. Even Reuchlin, in 1518, wrote to Cardinal Adrian that, since many people claimed that the Greeks were schismatics, it would be heretical to study the Greek language and literature,[57] an argument that undoubtedly found its supporters. In his inaugural address at the University of Freiburg in 1521, Conrad von Heresbach related that he had heard a monk preach that one should be careful to avoid the newly invented language of the Greeks since it was the mother of all heresies. Moreover, he understood that a book in the Greek language, called the New Testament, had been widely distributed and that "it is full of thorns and snakes".[58] Even in 1531 Melanchthon protested that the study of Greek was not yet popular because in the extreme view, it was considered the most contemptible thing in the world.[59]

Two important influences fostering humanism in university circles can be discerned: one had its source in Leipzig, the other in Erfurt. A third — and probably the most important influence on early humanism in Wittenberg — was the influx of personalities most closely associated with Italian humanism. It was customary for jurists to go to Italy, especially to Bologna, to finish or supplement their studies before accepting positions with princes or universities in their native country. Among the early law professors at Wittenberg there were three who had had their training in Italy: Petrus of Ravenna, Johann von Kitzscher and Christoph Scheurl. These three had more than their profession in common: Petrus of Ravenna, an Italian, left his country for good and entered the service of Duke Bogislaw of Pomerania, the duke who also recruited Johann von Kitzscher for his University of Greifswald; both Petrus and Johann von Kitzscher later left Greifswald for Wittenberg. Christoph Scheurl and Johann von Kitzscher met first when both were studying and teaching in Bologna.

Thus a community of experience and interests can be presupposed among these three men, expressing itself most clearly in their nationalism: their stay in Italy and the influence of Italian nationalism evoked in them great pride for their native or adopted country. All three were invited to come to Wittenberg by elector Frederick who justly expected from this move a splendid addition to the cultural life of his capital. Petrus of Ravenna and Johann von Kitzscher were among the first to create a freer atmosphere at the university; and with Christoph Scheurl we enter upon a different period in its growth. After 1507 the humanistic influence had become a real force, espressing itself not only through individuals but in the

---

56 *Der Briefwechsel des Conradus Mutianus*, p. 930.
57 Cf. Johannes Reuchlin, *Briefwechsel*, ed. L. Geiger (Stüttgart, 1875: Bibliothek des Literarischen Vereins in Stuttgart, 126), p. 283.
58 Quoted by Kluge, 'Die griechischen Studien', p. 13.
59 *CR* II, p. 557.

curriculum of the university and its whole environment; and it was largely due to Christoph Scheurl that this fundamental change took place.

Petrus of Ravenna, a native Italian, was born about 1448; he studied and taught at several universities in Italy, staying longest in Pisa and at Padua. His memory was phenomenal: he apparently knew all of Justinian's law code by heart, being able to quote it at any time.[60] When Duke Bogislaw came through northern Italy in 1497 on his return voyage from the Holy Land, he persuaded Petrus to come to his University at Greifswald. Petrus traveled by way of Innsbruck, where he gave several orations in the presence of Emperor Maximilian. In Greifswald he stayed for five years and with his son Vincentius lectured on law and attracted many students from all over Germany. After the death of his daughter Margareta in 1503, he considered returning to his native country, but instead accepted elector Frederick's invitation to Wittenberg. In 1503 he delivered his inaugural address, *De potestate pontificis maximi et romani imperatoris*, in which he glorified the emperor. This oration so impressed Frederick and the university faculty that they asked Petrus to stay. He seems not to have received a *lectura ordinaria* since he is nowhere mentioned in the *Album*. It may be that he chose to lecture *extraordinarie* because his professorship at Padua had not been given to anyone else, or because he did not want to offend Duke Bogislaw by accepting a professorship other than in Greifswald. Nevertheless, he now lectured extensively at Wittenberg on different religious and moral themes; These *sermones extraordinarii* to which elector Frederick and Duke Johann listened with intense delight, were immediately printed in Wittenberg.[61] Petrus' friends and colleagues in Wittenberg – Nikolaus Marschalk, Hermann Trebelius and Johann von Kitzscher – all added their own laudatory poems to his numerous publications. Petrus, reciprocating, added some of his verses to his friends' publications, among them Kitzscher's *Tragicomedia* and *Oracio Funebris*. When in 1506 the plague broke out in Wittenberg, Petrus left with a promise to return. He went first to Cologne, where he was received with as much enthusiasm as in Wittenberg and where he became involved in several controversies, especially against Hochstraten. Frederick the Wise was angry that Petrus had not kept his promise to return, but his pleas were of no avail. Petrus left Cologne in 1508 for Mainz where he again lectured in law and where he probably died in 1508 or 1509.[62]

Vincentius of Ravenna remained behind in Wittenberg, where he matriculated in 1503–1504[63] and became rector in 1504. He lectured in law until 1507 when he returned to his native Italy. In 1505 Vincentius published an oration full of praise for Wittenberg; he stressed the importance of eloquence and complimented Frederick on his university and on what he had done for the *humaniora* and the appreciation on fine arts there. He declared that the elector's court was composed of educated men and scholars and that the atmosphere of Wittenberg was congenial to students and teachers alike. This was one of those laudatory orations which, though abounding in exaggerations, best conveyed the spirit and aspirations

60 Cf. Th. Muther, *Aus dem Universitäts- und Gelehrtenleben im Zeitalter der Reformation* (Erlangen, 1866), p. 69.
61 *Ibid.*, pp. 371ff, for a list of Petrus of Ravenna's publications.
62 For Petrus of Ravenna's later life, cf. *ibid.*, pp. 95ff, 'Der Ausgang des Petrus Ravenna'.
63 Cf. *Album*, p. 10.

of the orator and his audience.[64] Both Ravennas, father and son, were the first genuine emissaries of Italian humanism at Wittenberg; their impact was of consequence since they left behind them a town and university that had tasted real humanism.

Dr. Johann von Kitzscher, the friend of many humanists, was a native of Saxony, from an old and well-established Meissen family and wealthy property owners. We know that he and his brother Friedrich received an excellent education; that Friedrich studied at Leipzig and then went to Siena where he received his doctorate of canon law. In 1492 he returned to Germany and in 1503 moved to Wittenberg, where he became professor of canon law.[65]

Most of the biographical facts about Johann von Kitzscher's life come to us from the introduction to his *Dialogus* which was one of the most important works printed by Hermann Trebelius in Wittenberg in 1504. Like his brother, he studied in Leipzig, where he arrived in 1478–1479, but did not stay long, since he had to return to his family's estates to administer them. When this career failed to appeal to him, he decided to return to his studies and went to Italy about 1490. In Rome he became a member of Cardinal Ascanio Sforza's humanistic circle; from there he went in 1496 to Bologna to complete his law studies. In Bologna Johann associated with the circle of Philippus Beroaldus (Senior) who was at that time the most beloved teacher of the *humaniora* in Bologna. An imaginary letter to Beroaldus in Kitzscher's *Dialogus* shows how completely he had come under humanistic influence in Bologna.

When Duke Bogislaw of Pomerania visited Bologna in 1497, the Germans at the university welcomed him with great celebrations. It fell to Kitzscher, then rector of the law faculties, to greet the distinguished visitor with a Latin oration.[66] Kitzscher so impressed Bogislaw that the duke asked him to come and teach law at Greifswald. On his way to Pomerania, Johann visited his old friends in Leipzig who urged him to describe Duke Bogislaw's journey to the Holy Land in a play; the result was the *Tragicomedia* which was published in 1501.[67] The play was dedicated to Bogislaw's son Georg of Pomerania. In typical Renaissance fashion much praise is lavished on the ducal house, and Bogislaw is put on a higher pedestal than were the Greek, Roman, Persian and Trojan heroes of antiquity. Petrus of Ravenna contributed several enthusiastic verses to the work of his friend, and so did his son Vincentius. Petrus' laudatory verses on Kitzscher in *Aurea Opuscula*[68] are but another token of the friendship between the two men. During his Greifswald residence, Kitzscher became involved in the diplomatic

64 Cf. Panzer, *Annales*, IX, 66, no. 4; Maria Grossmann, *Wittenberger Drucke, 1502 bis 1517*. Ein bibliographischer Beitrag zur Geschichte des Humanismus in Deutschland (Vienna, 1971), no. 26. Cf. also Charles G. Nauert, "Petrus of Ravenna and the 'Obscure Men' of Cologne; a case of pre-Reformation controversy", In: *Renaissance Studies* in honor of Hans Baron. Ed. Anthony Molho and John A. Tedeschi (De Kalb, Ill. and Florence, 1971), pp. 607-640.
65 Cf. *Rotulus doctorum Vittemberg profitentium*, in: Friedensburg, *Urkundenbuch*, p. 15.
66 Cf. G. Bauch, 'Dr. Johann von Kitzscher, ein meissnischer Edelmann der Renaissance', *NASG*, 20 (1899), 301.
67 Cf. Panzer, *Annales*, VII, 136, 2; Proctor, *Index*, no. 11319.
68 Cf. Panzer, *Annales*, VII, 142, 42.

negotiations between the Pomerian duke and the city of Stralsund.[69] But when his advice as to how to deal with the city proved unsuccessful, he fell into disgrace with Duke Bogislaw and decided to leave Pomerania for his native Saxony.

It was Vincentius of Ravenna, who first called Kitzscher to the attention of Frederick the Wise. He knew that Kitzscher's *Oracio Funebris*, composed at the death of Anna of Poland, second wife of Bogislaw, would appeal to Frederick on account of its high and sincere moral tone, and also for its accomplished style. To accentuate the plea for his friend, Vincentius added an elegy of his own, in which he praised Frederick for his political astuteness and great virtues, and for his interest in scholarship and the arts. He convinced Frederick to call Kitzscher to Wittenberg, where the elector took him into his personal service as secretary and chancellor. In this capacity he is described in the *Dialogus* of Magister Andreas Meinhardi. Kitzscher was concerned with university affairs, as for instance in establishing a printer in Wittenberg in 1503,[70] and probably also with church affairs, since he was provost of the *Allerheiligenstift*.

In Bauch's essay on Kitzscher the information concerning the years between 1506 and 1512 is scant; however, Hermann Freytag filled in the gap when he found that during this period Kitzscher was in the service of the Teutonic Order.[71] At that time Frederick of Saxony, a brother of Duke Georg of Albertine Saxony, was Grand Master of the Teutonic Order. When Frederick came to Saxony in 1507 to plead his cause in his controversy with the Polish king, he met Frederick the Wise whom he asked to intervene with the Pope on behalf of his order. In his capacity as the elector's chancellor, Kitzscher certainly met often with the Grand Master, who shared his interest in humanism. He persuaded Kitzscher to enter the service of the order, and in 1508 Kitzscher was appointed General Procurator of the Teutonic Order at the Papal curia. He arrived in Rome in 1508 and immediately began negotations between the Polish king, the Teutonic Order and the Papal court. When in 1510 the Saxon Grand Master died and the young margrave Albrecht of Brandenburg became his successor, Kitzscher continued in his service.[72] He no longer remained at the post in Rome but was entrusted with other diplomatic missions, one of which took him to the Polish court at Petrikau. There he gave his *Oratio ad serenissimum Polonorum Regem* in which he pleaded for King Sigismund's friendship with the new Grand Master of the Teutonic Order, the king's own nephew.

It seems probable that during this time Kitzscher was no longer in the official service of Frederick the Wise, though he kept in close contact with him. Kitzscher later returned to Altenburg, where he held a church prebend, and resumed his studies which he had neglected for some time. In order to pursue his interest in the

69 Cf. Thomas Kantzow, *Pommerania*, ed. H. G. L. Kosegarten, (2 vols., Greifswald, 1817), II, 282ff.
70 Cf. Friedensburg, *Urkundenbuch*, p. 6, where Frederick writes to Martin Polich von Mellerstadt and Johann von Kitzscher to confer with other members of the faculties about the possibility of calling a printer to Wittenberg.
71 Hermann Freytag, 'Dr. Johann von Kitzscher im Dienste des Deutschen Ordens', *NASG*, 28 (1907), 117–122.
72 Cf. F. Joachim, *Die Politik des letzten Hochmeisters in Preussen*. (2 vols., Leipzig, 1892–1895), I, 9.

history of the German nation, he wrote to the elector on May 8, 1514, asking him for the loan of several German chronicles, but Frederick was able to supply only one.[73] Kitzscher's desire to learn more of Germany's past may be seen not as an isolated wish but as a sign of the growing German nationalism among the entourage of Frederick the Wise.

In this period Kitzscher wrote the *Virtutis et fortune dissidentium certamen*,[74] an allegory in which *Virtus, Castitas and Temperantia* discuss how they have no home in this world, neither among the lower estates nor at the palaces of the secular and ecclesiastical princes. It is a highly critical and candid treatise on the abuses by high officers of the church and state, surprising in view of the fact that the treatise was allegedly intended for the eleven-year old son of Duke Johann, the heir apparent of electoral Saxony; but it ends on a conciliatory note.

Information on the life of Kitzscher after the year 1514 is almost completely wanting. A letter from a friend of Carlstadt mentions that Kitzscher was ill in 1518,[75] and from another letter it may be inferred that by 1521 Kitzscher had died.[76]

Kitzscher was indeed an interesting and a versatile personality, steeped in classical learning; his orations show imagination and independent judgement. He was aware of the emerging nationalism and critical of his own times, advocating a strong empire. That Frederick assigned him the high position he held for many years and enjoyed his company reflects the elector's own interest in the new humanistic tendencies and his desire to draw upon its representatives.

In these early years at the University of Wittenberg, the old methods were slowly giving way to the new. The *Doctrinale* of Alexander de Villa Dei, which had been written at the beginning of the thirteenth century and had become the basic text for the teaching of grammar in scholasticism in all of Europe, was replaced in Symon Steyn's philosophy course by a more recent grammar of the Italian humanist Johannes Sulpitius Verulanus.[77] The second edition had been prepared by Johannes Crispus (Krause) of Freistadt,[78] who had come to Wittenberg in 1502 and received his M. A. at the first commencement. He dedicated the work to Staupitz and Mellerstadt, praising them for their care of the university at Wittenberg, for their attempts to educate the youth in the right spirit and for the encouragements they had given to his preparation of this new grammar from the humanist point of view. As a consequence of this reform in the curriculum the new humanistic, factual and linguistic treatment of grammar replaced the traditional one with its emphasis on logic, metaphysics and scholastic arguments. Thus students could now learn this important discipline in a more progressive way, without reliance on the old scholastic explanations.

With the year 1507 what might be called the first phase of the infiltration of

73 Bauch, 'Dr. Johann von Kitzscher', pp. 313ff.
74 Cf. Proctor, *Index*, 11360.
75 Bauch, 'Dr. Johann von Kitzscher', p. 314.
76 Cf. Paul Kirn, *Friedrich der Weise*, p. 181, letter no. 6, Aug. 4, 1521. Bauch mistakenly considers the possibility of Kitzscher's death sometime after 1540; this he based on the mentioning of a Johann von Kitzscher in church visitations in 1540.
77 Cf. Bauch, 'Wittenberg und die Scholastik', p. 309.
78 Cf. *Album*, p. 4.

humanism at the newly founded university comes to an end. Attempts to introduce humanistic thought and learning had been hesitant — some of them tentative and short-lived. Nevertheless it is apparent that humanism existed side by side with the old scholasticism, that the study of Greek was well launched and on its way, and that Frederick the Wise was assiduous in bringing to the university as many men as possible who represented the new learning.

The spread of humanism throughout the university would proceed in the years which followed, needing nothing more by way of radical innovation.

CHAPTER IV

HUMANISM AT THE UNIVERSITY OF WITTENBERG
1507–1512

In the period 1507–1512 humanism, which had previously been the concern of a few vigorous individuals, emerged as a determining force in the life of the university and the acknowledged cultural ideal of the young scholars. Andreas Meinhardi's *Dialogus*, published in 1508, may be regarded as one of the first expressions of the new spirit.[1] At the request of Mellerstadt, Meinhardi had written this propaganda pamphlet glorifying the town of Wittenberg and its university as one of the great centers of the learned world. Of greatest significance for us is that in the *Dialogus* humanism is represented as the accepted mode of learning and thinking at Wittenberg. While the description did not entirely correspond to reality, the fact that humanism was considered a major attraction, indicates its potential and growing strength.

This was also the year of the arrival in Wittenberg of Christoph Scheurl, who became instrumental in introducing important changes in the statutes of the university and of the castle church. In his first years there Scheurl published the *Rotulus doctorum Vittemberge profitentium*:[2] a catalogue listing all the professors at the university and the subjects they taught (in some instances even the hours) with an introduction, emphasizing its high standards and its humanistic orientation and inviting students to come to the university.

In 1508 Jodocus Trutfetter, a representative of the *via moderna*, was called to Wittenberg which gained with him its first exposure to Occamism. In this same year also Martin Luther was transferred to Wittenberg by his Augustinian order to teach philosophy as a representative of the *via moderna*; he also studied theology at the university. Changes in the curriculum were slowly introduced in this period, thus preparing the way for more advanced study in the classical disciplines. A new approach in teaching grammar was already in practice, and in 1509 a modern translation of Aristotle by the Greek scholar Johann Argyropoulos was adopted; the study of geography was also introduced in the year 1509.

When Martin Luther came a second time to Wittenberg in 1512, the ground was well prepared for his new approach to the Scriptures; and even though he never professed to be a humanist or to be sympathetic towards the pagan elements in humanism, he made full use of the tools it offered, albeit for his own end.

I

When the University of Wittenberg opened its doors in 1502, 416 students matri-

1 *Dialogus illustratae ac Augustissime urbis Albiorenae, vulgo Vittenberg dicte* . . .Impressum Lips per Baccalaureum Martinum Herbipolensem . . . 1508.
2 Cf. G. Kaufmann, *Die Geschichte der deutschen Universitäten* (2 vols., Stuttgart, 1888–1896), II, 574–577; also Friedensburg, *Urkundenbuch*, pp. 14ff.

culated; the next year 258 more are listed, and the following term another 132 students entered – unusually large numbers for a newly-founded university. Many of the students belonged to ecclesiastical orders, especially to the Augustinian Hermits, and they came from different parts of Germany, the majority from Ernestine and Albertine Saxony; but many arrived from neighboring Silesia, Bohemia and Lausatia, and others from regions as far as Franconia, Swabia, Bavaria and Austria.

Although the first years seemed promising for the new institution, by 1505 interest in it had slackened and the registration dropped considerably: only 55 students entered in one term in 1505. When the University of Frankfurt a. d. Oder was established by Mellerstadt's old foe Wimpina in 1506, it was to be expected that this new center of learning in electoral Brandburg would draw many students away from the Elbe region. Also, in 1506 the plague broke out in Wittenberg and the university had to move to Herzberg. With these unfavorable circumstances to counter, it was essential that the authorities should find means and ways to increase the student body when the university returned to Wittenberg. At the invitation of Mellerstadt, still the most influential person at the university, Meinhardi prepared the *Dialogus*; it represents the first major effort of the Wittenberg humanists, to present the university as a center of humanism in the hope that it would draw the attention of the world to the university.

Magister Andreas Meinhardi,[3] a native of Pirna (in Albertine Saxony near the Bohemian border), matriculated at the University of Leipzig in 1493 where he received his B. A. in 1495 and his M. A. in 1501–1502.[4] He remained for several years in Leipzig, though apparently dissatisfied with conditions there. In a memorandum that he wrote for Duke Georg of Albertine Saxony in 1502, he criticized most members of the faculty, reserving approval only to those who taught 'poetry', the group to which he himself belonged. He also complained that the younger magisters were allowed to become members of the faculty only seven years after receiving the M. A. degree. He moved on to Wittenberg where he matriculated in 1504–1505 and two years later he was teaching "in litteris secularibus extraordinarie".[5] It was at this time that Meinhardi wrote the *Dialogus*, his only known existing work.[6] Its publication probably led to his appointment as city scribe of Wittenberg in 1508, an office which he kept until 1525; it is believed that he died the following year.

The title-page of the *Dialogus* is a woodcut showing the seal of the theological faculty of Wittenberg, St. Augustine in his bishop's robe, sustained by four angels and a closed book. The back of the title-page contains the expanded and long

3 There are several variants of the name: Meynardt, Meynhardt, Manhart, Mayner, Mynar. Cf. Müller, *Wittenberger Bewegung*, pp.,300–304.
4 Cf. Georg Erler, ed., *Die Matrikel der Universität Leipzig* (3 vols., Leipzig, 1895–1902: Codex Diplomaticus Saxoniae Regiae, II, 16–18), 1, 399; 2, 350 and 383.
5 Friedensburg, *Urkundenbuch*, p. 16.
6 For a very interesting discussion, see the article by Brandis, 'Italienische Humanisten in sächsisch – thüringischen Landen', *ZB*, 46 (1929), 277–296, where the author emphasizes Meinhardi's dependence on Boccaccio's *Genealogiae deorum* for his explanation of classical mythology. He also points out that Boccaccio was known and read in Wittenberg as can be seen by some books which were transferred from the Wittenberg library to the Jena library in the middle of the 16th century.

title. The work has 68 leaves, with the signatures, Aij – Nij; the last page gives the imprint, Martin Landsberg, 1508.

The first pages contain the introductory poem by Chilian Reuter of Meller-stadt,[7] followed by the dedication of the book to elector Frederick the Wise and an address to Mellerstadt. We learn that Mellerstadt had asked Meinhardi to write the *Dialogus*,[8] as a tribute to the flourishing university. The reader will find in the dialogue an account of the great deeds of the Dukes of Saxony and especially of Frederick the Wise, the founder of the university, and an enumeration of Witten-berg's great cultural attractions, its buildings and the collection of relics. Because of its literary excellence, the dialogue is meant to serve as an exercise book in Latin conversation for future students. At the end of the work are laudatory poems by two of the foremost Wittenberg humanists: Otto Beckmann and Richard Sbrulius.[9] This is further evidence that the humanists were considered more likely to draw students to Wittenberg than the representatives of scholas-ticism who were certainly numerically still in the majority.

The dialogue is between two students, Meinhard and Reinhard, who meet on the way from Dresden to Meissen. Reinhard is on his way to Cologne where he plans to take up his studies, Meinhard to the new University of Wittenberg, where he expects to study with its famous teachers in the magnificent town. The professors, poets and especially the theologians of Wittenberg are praised lavishly. There follows some general conversation until the towers of Wittenberg appear on the horizon.[10]

The following two chapters describe the dreams of Reinhard and Meinhard respectively. Reinhard tells the dream he had the night they had spent at an inn in Meissen. Then Meinhard relates his dream which is actually an interpretation of Reinhard's dream. The three dukes who appeared in it were the three princely brothers of the Ernestine house of Saxony: Archbishop Ernst of Magdeburg, Frederick the Wise and Duke Johann. Frederick's travels to the Holy Land are compared to Plato's alleged journey to Egypt, to Pythagoras' journey to the seers of Memphis and to Apollonius of Tyana's journey to Persia and India. The love between Duke Johann and Sophia of Mecklenburg is compared among others to that of Dido and Aeneas, Scylla and Minos. When Johann heard of the death of his wife Sophia, his laments are expressed in verses of Virgil.[11] (Meinhardi quotes Virgil and Boethius all through his work in order to show how highly these Latin poets are esteemed at Wittenberg. Meinhard continues his interpretation of the dream and enumerates twenty-six "novae universitatis conservatores", outstanding among whom is Christoph Scheurl, the then-rector.[12] Next we are introduced to the chancellor of the university, Goswin of Orsoy, and then follow the names of all the university professors. The list is headed, as is to be expected, by Johann von Staupitz and Martin Polich von Mellerstadt, which shows that even as late as 1507 they were still considered the most prominent professors of the faculty.

7 *Album*, p. 18.
8 Aiij
9 Niij
10 Reproduced in a woodcut on A vi.
11 C v (Virgil, *Aeneid*, I, 94–101).
12 Ciij

Then Meinhard lists all members of the faculty whom Scheurl had included in his *Rotulus*; he informs us of their positions and in some instances recites the courses they were teaching. Among them are the names of Jodocus Trutfetter, Chilian Reuther, Georgius Sibutus, Nicolaus Amsdorff and Ricardus Sbrulius. Then come the advisers and officials of Frederick's court. This detailed description of the university and the court made such an impression on Reinhard that he revised his original plans so that he might come to Wittenberg to study. His decision is further strengthened by a letter from Jupiter, delivered to him by Mercury in a dream at night, in which the chief god urges him to come to Wittenberg.

Chapter 6 opens with the two students in Wittenberg, visiting the castle church, on the one Sunday of the year (the Sunday of *Misericordia Domini*, i.e. All Saint's Day) when all the treasures and relics of the castle church are displayed. Kitzscher, the provost of the castle church, himself acts as their guide. Reinhard is speechless and is eager to learn more about the indulgences and privileges of the church. From the church the two visitors proceed to the castle, where many canvasses showing scenes from Roman history are exhibited: scenes from the lives of Scipio, Tarquinius Priscus, Marcus Antonius and others. The students continue to the quarters of elector Frederick, where they see the portraits of all the Saxon dukes; the legends to the pictures are brief poems giving the name of the person and his deeds. The enumeration of pictures, together with their legend, starts with Leupoldus (died 866), followed by the Billungs, Henry the Lion and the Ascanians; then follow the first Wettin elector, Frederick the Valiant, and the complete line of electors to Frederick the Wise. These descriptive poems are really meant to be lessons in history — Roman and Saxon. The poems, rendered in Latin, in the *Dialogus*, are obviously Meinhardi's own translations from the German original.[13] In Frederick's bedroom the students find pictures showing incidents from Greek mythology: stories of the Argonauts, Jason and Medea, and from the deeds of Hercules. In other parts of the castle the visitors find still more pictures and other objects of art.

In the *Dialogus* Meinhardi has provided the most minute contemporary description of the castle, and apparently a fairly accurate one;[14] the emphasis throughout is on the alleged humanistic atmosphere of the Wittenberg scenes. Language, comparisons, references all are saturated with classical allusions. Meinhardi makes the observation that Latin is becoming so popular in Wittenberg that even the peasantry of the neighborhood are speaking it.[15] Even when the visitors ask at the end of the sightseeing tour when the castle will be finished, they are told that Rome was not built in one day.

To Reinhard's questions about the leaders of the city of Wittenberg, Meinhard answers that they are fine persons, but that the real leaders are the beloved dukes Frederick, Johann, and Ernst. Here verses by the Breslau humanist Laurentius Corvinus supplement the praise of the three Saxon dukes.

Chapters 10—14, which are concerned with the matriculation and initiation of

13 G iij
14 Cf. Georgius Sibutus, . . . *torniamenta* . . . (Wittenberg, 1511). Cf. Panzer, *Annales*, IX, 68, 16; Proctor, *Index*, no. 11830; Sibutus here describes the castle in similar, though less detailed, terms.
15 H

the new student Reinhard, are considered one of the best sources on the origin of initiations and the concept of the *beanus*.[16] When the student is asked which authors he has read to prepare himself for the entrance examination, he answers: the *Doctrinale* of Alexander de Villa with three commentaries and other scholastic authors, among them 'Claus Narr', meaning the court clown of Frederick the Wise. Thus fun is poked at scholastic methods and their works. Elsewhere fun is made of the sacrament of confession: the theologian Prometheus poses as father-confessor, wearing the clothes of a cook instead of his usual robes. The student appeals to Jupiter for final deliverance from all the torments of initiations, which Jupiter promptly grants, and the student is finally accepted at the university.

In the next to the last chapter Reinhard, now properly initiated, goes out to see the surroundings of Wittenberg. He again has a dream in the fashion of a humanistic allegory that he tells to Meinhard. The goddess of hunting, Diana, and the goddess of wisdom, Athena, are taking him on a hunt all over the countryside. He learns the names of all the Roman nymphs and gods of the forest, of animals and trees — with the aid of frequent quotations from Boethius and Virgil. After having told his dream, the two students go to the university and the chapter ends with a short dialogue that reflects the actual state of affairs. Uppermost in the students' minds are the merits and status of the *via Thomae* and *via Scoti*. They come to no conclusion, but leave it that each system is well-founded in its own right.

The sixteenth and final chapter has two parts: the first presents a complete survey of the town of Wittenberg in such minute detail that a map could be made from this description.[17] The other part treats of the position of women in Wittenberg society. After reminding his friend that Troy was destroyed by a woman, Meinhard warns him never to trust women or make friends with them. He then tells the long story of the devil's marriage which he had heard from Vincentius of Ravenna;[18] the passage echoes Christoph Scheurl's speech of 1509[19] which ridicules women, declaring them worthless and comparable to priests, and makes direct references to the oration *An uxor sit ducenda* of his Bologna teacher Codrus Urceus. It seems strange enough that Wittenberg scholars thought it to be in good humanistic taste to show contempt for women.

In his picture of Wittenberg Meinhardi covered all areas of university life. Everyday life has been clothed in classical robes. The castle of the Saxon dukes becomes Jupiter's dwelling, the hills around Wittenberg the mountains of Apollo, and Wittenberg a new Rome! Of course, Wittenberg was not a new Rome — nor another Florence — and Meinhardi's description is more than an exaggeration. But the significance of this presentation is that Meinhardi and his sponsors felt that a Wittenberg steeped in classical antiquity, adorned with its works of art, displaying the world of classical mythology and taking for granted the knowledge of the ancient language was the best propaganda for attracting scholars and students.

16 These four chapters are printed in J. Haussleiter, *Die Universität Wittenberg vor dem Eintritt Luthers.* (Leipzig, 1903), 54–84.
17 Cf. Schwiebert, *Luther and his times,* chapters 6 and 7, where the author describes the town of Wittenberg in great detail and also gives several maps, partly reconstructed from Meinhardi's work.
18 Reprinted in Haussleiter, *Wittenberg*, pp. 85–88.
19 *Oratio doctoris Scheurli attingens litterarum prestantiam* . . . [1509], B vi and C j.

Such a picture leaves little, if any, space to scholasticism. We are reminded of the church only when the castle church is being described with all its privileges and treasures, of which Meinhardi is justly proud. At the same time he glories in the pictures of the classical scenes and the Latin verses he finds there. This coexistence and confusion of the new learning and the old is typical not only for Meinhardi's but for the general state of mind in Wittenberg. We know that in 1507 the teaching at the university still relied on medieval material used in the medieval manner. Yet humanism had made inroads into all ways of life. We only have to recall the ridicule aimed at the church in the initiation rites of the student and in the magnificent story of the devil's marriage; clearly, the old ways were no longer taken so seriously and were modified by the invasion of new classical and humanistic forces.

II

The year 1507, which we have labeled a turning-point in the story, also saw the arrival in Wittenberg of Christoph Scheurl, the most colorful personality yet to arrive on the scene. During his five years at the university the spirit of the institution changed considerably.[20]

Christoph Scheurl grew up in Nürnberg where his father, a native of Breslau, had married Helene Tucher of the old and prominent Nürnberg patrician family. In his home he met many famous princes and personalities of the time: Emperor Maximilian had been a guest in the Scheurl residence twice, in 1489 and 1491;[21] it was, as he later called it, a *Fürstenwirtschaft*. Scheurl and his brother Albrecht had as their tutor Leonhard Vogel, a Saxon from Coburg. From him they learned Latin and Greek and supplemented their school education at home. The brothers went to the University of Heidelberg in 1497[22] where Christoph matriculated in the faculty of liberal arts. Little is known of his Heidelberg days, except that he and his brother stayed at the house of Peter Siber, a Dominican professor of theology (later confessor to the Count of the Palatinate). Siber seems also to have taught in the humanities, with Scheurl probably in attendance, for many years later, writing from Bologna to Siber, he acknowledged that he had received from

20 Cf. Franz Freiherr von Soden, *Christoph Scheurl II und sein Wohnhaus in Nürnberg.* (Nürnberg, 1837), and his *Beiträge zur Geschichte der Reformation und der Sitten jener Zeit, mit besonderem Hinblick auf Christoph Scheurl II* (Nürnberg, 1855); Christoph Scheurl, *Briefbuch.* Ein Beitrag zur Geschichte der Reformation und ihrer Zeit; ed., F. v. Soden and J.K.F. Knaake (2 vols., Potsdam, 1867—1872; reprint Aalen, 1962). G. Bauch, 'Zu Christoph Scheurls Briefbuch', *NMGHAF* 19 (1898), 400—456; G. Bauch, 'Christoph Scheurl in Wittenberg', *NMGHAF* 21 (1903), 33—42; F.E.Streit, *Christoph Scheurl, der Ratskonsulent von Nürnberg und seine Stellung zur Reformation*, (1908; Wissenschaftliche Beilage zu dem Jahresbericht des Realgymnasiums mit Realschule zu Plauen, I, 5); Wilhelm Graf, *Doktor Christoph Scheurl von Nürnberg* (Leipzig, 1930: Beiträge zur Kulturgeschichte des Mittelalters und der Renaissance, 43).
21 Dr. A. v. Scheurl, 'Christoph Scheurl', *Mitteilungen des Vereins für die Geschichte der Stadt Nürnberg 5* (1884), 43.
22 G. Toepke, ed. *Die Matrikel der Universität Heidelberg,* I: 1386—1553 (Heidelberg 1884), 426.
23 Scheurl, *Briefbuch,* I, 2; I, 22.

the professor more help and encouragement than even from his own father.[23] Whether Scheurl's interests lay in the *via antiqua* or the *via moderna*, or whether the small signs of humanism at Heidelberg caught his imagination, it is impossible to determine.

After a stay of almost two years, Christoph, not quite seventeen years old, went to Bologna to study law. Unfortunately, from that period only twenty-five letters which he wrote between 1505 and 1507 are available in the *Briefbuch*. He traveled a great deal in Italy, especially during his early years there: in 1500 to Venice and Rome and, unable to resist, all the way to Naples. The time spent in Italy Scheurl considered as his *Wanderjahre*; he often commented later that he was fortunate to have spent so many years there, traveling from north to south and feeling that he was participating in the great Italian awakening. But his travels came to an end when his funds gave out. His father had been imprisoned as a consequence of a financial disaster in Nürnberg. It was only with help which Scheurl received from the Nürnberg city council, at the request of his uncle Sixt Tucher, that he was able to finish his studies in Italy. His developing passion for bookcollecting did little to relieve the financial strain.

In Bologna Scheurl studied not only law – but also *secularia studia*, and with even greater zeal than he applied to law. He explained to his uncle, whom he loved and respected above anyone else, that the study of the humanities would enable him to write the history of his time, which is lacking in historiographers, and thus gather immortal glory for himself.[24] Whenever the study of law becomes too tiresome he turns to secular subjects.

Scheurl's teachers were all Italians. In the first years Codrus Urceus was still teaching there,[25] and Philipp Beroaldus Senior was especially interested in and helpful to the German students at the university. Giovanni Garzoni,[26] who had studied with Laurentius Valla, taught philosophy, and it was his great interest in history which had a decisive influence on Scheurl's later work in this field, as Scheurl later acknowledged. Scheurl's teachers of law were Laurentius Campegius, the later Cardinal, and Johannes Crotus of Monteferrato under whose guidance Scheurl published his first works. When Scheurl was teaching in Wittenberg he sent many of his students to his former teachers at Bologna. Scheurl was proud to have been educated in Italy, and even that he pronounced Latin in the Italian way.[27]

Scheurl's earliest known oration – and the one that made him famous immediately – he delivered in Bologna in 1505.[28] The occasion for this speech,

24 *Ibid.*, I, 16.
25 Cf. L. Geiger, *Renaissance und Humanismus in Italien und Deutschland* (Berlin, 1882: Allgemeine Geschichte in Einzeldarstellungen, II, 8), p. 183.
26 *Nouvelle Biographie Génerale*, 'Garzoni'; it is interesting that Garzoni later wrote on German history. *De rebus Saxoniae, Thuringiae, Libonotriae, Misniae et Lusatiae et de bellis Friederici Magni libri duo.* (Basel, 1518). Cf. Panzer, *Annales*, VI, 205, 220. This work was dedicated to Frederick the Wise.
27 Bauch, 'Christoph Scheurl in Wittenberg', p. 36.
28 Cf. Panzer, *Annales*, VI, 325, 46. Maria Grossmann, 'Bibliographie der Werke Christoph Scheurls', *Archiv für Geschichte des Buchwesens* 10 (1969), no. 19. For the variants of the two editions, cf. R. Kautzsch, 'Des Chr. Scheurl *Libellus de laudibus Germaniae*', *RK*, 21 (1898), pp. 286–287.

the *Libellus de laudibus Germaniae et ducum Saxoniae*, was the appointment of Dr. Ketwig, a Saxon scholar, as rector of Bologna University. The speech itself is no longer extant, but an expanded text, published in book form in Bologna in 1506, is preserved. The second edition (1508) was dedicated to Frederick the Wise.

Scheurl opens his oration with praise for the University of Bologna as the leading institution in the field of law in all the world. He then emphasizes the importance of laws, which he called the foundation and walls of every state, and praises the jurists as the true philosophers and real leaders of the states. Then he speaks briefly of the role a rector plays in a university; then of the new rector; and, finally, he comes to the real subject of his oration: Germany. He notes that Germany has been neglected by the historians, although its role in history has been of great importance. He speaks of the countryside – the Alps, the big rivers and mountains, the fertility of the soil, the mild climate, the vineyards that stretch all over the country. The Germans of his day he characterizes as helpful, friendly and hospitable.

Certainly, prior to the introduction of Christianity Germany had looked differently, like a pagan country without civilization. With the introduction of Christianity the Germans had become humanized. Scheurl speaks of the early Germans, of the tribes, *mores*, clothes and names. It was the German tribes that had defeated most other nations; even Caesar would never have been able to conquer Gaul without German help. Not only in war but in peace also, the Germans had been magnificent. Scheurl mentions some great Germans and their achievements: Albertus Magnus, Otto von Freising, Johann Gutenberg, and cites several laudatory poems on the Germans by his friends, Sbrulius and Sebastian Brant, and by his teacher Philipp Beroaldus. He tells us that Beroaldus is of the opinion that the knowledge of the German language is indispensable, since it is next to Latin the most important language. Then follows an outline of the history of the empire, starting with Caesar and Augustus, the Roman emperors, and on to Charlemagne, Otto I, and finally the Habsburgs. In typical humanist fashion Scheurl builds up a genealogy of the aristocratic families of Germany. He claims that the Italian aristocratic families are actually of German origin and thus, by the alchemy of genealogy, the German noble families become the oldest of the world.

Scheurl finally discusses his own native city, Nürnberg. He speaks of its Roman origin, its beauty, its morals and piety, its inhabitants, its buildings and palaces and the flourishing trade of the "German Venice". Its great citizens find special mention: Willibald Pirckheimer, Sixt Tucher and, above all, Albrecht Dürer.

In the final portion of his speech Scheurl turns to the Saxon dukes. He gives a short history of the house of Wettin and then goes on to praise Frederick the Wise, who had recently founded the University of Wittenberg as an asylum for genuine scholarship. Frederick has transformed the town of Wittenberg from a brick city into a city of marble; he had a magnificent church built and endowed it with many privileges and relics. Frederick, aside from his deeds, is a just prince and a friend of scholars; he appreciates music, has the ability to read fast and can write beautifully and with great ease.

We know that Scheurl, in his historical knowledge and interpretation, drew heavily on the earlier works of two German humanists: Heinrich Bebel and

Conrad Peutinger. But this only goes to show that he was well read in contemporary literature as well as in classical authors. It is a well-constructed speech with many quotations; it is a speech of intense German patriotism, delivered on Italian soil before students, teachers and interested people from all countries of Europe. It almost seems that a few years earlier no German in Bologna would have dared to give a speech in praise of Germany; there is a new audacity in this fact. Another interesting feature is that Scheurl brought a little territory in the east of Germany to the attention of an audience that had most likely never before heard the name of Saxony.

When Scheurl's father had met Frederick the Wise at the Diet of Cologne in the summer of 1505, the elector had promised to give his son a lectureship at the University of Wittenberg.[29] In that same year Scheurl informed his uncle Sixt Tucher of this possibility,[30] and by September 1506 negotiations were concluded. Sixt Tucher thought that his nephew should proceed directly to Wittenberg but Scheurl decided to finish his doctorate in Bologna rather than get it at Wittenberg. He considered his appointment only a temporary solution to his future ambitions; his hope was that one day he could serve his native city of Nürnberg.

The time he was still to spend in Bologna was in fact of great value to his education as a historian; just at this time Bologna was in an uproar, having lost its rulers. Scheurl gained insight into the political situation and realized to how many mishaps governments were exposed. At that time, also, Pope Julius II visited Bologna and dazzled the spectators, Scheurl among them, who however took notice not only of the splendour of the Pope's appearance but also of the evil rumors about his entourage.[31] Scheurl was a sharp and cool observer, although his attitude towards the emperor lacked objectivity: he glories in the victories of Maximilian and rages against the French whom he mistrusts and despises.

His most burning ambition was fulfilled when, in December 1506, he received his doctor of law at Bologna.[32] The commencement was magnificent, attended by the Pope, who happened to be in town, and by many famous men, among them Johann von Staupitz, who was on his way to Rome. It was a fitting conclusion to Scheurl's Italian years, so richly filled with experiences and with learning. Now he would have to prove himself an educated man.

Scheurl proceeded to Wittenberg by way of Nürnberg where he visited his mother for a week; in Weimar he was disappointed because the elector, being ill and fearing the plague, was evading all visitors and did not receive him.[33] Staupitz made the necessary arrangements, and on April 13, 1507, Scheurl started lecturing at the University of Wittenberg.[34]

Scheurl must have been disappointed at what he found there. He had grown up in prosperous and educated Nürnberg, he had seen Italy and its cities in their Renaissance splendor; without real knowledge he had praised Wittenberg out of all proportions. He now found a small town of about twenty-five hundred people,

29 Bauch, 'Scheurl in Wittenberg', p. 34.
30 Scheurl, *Briefbuch*, I, 4.
31 *Ibid.*, I, 23.
32 *Ibid.*, I, 25.
33 *Ibid.*, I, 26.
34 *Album*, p. 20

most of them uneducated and working in the fields. In a letter written to Sixt Tucher three weeks after his arrival in Wittenberg, Scheurl describes his feelings; he is longing for the cities of Italy and all their beauty; the people in Wittenberg are drunken, crude and quarrelsome;[35] he feels the strong contrast they make to the Italians, and he feels lonely and cut off from the big world.

But at the same time Scheurl was getting used to his new environment. He had the gift of making the best of almost any situation; he was easily enthusiastic and he transformed his thoughts quickly into actions; thus he started a very energetic university career. Circumstances helped him: he had come from Italy, and his orations had spread his fame before his arrival. The University of Wittenberg had as yet little tradition, and few well-known teachers were there. His knowledge, his style and his lectures made him realize how much better trained he was than his colleagues; his self-confidence grew and he felt himself superior. He told Sixt Tucher how everybody had gathered to listen to his inaugural address since his fame had gone before him.[36]

III

Three weeks after his arrival Scheurl was elected rector of the university.[37] In May 1507 he published the famous *Rotulus doctorum Vittemberge profitentium*; in the introduction to this course directory Scheurl tried to make as much propaganda as possible for the university; this document was intended for distribution not only at Wittenberg but in all of Germany. As was his habit, he exaggerated enormously: students should come to Wittenberg where the climate is excellent, the citizens are educated and favorably inclined to studies and students, it is cheap to live and everything is conducive to study. High praise is showered upon Frederick the Wise. Then, patterned after the practice at Italian universities and especially Bologna, Scheurl gives the catalogue of professors and their lectures. He sent his *Rotulus* to every corner of the land[38] to make propaganda for his university and also to show himself off as its rector and to call attention to the success he had already made in Wittenberg.

The list of the faculty is impressive. At the head are the teachers of sacred theology, beginning with Staupitz and Mellerstadt; the third to be mentioned is Jodocus Trutfetter, the representative of the *via moderna* in Wittenberg and later a good friend of Scheurl. Then we find a list of teachers of canon law, among whom appears Scheurl himself. The medical faculty is represented by only three members, also headed by Mellerstadt. Then follow the faculties of philosophy and humanities, the former strictly divided into two groups, one representing the Scotists, and the other the Thomists; among the Thomists are Carlstadt and

35 Scheurl, *Briefbuch*, I, 26.
36 *Ibid.*
37 Bauch, 'Scheurl in Wittenberg', p. 26; *Album*, p.21.
38 Cf. Grohmann, *Annalen*, II, 79–84; Friedensburg, *Urkundenbuch*, no. 17. Panzer, *Annales*, IX, 66, 6. Scheurl, *Briefbuch*, I, 36, 37. Bauch, 'Zu Christoph Scheurls Briefbuch', no. 38a, where Scheurl sent a *Rotulus* to Leipzig in 1509; thus we could assume that more than one *Rotulus* was published, though there is no certainty.

Chilian Reuter; among the Scotists Amsdorf and Symon Steyn, the latter lecturing on the grammar of Sulpitius.

The faculty of the humanities lists thirteen members – among them Scheurl, Sibutus, Meinhardi and Wolfgang Mellerstadt, the son of Martin. These men, different as they were one from another in intellectual status and importance in the university community, were all engaged in furthering the study of the humanities at Wittenberg. Thanks to the *Rotulus* we know their names and the nature of their appointments. Since they can properly be considered the real protagonists of humanism in Wittenberg, as much relevant information as possible has been gathered concerning their backgrounds, activities and interests.

Magister Balthasar Phacchus[39] who heads the faculty of the humanities was the successor to the chair of 'poetics' vacated by Hermann von dem Busche. A native of Vacha (Hesse), he matriculated in 1502 in Wittenberg and received his M.A. at the first commencement in 1503; he stayed in Wittenberg as lecturer in the humanities until his death in 1541, without ever achieving any particular fame. According to the *Rotulus* he read on Valerius Maximus and Virgil in the mornings and Sallust's *Bellum Jugurthinum* in the afternoons. Later he lectured mostly on Virgil, but in 1520 he treated Erasmus' *Praise of Folly*. Phacchus was a friend of Hutten who celebrated him as 'patriae nova gloria nostrae,'[40] and when Hutten came to Wittenberg in 1511 he stayed at Phacchus' house.[41] He seems to have been a quiet and passive personality who easily weathered all the changes at Wittenberg during his lifetime.

Next in the list is Scheurl, lecturing on Suetonius, and then Georgius Sibutus, lecturing on Silius Italicus.[42] Sibutus was born in Thuringia and had probably been a student of Celtis in Vienna; he was a friend of Hermann von dem Busche who added some verses to Sibutus' *Panegyricus* with which he celebrated emperor Maximilian's arrival in Cologne in 1500.[43] At Wittenberg he interpreted Silius Italicus' *Punica*, a book in seventeen parts, glorifying Scipio against Hannibal. He also lectured on his own work, the *Silvula in Albiorim illustratam*,[44] a poetic dialogue praising Wittenberg, which had been first recited in the presence of the elector and the student body and faculty. Afterwards the author had it printed to interpret it with his classes. Sibutus published several smaller works written in the worldly-erotic fashion that was beginning to be introduced in Wittenberg; he also added many poems to his friends' works, several in praise of elector Frederick; he was the center of a small circle of humanists that had a strong impact on university life at that time.

Among the magisters listed in the *Rotulus*, the most outstanding is Christian Beyer.[45] A native of Franconia, he had studied at Erfurt, where he received his

---

39 *Album*, p. 4
40 Ulrich von Hutten, *Opera Ulrichi Hutteni equitis Germani*, ed. Eduard Böcking (7 vols., Leipzig 1859–1870), III, 67.
41 Cf. D. F. Strauss, *Ulrich von Hutten* (Bonn, 1895), pp. 52ff. and P. Kalkoff, *Ulrich von Huttens Vagantenzeit und Untergang* (Weimar, 1925), pp. 117ff.
42 For a short appreciation of Sibutus from a literary point of view, cf. Ellinger, II, 63–64.
43 Cf. Panzer, *Annales*, VI, 356, 85; IX, 420, 85.
44 Cf. Panzer, *Annales*, VII, 233, 937.
45 Cf. Müller, *Wittenberger Bewegung*, pp. 246–253.

B.A. in 1502.[46] According to the *Rotulus* he was teaching humanities, but he turned from this discipline to the study of law, receiving his bachelor of law in 1507 and his doctor of law in 1510. He succeeded to Scheurl's chair in the faculty of law when the latter moved to Nürnberg in 1512. Beyer was dean of the law faculty several times; he was also active in the elector's courts and spent much time traveling in connection with jurisdictional disputes; also he took part in the administration of the town of Wittenberg, of which he became mayor in 1513. Beyer associated at Wittenberg with Scheurl and Beckmann, and added many poetical contributions to their works — as for instance, to Scheurl's *Oratio attingens* and to Beckmann's *Panegyricus.* One can count Beyer at Wittenberg among the humanists,[47] but, in contrast to his friends, he later espoused the cause of the Reformation. Today it is still remembered that in 1530 it was he who read the German version of the Augsburg Confession before the emperor and the assembled diet.

Another magister lecturing in the humanities was Mauritius Magdeburgensis, better known as Moritz Mette.[48] He probably studied in Leipzig before coming to Wittenberg, where he received his M.A. in 1503, his *baccalaureus biblicus* in 1505, his *sententiarius* in 1507 and his licentiate of theology in 1510.[49] He later became provost in Schlieben where the church had been incorporated into the university organization. He was a quarrelsome man and made a great deal of trouble for his parishioners and for the church itself, especially since he was a staunch enemy of the Reformation. So incapable was he of taking care of his office that Frederick the Wise had often to intercede on his behalf and finally dismissed him from the church. In 1525, after Frederick's death, he went to Magdeburg and became canon of the church of St. Sebastian.

Georgius de Staffelstein, better known as Georg Elner,[50] also taught *humaniora* according to the *Rotulus*; he had received his B.A. in Leipzig in 1498; in 1504 he came to Wittenberg,[51] in 1505 he received his M.A. and from that date on taught humanities. Twice he was dean of his faculty, in 1511 and in 1519—1520, and in 1514—1515 he was rector of the university. He also studied theology and received the theological degrees from Wittenberg.[52] As a teacher of humanities he is praised by Meinhardi in his *Dialogus.*[53] Later he lectured in Thomistic philosophy; but, although a friend of Carlstadt, he did not follow him in his radical turn. Elner remained quiet, doing his duties in Wittenberg, a neutral in the midst of the battles of churches and personalities. His friends were mostly reformers; his best friend was Johann Mathesius. In 1543 he died, a friend of the Reformation.

Magister Udalricus Erberer, better known as Ulrich Erbar,[54] another teacher of the

---

46   Cf. *Acten der Erfurter Universitaet*, vol. 2, p. 217.
47   He was an advisor to Frederick the Wise and later to elector Johann; in 1528 he became chancellor of electoral Saxony.
48   Cf. Müller, *Wittenberger Bewegung*, pp. 390—394.
49   *Liber Decanorum*, pp. 2ff.
50   Müller, *Wittenberger Bewegung*, pp. 272—276.
51   *Album*, p. 13.
52   *Ibid.*, 53; *Liber Decanorum*, pp. 11ff.
53   C iv.
54   *Album*, p. 8; Friedensburg, *Geschichte*, p. 86.

humanities, had studied since 1503 in Wittenberg, where he received his M.A.; he then turned to the study of medicine, and later was appointed professor in this subject; while he was rector of the university in 1511–1512, he was murdered by one of the students whom he had dismissed for disciplinary reasons.

Wolfgang Mellerstadt, the son of Martin Polich von Mellerstadt, was one of the first to matriculate in Wittenberg, where he studied law.[55] In 1508, while teaching humanities, he left Wittenberg, at the suggestion of Scheurl, to continue his legal studies at Bologna. He never returned to Wittenberg since he, too, was murdered – in 1511, by a Swiss student at Bologna who thought Mellerstadt had insulted him.[56]

Johannes de Feldkirchen, known as Johannes Dölsch von Feldkirch,[57] having studied first in Heidelberg, matriculated in Wittenberg in 1504,[58] where he received his B.A. the same year and his M.A. in 1506. He also studied theology and in 1509 became *biblicus* and in 1511 *sententiarius*. He was rector of the university in 1516–1517;[59] in 1521 he received his degree of doctor of theology. He was well known for having collected a magnificent library of his own.[60] He lectured *in via Scoti* but later followed Luther; his lectures in 1512 on the Gospel of Luke were already in the spirit of the reformed. He died in 1523.

Another member of the faculty of arts was Johannes Gunckel, or Stöb; twice he was rector of the university in the summer of 1518 and in 1528–1529.[61] Two other members were Kaspar Kanzeler of Bischofsheim[62] who had matriculated in 1503 and Wilhelm Sedelarius who had matriculated in 1506–1507.[63]

To what extent certain customs initiated by humanism had become part of university life by 1508 is shown by the official position of the *poet laureate*[64] as a member of the faculty of arts. In the seating arrangement he was allowed to sit in the last row next to the masters of the liberal arts. The *laureatus* was considered the equivalent of the M.A. The ordinary poet, the *poeta conductus* such as Ricardus Sbrulius, had to undergo all the regular examinations in order to prove himself the equal of the other members of the faculty. Actually in Sbrulius' case the authorities had to give consideration for poetic abilities where general knowledge was wanting.

Thus the *Rotulus* has transmitted to us the basic information concerning the composition of the faculty of humanities. Its three leading members, Phacchus, Scheurl and Sibutus, were humanists, as were most of the minor members and the poets attached to the faculty. Whatever the intellectual caliber of these men and however *pro forma* their idea of humanism, they were exponents of the great new movement at the university.

One development in the faculty of philosophy and theology deserves attention

55 *Album*, p. 2.
56 Bauch, 'Zu Christoph Scheurls Briefbuch', p. 406.
57 Cf. Friedrich Kropatschek, *Johannes Dölsch aus Feldkirch* (Greifswald, 1898).
58 *Album*, p. 13.
59 *Ibid.*, p. 63.
60 Friedensburg, *Geschichte*, p. 78.
61 *Album*, pp. 72, 132.
62 *Ibid.*, p. 8.
63 *Ibid.*, p. 19.
64 Friedensburg, *Urkundenbuch*, p. 24.

for its significance in the spread of humanistic tendencies within the university. The usual distinction found in the late Middle Ages between the *via antiqua*, as referring to Thomism and Scotism, and the *via moderna*, as referring to Occamism, does not apply to Wittenberg during the first five years of the university's existence. At the beginning only the *via antiqua* was taught and, when speaking of the 'two ways' at Wittenberg, one meant Thomism and Scotism.[65] The introduction of the *via moderna* as it was taught by Jodocus Trutfetter (mentioned in the *Rotulus* as teaching theology) came later.[66]

When Scheurl became dean of the faculty of law in 1508, elector Frederick asked him to draw up new statutes for the whole university.[67] He patterned his proposals partly on the statutes of Bologna, but mainly on those of Tübingen.[68] In addition to these general regulations, each faculty was to receive its own statutes. Thus the organization of the university, from the formal point of view, was completed in the sixth year of its existence. In the new statutes of the faculty of theology, the 'third way', the *via moderna*, was for the first time officially acknowledged as a part of the curriculum.

The *via moderna* had been introduced at Wittenberg in the course of the general reorganization of the university after its return from Herzberg in 1506. At that time elector Frederick decided to add to the philosophy faculty a representative of the Nominalist school, in the person of Jodocus Trutfetter. One of the most eminent proponents of this school, 'Doctor Eisenach' as he was called, after his native town, had received his B.A. at Erfurt in 1478, his M.A. in 1479, and in 1504, his doctor of theology.[69] He considered Johann Buridan and Gabriel Biel, both 'orthodox' Occamists, as his most important teachers,[70] and he was well acquainted with the works of classical authors and Italian humanists. Trutfetter had become a prominent member of Erfurt University when, to their disappointment, he followed the call of Frederick the Wise to Wittenberg.

---

65 For a discussion of this problem (though not at Wittenberg), cf. Gerhard Ritter, *Studien zur Spätscholastik*, II. *Via antiqua* und *via moderna* auf den deutschen Universitäten des XV. Jahrhunderts (Heidelberg, 1922: Sitzungsberichte der Heidelberger Akademie der Wissenschaften, philosophisch-historische Klasse, 1922, 7. Abhandlung).

66 In the statutes of 1508 we find: 'via Thomae, Scoti and Greogorii', as Friedensburg, *Urkundenbuch*, p. 53, no. 26, published it. He adds that the *Codex Scheurl* as well as the *Dekanatsbuch* of the philosophical faculty had it that way but he also adds: 'Guilelmo [von Occam]?' Substantively it does not matter since it is either Gregor of Rimini or William of Occam, both 'modernists'.

67 Friedensburg, *Urkundenbuch*, pp. 18–58; also Bauch, 'Scheurl in Wittenberg', p. 37. In order to help in financing the university, another administrative change was introduced, largely on the advice of Scheurl; it was decided to connect the *Allerheiligenstift* with the university, to expand the number of members of its chapter to twelve and to incorporate several churches around Wittenberg into this same chapter. Thus a broader financial basis for the university was created, since the incumbents of the spiritual offices of the chapters were also to serve as professors at the university; several professorships were thus supported from the chapter's treasury. Staupitz was sent to Rome where he received the Pope's approval of the plans for reorganizing the chapter. Cf. also Israel, *Wittenberger Universitätsarchiv*, no. 83.

68 Cf. Luther, *WATR* IV, no. 4074: '... wie den Wittenberg sein universitet hatt von Thubingen genummen'. [1538]

69 Cf. Gustav Plitt, *Jodocus Trutfetter von Eisenach* (Erlangen, 1876).

70 Cf. F. W. Kampschulte, *Die Universität Erfurt in ihrem Verhältnis zu dem Humanismus und der Reformation* (2 vols. Trier, 1858), 43–45.

Immediately upon his arrival there in 1507 he became rector of the university[71] and later served twice as dean of the faculty of theology. Because there were no textbooks for his courses in Wittenberg, Trutfetter immediately had one of his own works reprinted for his students' use.[72] This edition was introduced by a laudatory poem by Georg Sibutus which mentions that Trutfetter from the beginning befriended the humanists in Wittenberg as he had done in Erfurt where he was among the friends of Nikolaus Marschalk and Maternus Pistoris. We known little of Trutfetter's actual teaching career in Wittenberg; Meinhardi in his *Dialogus* calls him 'humilis, iustus, a mundo segregatus et deo dicatus',[73] and Scheurl who says that he taught according to the *via moderna*[74] loved and respected him — their friendship was continued in their correspondence long after both had left Wittenberg.

However, the representatives of the *via antiqua* — especially Mellerstadt, the leader of the Thomists — resented this intrusion by an exponent of the *via moderna* and were also jealous of the general esteem Trutfetter enjoyed at Wittenberg. Even in his own department he suffered from the general animosity of his colleagues. Frederick the Wise was unable to prevent Trutfetter's return to Erfurt in 1510 when he was called there as *canonicus Beatae Virginis*;[75] he also resumed his work at the university there. Trutfetter's place in Wittenberg University was not filled, and the Thomists and Scotists were again in exclusive control of the philosophical faculty. His place as archdeacon in the cathedral chapter was taken by Carlstadt, the Thomist, another victory for the *via antiqua*.

Another representative of the *via moderna* arrived at Wittenberg, though only for one year: Martin Luther, a former student of Trutfetter at Erfurt, was transferred by his order to the Augustinian convent and the University of Wittenberg in 1508. He succeeded to the chair vacated by Wolfgang Ostermayr who had taught the Nicomachean Ethics. Luther was also enrolled as a student of theology and received his *baccalaureus biblicus* in 1509.[76] In that same year he began to teach theology, at the same time preparing himself for the degree of *sententiarius* — a schedule so demanding that he complained often about it — when he was recalled to his Erfurt convent.

IV

In 1508 Scheurl had the second edition of his *Libellus de laudibus Germaniae et ducum Saxoniae* published in Leipzig. There were few changes from the first edition except that he added an important reference to Albrecht Dürer, praising him above any other artist of his time and claiming that the artists in Italy, where Dürer had just traveled, agreed with his judgement.[77]

71 *Album*, p. 24.
72 *Epitome seu breuiarium logice ingeniose discipline* . . . [Erfurt, 1507].
73 C iv.
74 Scheurl, *Briefbuch*, I, 80.
75 *Ibid.* p. 42.
76 For Luther's year in Wittenberg, cf. K. Bauer, *Die Wittenberger Universitätstheologie und die Anfänge der deutschen Reformation*. (Tübingen, 1928); Otto Scheel, *Martin Luther*. Vom Katholizismus zur Reformation (2 vols., Tübingen, 1917).
77 Cf. Soden, *Beiträge*, pp. 16–17.

Scheurl made a public speech on the occasion of the promotion of Johann von Leimbach, electoral councillor and treasurer.[78] His next oration, and one of his most famous, was the *Oratio doctoris Scheurli attingens litterarum prestantiam*,[79] in recognition of the promotion of Ulrich Dinstedt and Caspar Schicker, on November 16, 1508. After a long dedication to Cranach, Scheurl proceeds to a discussion of the advantages of scholarship. He starts with Plato's idea that only philosophers are qualified to rule the states: Frederick the Wise is such a ruler. All princes, says Scheurl, are indebted to scholars for their education, and if it were not for historians their names would be forgotten. Thus one remembers the Roman emperors because of Suetonius' works and Alexander the Great on account of Plutarch and Quintus Curtius. It is therefore deplorable that the Germans have had no historiographers (a theme which Scheurl also developed in his *Libellus*). Roman historiography should be imitated in Germany and the study of history as an indispensable discipline should be pursued. Scheurl quotes Cicero: if we do not know about our past, we shall always remain children. History is as the light of truth, the educator of life, the herald of the past.

The second part of the oration is devoted to praise of Wittenberg and its castle church. Scheurl relates its history, the origin of the church and the relations, only recently defined, between the cathedral chapter and the university. He showers praise on several members of the university, singling out Carlstadt as a scholar of Latin, Greek and Hebrew, a great philosopher and Thomist, and an individual of unimpeachable character and lovable personality. Scheurl ends with a passage in which he speaks about women and the contempt everyone in Wittenberg should have for them. Several works were appended to the speech: a letter of Scheurl, of May 15, 1509, to Ulrich Dinstedt; a poem by Christian Beyer in praise of Lucas Cranach and Scheurl; a poem by Sbrulius and another by Carlstadt (with a Hebrew quotation in Latin transliteration); and two poems of Otto Beckmann dedicated to Scheurl and the printer Symphorian Reinhart. A magnificent speech in excellent Latin, it conveys a strong impression of Scheurl's warm German nationalism in conjunction with Italian humanism — the two attributes serving the intellectual interests of the university. No German who had not been to Italy could have given a speech with such width and breadth of thought as could only have come from across the Alps.

Scheurl, as overworked as he was,[80] looked for still more assignments, partly for financial reasons and partly because his university work did not satisfy him completely. He became a consulting jurist to the electoral court and often gave advice on diplomatic and administrative matters. He traveled on official business to Leipzig, Halle, Naumburg and Torgau.[81] In 1508 he became a member of the elector's court, thereby adding still more to his duties.

Scheurl's oration which was best known to his contemporaries, was probably the one on priesthood.[82] Dedicated to Johannes Scheurl, a relative in Breslau, the

78 Cf. Panzer, *Annales*, IX, 487, 229b Grossmann, 'Scheurl', no. 22.
79 Cf. Panzer, *Annales*, VII, 164, 263; Proctor, *Index*, 11284; Grossmann, 'Scheurl', no. 24.
80 Scheurl, *Briefbuch*, I, 26; Bauch, 'Scheurl in Wittenberg', p. 38.
81 Scheurl, *Briefbuch*, I, 41; Bauch, 'Zu Christoph Scheurls Briefbuch', p. 404.
82 This work went through many editions. Cf. Panzer, *Annales* VII, 172, 342; 449/50, 74; 451, 84; 453, 97; 135, 27. Grossmann, 'Scheurl', 27, 28, 29, 30 31, 32, 33, 34, 35.

speech was delivered when a priest, named Andreas, received his *baccalaureus iuris*. Scheurl's thoughts are neither original nor especially remarkable: whoever loves God respects his priests. From his study of history Scheurl had learned that never had the priesthood been so much in contempt. He gives examples of how priests were honored in Egypt, India and Ethiopia. He displays his knowledge of classical times by lavish use of references to Cambyses, Hercules, Rome, Xenophon, Caesar, Constantine the Great, Alexander the Great. Among the Germans he mentions Rudolf von Habsburg, Maximilian and the Habsburgs in general. As did the ancients, so should Wittenberg honor its God and its priests and follow the great examples of the two princes who head the Saxon state. Contempt for religion has always been punished (again he illustrates with examples from ancient history). Scheurl also draws on biblical knowledge: the bad priests (and he cautiously assumes that there may be some) have to be respected too, since, as Paul taught, it is not up to everybody to pass judgment and to criticize those who preach the word of God; judgment should be left to God rather than to man.

In this speech one can only find complete agreement with the Catholic dogma. Whether this was Scheurl's real opinion is open to question. He may have been forced to reaffirm his faith in the Roman church for several reasons: his association with the 'poets' and humanists had made him suspect to some of the more orthodox members of the church;[83] and his Italian experiences may have been looked upon with displeasure by some of his colleagues. For all that, the oration is encrusted with the typical humanist barnacles: a poem by Sbrulius to Johannes Scheurl at the beginning; then a dedicatory letter to Johannes Scheurl by Scheurl himself. To the end are appended a poem by Aesticampianus, a letter from Beckmann to Scheurl, and to Scheurl's aunt. It is entirely compatible with Scheurl's character to give an 'orthodox' speech and then have his humanist friends adorn it. This mixture of tradition and the new learning Scheurl carried on through most of his life. He himself looked after the distribution of his latest work according to his letter of August 25, 1513, to Trutfetter; more than one thousand copies were circulating in Nürnberg.[84]

This is the last extant speech of Scheurl's in Wittenberg. Meanwhile he had kept up his connections with Nürnberg and with Sixt Tucher. When, in 1511, the city council again inquired under what conditions Scheurl would return, he went to Nürnberg and, after negotiation, accepted their appointment as consultant.[85] His ambitions had finally been realized – he was to serve his native city in an official capacity. In a letter to Spalatin in 1515[86] he explained why he did not return to Wittenberg although he had received an offer from Frederick the Wise; he considered it his fate to have had to leave Wittenberg and return to Nürnberg. But he acknowledged himself a student of the Wittenberg school and a faithful servant of its ruler, and he longed to go back to Wittenberg and visit with friends. Three years later Scheurl confessed in a letter to Melanchthon[87] that he owed to Wittenberg as much as to Nürnberg, that he loved its people as much as his own Nürn-

83 Scheurl, *Briefbuch*, I, 56.
84 Cf. Bauch, 'Zu Christoph Scheurls Briefbuch', p. 420, 422, 423.
85 Cf. Bauch, 'Scheurl in Wittenburg', p. 40.
86 Scheurl, *Briefbuch*, I, 92.
87 *Ibid.*, II, 173.

bergers and that he thought that God had chosen Wittenberg as his favorite abode. It is understandable that although Scheurl, while in Wittenberg, complained of many things about his life there, in retrospect he should have cherished it; it was here that he had finished his many student years, that he had proved himself and enjoyed an obviously brilliant success. His impact on university life at Wittenberg had been of real consequence and he was justified in his claim that he had changed the face of the Wittenberg republic of scholars.[88] He had been acknowledged as the leader of the humanists and praised and admired; but the horizon had been too limited to satisfy his ambitions. He needed a wider scope and a more advanced stage of culture for the exercise of his interests and abilities. In Nürnberg he found what he sought and he remained there, active and alert, till his death in 1542.

V

Scheurl's closest friend was Otto Beckmann.[89] Although Beckmann repeatedly stressed the value of scholastic methods, he wrote poems in the style of the humanists and made orations in praise of the *humaniora*. His reputation as representative of humanistic studies at Wittenberg was actually so great that Melanchthon dedicated to him his famous inaugural address – *De Corrigenda adolescentiae studiis.*[90]

A native of Wartburg in Westphalia, Beckmann had studied at Deventer under Alexander Hegius and matriculated later at Leipzig in 1500 where he became a student of Hermann von dem Busche, receiving his B.A. in 1502.[91] After living for a time in Halberstadt, he came to Wittenberg in 1507 under the rectorate of Scheurl.[92] He received his M.A. in 1508; in 1510 he entered the faculty of arts, and at the same time studied law, though it was not till 1517 that he received a degree in law and taught the subject in Wittenberg.

The earliest publications of Beckmann were some Latin verses dedicated to his teacher, Hermann von dem Busche. Others of his Latin poems he added to Meinhardi's *Dialogus* and to Scheurl's *Oratio attingens*; also, when entrusted by the university with the publishing of Mellerstadt's *Cursus physicus* in 1514, Beckmann added as an introduction some of his own poems, praising Mellerstadt's scholastic ways of thinking – and this in spite of Mellerstadt's own apology in his introduction for the scholastic form of his work and his statement that he did not intend in any way to slight the *humaniora*.

In 1509 Beckmann published his *Panegyricus*[93] and in 1510 his most famous oration, the *Oratio in laudem philosophiae ac humaniorum,*[94] to which Sbrulius

88 *Ibid.*, I, 37.
89 No monograph on Otto Beckmann has been written. The best treatment is still N. Müller, *Die Wittenberger Bewegung*, pp. 224–237.
90 *CR* II, col. 15–25.
91 Erler, *Matrikel der Universität Leipzig*, I, 433.
92 *Album*, p. 23.
93 Cf. Panzer, *Annales*, IX, 67, 9; Proctor, *Index*, 11829; Grossmann, *Wittenberger Drucke*, no. 50.
94 Cf. Panzer, *Annales*, IX, 68, 14; Grossmann, *Wittenberger Drucke*, no. 57.

added some laudatory poems of his own. In this commencement speech Beckmann praises the university, the new statutes of 1508 and especially the founder for providing so generously for the university, thus placing it in a position to attract outstanding teachers. Although the professors have to teach the old 'barbarian' dialectics, they implant in their students such a love for the new rhetoric, the mother of all studies, that the instruction is easily compatible with the new *virtus litteraria*. Beckmann especially singles out the fact that the students receiving their B.A. are proficient in poetry. In 1510 Beckmann gave another oration before the faculty of arts, the *Oracio in laudes sanctissime*.[95] Several other works of his were published during these Wittenberg years, among them poems to Andreas Crappus' work *Modus vitandi peccata*.

Beckmann's correspondence with Scheurl was extensive, as can be seen from the *Briefbuch*; like Scheurl, Beckmann considered that the gap between humanism and scholasticism could be bridged and tried, all through his early life, to merge the two constructively. But he was neither a forceful advocate nor a courageous fighter in the cause of humanism. He was a friend to everybody and showed understanding for every point of view. His importance for Wittenberg lies in his personality rather than in any particular work or deed.

One of the more prominent members of Scheurl's humanist circle was Ricardus Sbrulius.[96] A native of Friuli, Italy, he was born probably around 1480. He wrote poems, mostly lyrics, but his works were certainly not of high caliber. In his *Theocharis* (1514), a passion epic,[97] he combined classical and biblical subjects. Among the verses he added to contemporary works were numerous poems addressed to princes or well-known scholars; one of these, dedicated to Frederick the Wise, was at the beginning of his *Cleomachia*.[98] When Frederick invited Sbrulius, whom he had met at the Diet of Constance, to Wittenberg in 1507 the poet wrote a panegyric praising the elector and prophesying (mistakenly) that he would become Roman King and Emperor. At Constance he had also dedicated a long poem to emperor Maximilian on his arrival there. Similarly he celebrated Charles V in 1520. Sbrulius stayed in Wittenberg from 1507 till 1513 as *poet laureate*;[99] he made many friends, among them Scheurl, who called him his Ovid and to whom he addressed many letters. Sbrulius was often criticized for preferring contemporary authors to classical ones. He seems to have been criticized likewise for his private affairs — and admonished by his friend Scheurl — which created for him a number of enemies. Hutten labeled him an unscrupulous itinerant poet, one of the 'homines extreme leves et futiles', and Eobanus Hessus also expressed his hostility. Probably his personal conduct accounted in part for his departure from Wittenberg in 1513.

The change in the curriculum which substituted the new grammar of Johannes Sulpitius Verulanus for the *Doctrinale* of Alexander de Villa resulted in the furthering of humanistic ideas. In 1509 a new translation of Aristotle's *De Anima*

95 *Ibid.*, no. 58.
96 For the best literary appreciation, cf. Ellinger, *Geschichte der neulateinischen Literatur* I, 350ff, and II, 58ff.
97 *Ibid.*, I, 350.
98 Cf. Bauch, *Universität Erfurt*, p. 114; Grossmann, *Wittenberger Drucke*, no. 65.
99 *Album*, p. 21.

by the Greek scholar Johannes Argyropylos was published in Wittenberg, which, being in modern Latin, could be used by the Wittenberg professors with greater ease than earlier translations. Chilian Reuter had it printed as a textbook for use in his philosophy course in 1509.[100] Chilian Reuter had come from Cologne in 1505 and, according to the *Rotulus* of 1507, was teaching philosophy *in via Thome*. In spite of his scholastic teachings he preferred this new translation inspired by humanistic scholarship; because of its eloquence and oratory and also because the commentaries were superbly written, he said, with none of the ugly barbarisms and empty phrases of earlier translations.

In 1509 the curriculum of the faculty of arts was expanded to include a course in geography; its first lecturer was Bartholomaeus Stenus, a Silesian humanist.[101] At Cracow, where he received his B.A. and M.A. in the humanities, he had also lectured in the humanities, on Statius, Cicero and Aristotle. In 1508 he is entered in the Wittenberg matricles;[102] he had come as a private tutor with several Silesian young noblemen among whom were the sons of Vogel, the earliest teacher of Scheurl. Thus Scheurl came in contact with Stenus and procured for him the new chair in geography. As a textbook for his course Stenus chose Pomponius Mela's *Orbis Pictus*; he had it printed in Wittenberg[103] and dedicated this edition to the university. He added a *praelectio* and an introduction to his course, enumerating his own qualifications for the lectureship as well as discussing former teachers and scholars in the field and the use of geography for generals, politicians, merchants, poets and historians. He concluded with a poem praising Pomponius Mela.

In 1509 he gave an oration in honor of St. Catherine, the patron saint of the faculty of arts linking her to his own discipline by claiming Alexandria as her probable birthplace. Stenus left Wittenberg for Leipzig in 1512 and soon thereafter returned to his native Silesia where he wrote a history of Silesia and Breslau. He died probably around 1520. Although his personal impact on Wittenberg was not great, a precedent had been established with the introduction of the discipline of geography into the curriculum; yet no successor to this chair was appointed.

A further innovation in the curriculum occured in 1514 when a chair for the teaching of mathematics was established, making it a discipline independent of metaphysics.[104] The statutes prescribed that since it is the very fundament of all other sciences, mathematics should become a mandatory subject to take in preparation for the B.A. The first teacher of the subject was Bonifazius Erasmi de Rode from Zörbis,[105] who became dean of the philosophical faculty in 1515.

In the years 1507–1512 two men who would shape the history of the Reformation to a considerable degree made their appearance in Wittenberg. They were Carlstadt, the 'Thomist', and Spalatin, whose impact on the life of the university was felt more than a decade later.

Reviewing the years, we find that the major contribution to humanism in this

100 Cf. Panzer, *Annales*, IX, 67, 11; Grossmann, *Wittenberger Drucke*, no. 48.
101 Cf. Bauch, 'Beiträge zur Litteraturgeschichte des schlesischen Humanismus I', *Zeitschrift des Vereins für Geschichte und Alterthum Schlesiens*, 26 (1892), pp. 225ff.
102 *Album*, p. 25.
103 Cf. Panzer, *Annales*, IX, 67, 7; Grossmann, *Wittenberger Drucke*, no. 54.
104 Cf. Friedensburg, *Urkundenbuch*, pp. 56ff.
105 Cf. Friedensburg, *Geschichte*, p. 107.

period was made by Christoph Scheurl. All new institutional as well as general innovations were initiated by him and his enthusiasm for the new learning carried others, less educated, less sensitive, along. Humanism had made inroads in the university, and personalities of humanistic leaning had been accepted into the university community as permanent members.

CHAPTER V

HUMANISM DURING LUTHER'S EARLY YEARS AT WITTENBERG

The humanism that had been developing at the University of Wittenberg in the decade between 1502 and 1512 turned in a different direction during the succeeding five years. Early humanism in Wittenberg had been aptly called a 'scholastic-academic' humanism.[1] As important as these early humanistic endeavours were in preparing the ground, they were not capable of changing the official atmosphere at the university decisively. The real defeat of medieval scholasticism was to come not from a study of pagan antiquity but rather from a study of the Christian classics, of the Church Fathers, especially Augustine, and above all from the study of the Bible itself. But without the spade work of the early humanists, and especially of Faber Stapulensis, Reuchlin and Erasmus, the return to the sources, which was a prerequisite to the reform of the Christian church, would have been greatly retarded. Thus Luther found the necessary tools for his study and interpretation of the Scriptures prepared by humanists and available at Wittenberg.[2]

I

In the period 1512–1517 the influence of Leipzig on the intellectual life of Wittenberg seems to have decreased. Leipzig had become the rallying point of conservatism under the rule of Duke Georg of Albertine Saxony, a staunch supporter of the papacy. The few humanistically inclined teachers at Leipzig, among them Aesticampianus and Mosellanus, were eager to transfer to Wittenberg. The atmosphere there, however, was no longer so attractive to Italian-trained students; it had become too 'Christian' for that. Although Erasmus, Faber Stapulensis and Reuchlin had been to Italy, they developed their own 'native' northern humanism which was more Christian than pagan, their interest centering in the Bible, its translation and interpretation. However, they dit not follow Luther in his reform movement; all three were scholars who remained within the Roman Catholic Church, though they were critical of many of its aspects. They were not fighters for what was proclaimed the cause of religious freedom but rather remained quiet scholars, who detested violence in all its forms.

The most fruitful contacts maintained by some of the Wittenberg scholars during

---

1 Cf. M. Steinmetz, 'Die Universität Wittenberg und der Humanismus, 1502–1521', in *450 Jahre Martin-Luther-Universität*, I, 112ff.
2 This chapter will not discuss Luther the theologian but rather Luther the professor at Wittenberg University who, by his teachings and influence on students and teachers alike, transformed the university within a few years into a 'Protestant' university. This final transformation, however, is outside the scope of this study; it is only the preparatory steps that will be discussed here. The later history of the University of Wittenberg belongs in a discussion of the Reformation proper.

these years were with the humanist circle at Erfurt. Johann Lang, who had introduced Luther to the Greek language, and Luther himself, came from Erfurt. As a result of the Erfurt influence private teaching and tutoring of Greek and Hebrew began at Wittenberg, having been introduced by Marschalk who, just before coming to Wittenberg, had reprinted Aldus Manutius' *Introductio ad litteras hebraicas* in Erfurt.[3] Like Marschalk, Carlstadt and Tileman Conradi knew some Hebrew.

The person around whom humanists as well as future reformers rallied in the years 1512–1517 was Georg Spalatin. Among his most intimate friends was Scheurl who, not content in Wittenberg, was aiming for a position in his native Nürnberg. We can recognize it as a typical humanistic euphemism when Scheurl writes to Spalatin that the latter's presence in Wittenberg might induce him to remain there.[4] Spalatin was able to use Scheurl's library during these few months of their common stay in Wittenberg and even after Scheurl left, Spalatin had not returned all the books.[5] It was through Scheurl that Spalatin also became acquainted with Beckmann, Beyer and Carlstadt; Johann Lang, whom he already had known at Erfurt, he met in Wittenberg again and this friendship brought Spalatin in contact with Luther.

Johann Lang, a native of Erfurt, entered the university there in 1500 and became a student of Nikolaus Marschalk. In 1507 Lang entered the Augustinian convent at Erfurt, where he studied the *humaniora* and Greek; Luther, who entered soon thereafter, apparently did not know Lang well before his return to Erfurt in 1509. In 1511 Lang, together with Luther, was transferred by his order to Wittenberg where he received his M. A. in 1512; here he lectured on Aristotle and tutored the Greek language. It was from him that Luther learned the fundamentals of Greek. Mutian later on mentions that Lang owned approximately six hundred Greek books.[6] In 1516 Lang was transferred back to Erfurt where he became the reformer of the city.

Luther was transferred to Wittenberg in 1511 again by Staupitz, who had by then decided to resign from his *lectura in Biblia* and make Luther his successor. In Erfurt Luther was a student of Trutfetter, who had introduced the *via moderna* at Wittenberg and it was this *via* which Luther represented.[7] In order to be eligible for this position Luther had to get a doctorate in theology, which he received in October 1521.[8] At that time he was just an Augustinian monk who had received the same training as every other student of philosophy and theology; his promotion to the doctorate finds no particular mention in the *Liber Decanorum*[9] nor is there a record of any distinction which would officially single him out.

Thus we find, at the end of the year 1512, Spalatin, Lang and Luther at Wittenberg: the three friends who, during the next few years, would work together to go back to Christian sources and uncover what they considered original Christianity in its true sense.

3 Cf. Proctor, *Index*, 11232.
4 Cf. Scheurl, *Briefbuch*, no. 55.
5 Bauch, 'Zu Christoph Scheurls Briefbuch', pp. 423–425.
6 *Mutians Briefwechsel*, 567.
7 Cf. Herbert Rommel, *Über Luthers Randbemerkungen von 1509/10*, (Kiel, 1930) 1930)
8 Cf. H. Steinlein, *Luthers Doktorat* (Leipzig, 1912)
9 *Liber Decanorum*, p. 12.

In his more than thirty years in Wittenberg, Luther lectured only on the Bible. The original intention of the chair for the *lectura in Biblia* had finally been realized. In the Middle Ages lectures on the Bible focused on the medieval commentators of the Bible; when Luther discarded this concept, he revolutionized the teaching of the Bible and fulfilled the ambitions of the humanists: *ad fontes*. He started with the interpretation of the Psalms (1513–1515) and continued with Romans (1515–1516), Galatians (1516–1517) and Hebrews (1517–1518). These were his lectures prior to the posting of his 95 theses in 1517.

Each series of lectures is divided into two parts: *glossae* and *scholia*. First Luther had Grunenberg print the part of the Bible that he was going to interpret in the vulgate translation, with wide margins and spaces between lines for notes. These notes, the *glossae*, he dictated to his students. The interpretations of important texts, the *scholia*, were put into separate notebooks at a later date. This division, which is typically medieval,[10] Luther used until 1517; it can be seen most clearly in his lectures on Galatians.[11] In his second lectures on the Psalms, the *Operationes in Psalmos* (1519–1521) he gave up this method altogether.

A closer examination of Luther's early lectures reveals that, even though the form and the exegetical tradition are medieval, he makes full use of all the humanistic publications of his time. Since he did not know Greek and Hebrew well until he met Melanchthon, he relied on humanistic translations and put medieval and humanistic exegeses side by side.[12] Before Erasmus' publication of the New Testament Luther used most heavily Faber Stapulensis' two publications: the *Psalterium Quincuplex* (1509)[13] and the *Epistola Divi Pauli* (1512).[14] Already the order in which Luther treated the Biblical books reminds one of the sequence the French humanist chose. In his commentaries Faber Stapulensis had attempted to introduce a new method of exegesis which enabled him to break away from the traditional method of the fourfold interpretation of the Bible. The 'literal' sense is no longer important but is replaced by a 'prophetic' sense, i.e. inspiration; for him the Psalms speak of Christ and not of David. In particular Faber Stapulensis shows strong criticism of the Roman Church, its merit system and its sacramental system.

Next to Faber Stapulensis' works Luther relied on Reuchlin's *De rudimentis*

10 Cf. H. v. Schubert's introduction to the first edition of Galatians, in *Abhandlungen der Heidelberger Akademie der Wissenschaften*, Phil.-hist. Klasse, 5 (1918)
11 Cf. *WA* 57, Abteilung II.
12 Among a large literature on the subject, cf. K. A. Meissinger, *Luthers Exegese in der Frühzeit*. 1. Teil (Leipzig, 1910); W. Schwarz, *Principles and Problems of Biblical Translation* (Cambridge, 1955)
13 Cf. Panzer, *Annales*, VII, 538, 331. Cf. for the importance of this work for Luther: M. Mann, 'Erasme et les débuts de la Réforme française (1517–1536)', *Bibliothèque littéraire de la Renaissance*, 22 (1934), 14ff.; and the preface to the edition of Luther's notes on the Psalms, in *WA* IV, pp. 463–464. Luther's copy of Stapulensis' work is preserved and his notes in it bear witness to the fact that he used it for the preparation of his lectures on the Psalms; cf. *ibid.*, pp. 465–526.
14 This work contained only selections in Greek. When Erasmus' New Testament was published in 1516, Luther at once made use of this edition.

hebraicis[15] and his *In septem psalmos poenitentiales*.[16] When Reuchlin published the former work in 1506 it marked the beginning of a new epoch: from this date on it was possible to learn Hebrew in Europe.[17] Soon Reuchlin realized that his Hebrew grammar and dictionary was of no great use so long as there were no Hebrew books for the students, and for that reason he published the *Septem Psalmos* in 1512. As early as 1488[18] Reuchlin said that he had learned Greek and Hebrew in order to read the Holy Scriptures in the languages in which they are believed to have been originally composed under God's inspiration, as he considered translations from the original to be the best, he preferred the Greek and Hebrew texts of the Bible to the Vulgate. Twenty-five years later he still expresses doubts about translations which have caused many errors; he therefore prefers to read the New Testament in Greek, and the Old Testament in Hebrew.[19] Thus he asserts that errors were possible in the Vulgate translation. For him only the Bible in its original language is the real authority. It is obvious that there was no place in Reuchlin's philology for the philosophy of the schoolmen and that it meant questioning and doubting the whole of medieval tradition and the Vulgate. Reuchlin established the principle that philology is an autonomous discipline and that conclusions drawn from medieval theologians lose their validity if the philologist can prove the inaccuracy of the text on which the medieval commentator relied. However, it seems that Reuchlin failed to realize the dangerous implications of what he was saying: the Vulgate was declared inaccurate and therefore no longer valid and the whole basis of medieval theology was shown to be fallible. Yet, Reuchlin remained opposed to Luther's interpretation and doctrines and died as a member of the Roman Church.

Luther had purchased Reuchlin's work in Erfurt,[20] and references to Reuchlin can be detected in his notes to Lombard's *Sententiae*.[21] As Luther had very little knowledge of Hebrew at the time of his early lectures, Reuchlin's work offered him a general introduction to the language and gave him a notion of a Biblical exegesis based on the original text.

It was in connection with the Reuchlin controversy with the Cologne faculty that Luther came in contact with Spalatin for the first time. Spalatin had asked Mutian for his opinion on the feud between Reuchlin and the Cologne Dominicans; Mutian apparently was too outraged to answer, but asked Urbanus to write for him.[22] Soon after, Mutian must have written himself since only a few weeks later Reuchlin thanked him for his support, informing him also that Spalatin had gone on a campaign on his behalf; Frederick the Wise had written and promised special help.[23] It is understandable that Frederick, who might have considered

15 Cf. Panzer, *Annales*, VIII, 288, 9; Proctor, *Index*, 11754.
16 Cf. Panzer, *Annales*, VIII, 323, 16.
17 Cf. Schwarz, pp. 61ff., for the background of Hebrew studies in Europe; also L. Geiger, *Das Studium der hebräischen Sprache in Deutschland* (Breslau, 1870), pp. 17ff; L. Geiger, *Johann Reuchlin* (Leipzig, 1871)
18 Reuchlin, *Briefwechsel*, no. 15.
19 *Ibid.*, no. 163.
20 Scheel, *Luther*, p. 227.
21 *WA* IX, 82.
22 *Mutians Briefwechsel*, 270.
23 *Ibid.*, 303.

interfering in the struggle between Reuchlin and the Dominicans to prevent a conviction of Reuchlin, now turned towards his humanist advisor Spalatin for information. As a consequence Spalatin had written to Johann Lang at the end of 1513 or early in 1514 to find out what Lang knew about Luther's views on the controversy[24] and specifically whether Luther had seen Reuchlin's and his foes' books; if not, he wanted Luther to read the material in question and to convey to him his own views on the matter. Luther answered in a direct letter to Spalatin in which he unequivocally took Reuchlin's side and saw no danger in Reuchlin's views. At this point Luther used Reuchlin's works and even took Reuchlin's side without being fundamentally in sympathy with him or with humanism in general. He realized that Reuchlin's enemies were limited, prejudiced and followed blindly the medieval scholastic tradition; what he apparently did not see clearly was that Reuchlin's comrades, the writers of the *Epistolae obscurorum virorum*, the Huttens and Sickingens, were basically just as much at odds with him as were his foes.[25]

It is interesting that Spalatin did not rely on his own judgment but inquired from the humanist friends at Gotha and the professor of theology as to their judgment. From this point on he influenced Frederick as much as he could in favor of Reuchlin. The elector had written several letters at the beginning of 1514 in support of Reuchlin[26] and it might have been partly due to his influence that no final judgment was yet made in the case. Spalatin now proceeded as he did later in the Luther controversies: he influenced Frederick quietly and intensely and supported him in views that coincided fundamentally with his own.

This correspondence between Luther and Spalatin marks the beginning of a life-long friendship; more than four hundred of Luther's letters to Spalatin are extant, but unfortunately only a few of Spalatin's; the content, however, of many can be deduced from Luther's letters, which also reflect the course the reform movement took. Soon Spalatin was completely captivated by Luther: Johann Lang wrote to Mutian in 1515 that Spalatin adores Luther like an Apollo.[27]

Lang's edition of the *Enchiridion Sexti Philosophi Pythagorici*[28] published in 1514, was an open attack on scholasticism. In the introduction he quoted Plato and, as an adherent of the new learning, criticized all those who would prevent Christians from reading secular works and would limit their reading to Occam, Scotus and authors of the same tradition. He made an even stronger attack in the introduction to his edition of two letters of Jerome.[29] The choice of letters is interesting and revealing: on the status of secular knowledge and on the education of young ladies. He again speaks out against those who want to read only scholastic authors and those who prefer Occam to Jerome, Scotus to Augustine and Capreolus to Ambrius. It is significant that here Lang does not oppose the schoolmen with pagan-classical authors, but rather with the most prominent representatives of early Christianity. One might well recognize here the influence of

---

24 *WAB* I, 7.
25 *WAB*, I, 24, 25, 50.
26 Cf. Höss, *Spalatin*, p. 78.
27 *Mutians Briefwechsel*, 490.
28 Cf. Panzer, *Annales*, IX, 69, 22; Grossmann, *Wittenberger Drucke*, no. 94.
29 *Ibid.*, no. 99.

Luther on Lang. Lang also announced lectures on the Bible and in 1515 he read on Ecclesiastes and Titus. At the end of Lang's stay at Wittenberg, humanism at Wittenberg was changing its focus from the classical authors of antiquity to the biblical foundations of Christianity. In 1516 he returned to Erfurt as prior of the convent there.

From 1516 on Luther's exegesis was probably influenced chiefly by Erasmus' edition of the New Testament. Without being conscious of the fact, he used the greatest humanist's tool to round out his Biblical studies, which he would shortly turn into a weapon against that very humanist.

Erasmus learned Greek after his return from England early in 1500 and he then prepared an edition of the *Adagia*. In 1504 he wrote that he regretted having published the edition because of his former ignorance of Greek.[30] By 1500 he was also interested in preparing commentaries on Jerome; when he compared the Greek text of some Psalms with the Latin wording of the Vulgate, he discovered discrepancies between them, and he realized the importance of his discovery. He pointed out that a mistranslation will be the basis for a theological misinterpretation; a theologian must therefore have a thorough knowledge of Greek.[31] He quoted, as a defense for his daring proposition, the *Decreta* of the church council of Vienne of 1311–1312, a statement that he would use for many years whenever he was attacked. In the *Decreta* it was stated that at a university there should be some persons capable of teaching Hebrew and Greek, inasmuch as without this knowledge sacred literature could not be fully understood. Erasmus thus announced that he had the authority of a Pontifical Council on his side.

One of the points on which Luther would disagree with Erasmus even at that early time was that the knowledge of Greek, if not combined with spiritual qualifications, could further the study of the Bible. To Erasmus, works of literature and theology were equally open to his method of philological and grammatical interpretation.

In 1505 Erasmus published Valla's *Adnotationes*, which maintained that in principle the New Testament in the original Greek was to be preferred to the Latin Vulgate, and that it was futile to expound the New Testament without the knowledge of Greek. In the preface to his edition Erasmus points with scorn to the devotees of the inspirational theory who create a new honor for the theologian: these are the only people who are privileged to speak incorrectly.[32]

Erasmus' 1516 edition of the New Testament is an important milestone in the history of Biblical studies since it is the first complete edition with a Greek text and a translation based on it. It was printed by Johannes Froben at Basel in February 1516, with the Greek and Latin texts of the Bible printed side by side; at the end of the work Erasmus explained why the new version differs from the Vulgate. Several Greek manuscripts were compared in order to discover the variants; he attempted to verify the readings of the Vulgate by means of old Latin manuscripts, using the Church Fathers as independent sources for the early text of the Vulgate; the philological method was to be applied throughout the prepara-

---

30 *Opus Epistolarum Des. Erasmi Roterodami*, ed. P. S. Allen and H. M. Allen, and H. W. Garrod (12 vols., Oxford, 1906–1958), I, 181.
31 *Ibid.*, I, 149.
32 *Ibid.*, I, 182.

tion of the new text, and his aim, he declared, was to return to the holy truth which had been vitiated by man; also he wanted to restore the text of the Bible to its original wording as read by the early Fathers of the Church who, to Erasmus, are the representatives of the old theology.

Erasmus recognized that no reasoning is valid against those who advocated the inspirational method of translation. Since their fundamental attitude was so different from his own, no understanding with them was possible; here is the very basis of the disagreement between him and Luther: Erasmus believed that man can be changed through learning and that he can thus come to an understanding of the word of God; his was a rational approach to religion.

Luther, in contrast, believed in the inspirational view of the understanding of the Bible. Nobody can understand God's word without God's grace, and no one who uses merely secular knowledge is able to understand the Bible. Luther had in common with the humanists his antagonism to scholasticism, but for reasons of his own. Erasmus rejected the scholastic approach because, due to ignorance of the original languages, it could not lead to an understanding of the Bible. Luther rejected scholasticism which, he maintained, injected human doctrine and human thought into theology, whereas only God's grace could lead to an understanding of the Scriptures.

Yet immediately upon publication of Erasmus' New Testament Luther used the new text, drawing the students' attention to variants which he found in it, even though he still continued to use the Vulgate as text in his lectures. He followed Erasmus in philological details and thus used the technique of humanistic scholarship, but for purposes of theological interpretation. Erasmus, on the other hand, was concerned solely with a philologically sound text. The inadequacy of Erasmus's learning, according to Luther, was that it could lead him only to a human understanding but not to a theological or inspirational understanding.[33] Luther found himself less sympathetic with Erasmus every day; his knowledge of languages do not make him a correct interpreter of the Scriptures.[34] To illustrate his argument, Luther refers to Augustine whom he considered superior to Jerome as an interpreter, even though Augustine did not know Greek and Hebrew. Thus some of Erasmus' interpretations, however correct grammatically, cannot be valid, since he is not a theologian. 'The right faith' is a requirement for understanding the Bible, and only that will bring out the true meaning of the words. Erasmus was in essential agreement with Jerome, while Luther followed Augustine; Erasmus was attracted by Jerome because the latter had a knowledge of classical literature and had made such learning a prerequisite for real education and religion; he was fascinated by Jerome's style and language. Luther came to Augustine through his theology, through his biblical concern.

To understand the impact of humanism on pre-Reformation Wittenberg, it is important to delineate the difference between Luther, in this early stage of his theological formation, and Erasmus. Luther succeeded in cutting the ground from under scholasticism. Yet a wide gap separated him from the humanists at Wittenberg who attempted to remove themselves from scholasticism by way of classical

33 *WAB* I, 27.
34 *Ibid.*, 35.

antiquity. Classical antiquity actually had very little meaning for Luther since it had no connection with the Cross.

III

Thus, within a few years, Luther discovered what he considered to be the only and true Christian religion. At the same time, the University of Wittenberg changed, under the impact of his strong and fascinating personality, from a university where the two opposing forces, scholasticism and humanism, had reached a kind of balance of strength, to a university where there was hardly any place for either movement. Both were submerged by the reform of the Christian Church, as conceived by Luther and his adherents. Before this could happen, however, certain additional preliminary steps were necessary to prepare the university and faculty for acceptance of Luther's way of life and thinking.

Luther was able to win over the members of the theological faculty one by one. At his examination for *sententiarius* in September 1516, Luther's pupil Bartholomäus von Feldkirch defended the thesis that according to Augustine it is impossible to fulfill God's command without the grace of God. The two opposing professors, Lupinus and Carlstadt, the violent defender of Thomism, objected violently.[35] Anxious to clarify the problems brought up by Bartholomäus and hoping that he would be able to reaffirm his position, Carlstadt journeyed to Leipzig in 1517 to secure an edition of Augustine to buttress his argument.[36] But upon studying Augustine he found that his own was the wrong interpretation and after initial hesitation, he acknowledged that Luther was right. Now he became just as violent an adherent of Luther's views as he had previously been of Thomism.[37]

At this time Nicolaus von Amsdorff, who had been a Scotist until this time, also became an ardent supporter of Luther. And in September 1517 the disputation of Luther's student Franz Günther of Nordhausen,[38] defended Augustine against Pelagius; his teaching on free will and grace were contrasted with those of Scotus, Occam and Biel; the Schoolmen were represented as teaching the false religion and Luther's pupil stressed the individual's inner attitude towards God as the most important factor in man's relation to God. This disputation took place just one month before the posting of Luther's own theses. Luther had already written to Lang on May 18, 1517:

> Our theology and St. Augustine are continuing to prosper and reign in our university through the hand of God. Aristotle is declining daily and is inclining toward a fall which will end him forever. It is remarkable how lectures in the *Sentences* are despised.[39]

35 Cf. *WAB* I, 26; also *Liber Decanorum*, p. 19.
36 Cf. H. Barge, *Andreas Bodenstein von Karlstadt* (2 vols., Leipzig, 1905), I, 73.
37 Cf. Th. Kolde, 'Wittenberger Disputationsthesen aus den Jahren 1516 bis 1522', *ZK* 11 (1890), 448ff.
38 Cf. *WA* I, 224ff; *Liber Decanorum*, p. 20; *WAB* I, 45.
39 *Ibid.*, 41; this translation is taken from Schwiebert, *Luther*, p. 296.

As a natural consequence of these discussions and events, the faculty of the university became dissatisfied with the curriculum. Elector Frederick sent several of his advisors to Wittenberg in 1516 to check on the progress of lectures and examinations. He was also interested in the financial state of the university; on April 9 of that year the university senate had sent a long report to Frederick, pointing out the precarious state of the university's finances. Actually only the theological lecturers were assured of their salaries, by virtue of their membership in the chapter of the castle church; for no others was any regular income provided. The university senate also made a strong plea for an expansion in the profane disciplines: two professorships for the faculty of medicine, two for civil law, and five or six for the faculty of arts. Frederick responded immediately with a request for more information.[40] The university answered with more demands for expansion and issued a new list of professors and lecturers and the subjects they were teaching. The make-up of the courses had not changed much, except for personalities, compared with the *Rotulus* of 1507; now Luther stood at the head of the faculty of theology; the *humaniora* were covered by Balthasar Phacchus and Otto Beckmann.

It is not known how Frederick reacted to the faculty's report, but that he pursued the matter is evident from another visitation that took place in 1517.[41] Special complaints had been made by the faculty of law about some of their members' frequent absences from their lectureships and other irregularities. These professors were too busy making money in private practice to give their university lectures – a state of affairs apparently not unusual in law schools. Frederick sent two of his advisors, Fabian von Feilitsch and Hans von Taubenheim, to Wittenberg to negotiate with the university authorities and the castle chapter. They had been preceded by Spalatin, who in 1516 had become Frederick's private secretary and advisor in university affairs. The idea of a general university reform took shape in Frederick's and Spalatin's minds and they invited prominent members of the faculty for advice.[42] This reform, closely connected with Luther's teachings, took place in 1518.[43] Luther asked that teachers of Greek and Hebrew be provided – a suggestion that was implemented with the arrival of Melanchthon and Boeschenstein at Wittenberg. A letter from Luther to Jodocus Trutfetter elucidates the nature of his relation to humanism. As for the curriculum, it was his opinion that the reform of the church was impossible unless all the remnants of scholastic teachings of theology, philosophy and logic were eliminated and replaced with other studies.[44] For Luther the university reform was only a means to an end, the presupposition for the success of the reform of the church. The introduction of Greek, originally a major aim of humanism, was to serve a completely different function.

In summary, then, humanism played a major role in the development of the University of Wittenberg from the very outset. At the beginning hesitant and in the background, it was represented by only a few northern humanists; it then assumed

40 Friedensburg, *Urkundenbuch*, p. 76.
41 *Ibid.*, p. 83.
42 Cf. *WAB*, I, 63.
43 Friedensburg, *Urkundenbuch*, p. 85.
44 *WAB*, I, 74.

status when under the influence of Christoph Scheurl and his circle it became the dominant way of thought among the younger generation. However, humanism never had a chance to develop fully; as it was ready to take over some of the functions and positions of the entrenched scholasticism, an abrupt interruption came from a new quarter. On his journey towards the revolutionary restoration of what he considered Christianity should be, Luther estranged almost every humanist in Germany except Melanchthon. Attempts were made to separate Melanchthon and Luther; Erasmus warned Melanchthon of the enemies of the *bonae literae*;[45] when Reuchlin was unable to persuade Melanchthon to leave Wittenberg for Ingolstadt, he disinherited his grandnephew.[46] Others tried also to tell the world that Melanchthon was not living in peace with Luther. The humanists, well aware of the deep gap that separated them from Luther, realized that unless they could reconquer some of the territory that Luther had won, their cause would be buried under the impact of the Reformation.

The Wittenberg university reform and the beginnings of the German Reformation did stem from the same sources. When Luther started his *lectura in Biblia* in 1512, scholasticism and humanism were fighting each other for dominance. But the new theology that evolved from Luther's pulpit was victorious over both ways of thinking. Luther had learned from humanism, especially after Melanchthon's arrival in Wittenberg, and also from scholasticism; the reformer Luther, however, arrived at his conclusions through his new exegesis and hermeneutics of the Scriptures. Melanchthon and his humanism succumbed to Luther's Christianity.

Melanchthon, who could well be considered the synthesis of humanism and Lutheranism, soon realized that with Lutheranism much of what was valuable in humanism was doomed. From 1522 on he did not cease to lament the decay in education and the contempt that the new theologians showed for humanism. Melanchthon foresaw a new scholasticism, the rise of which could only be prevented by a combination of humanism and theology. His prophecies came true in the second part of the sixteenth century when Lutheranism became petrified in orthodoxy and fought against the very ideas of Melanchthon.

45 Desiderius Erasmus, *Opus epistolarum Des. Erasmi Roterodami*, ed. P. S. Allen, H. M. Allen, and H. W. Garrod (12 vols., Oxford, 1906–1958), III, 538.
46 Reuchlin, *Briefwechsel*, 280a.

CHAPTER VI

THE DEVELOPMENT OF PRINTING, 1502–1517[1]

At the time the University of Wittenberg was founded, the desire and the need for a printer and a printing press was felt in university circles. The initiative for the establishment of a press may have come from Martin Polich of Mellerstadt, the first rector of the university. In his many controversies at the University of Leipzig, especially with the physician Simon Pistoris and the theologian Konrad Wimpina, Mellerstadt had learned the value of printed material in intellectual battles.[2]

Nikolaus Marschalk

Nikolaus Marschalk,[3] who was to be the first printer in Wittenberg, came from the humanistic circle at Erfurt in 1502. He had worked for and with the Erfurt printer Wolfgang Schenck and in 1501 had established his own private printing press, probably with Schenck's types. In Erfurt Marschalk had been instrumental in the printing of the *Interpretamentum leue in Psellum* in 1499.[4] He brought to Wittenberg his enthusiasm for the Greek language and for classical antiquity; it is therefore not surprising that the first book he printed in Wittenberg included Greek letters. As a university professor he gave the first commencement speech of the faculty of arts in 1503[5] on the subject of the Judgment of Paris, which he interpreted with references to Greek mythology and philosophy, introducing the goddesses, Aphrodite, Hera and Athena, (in the manner of a Lucanian dialogue,)

1 For an exhaustive list of imprints, cf. Grossmann, *Wittenberger Drucke.*
2 Concerning this controversy at Leipzig, cf. Bauch, *Leipziger Frühhumanismus.*
3 Cf. Werner Bake, *Die Frühzeit des pommerschen Buchdrucks im Lichte neuerer Forschung.* Ein Beitrag zur deutschen Buchdruckergeschichte mit Wiedergabe zweier pommerscher Drucke vom Jahre 1537, Pyritz, 1934; Bauch, 'Die Anfänge des Studiums', pp. 75–98; Bauch, *Universität Erfurt*; Bauch, 'Wolfgang Schenck', 354–409; Ellinger, *Geschichte der neulateinischen Literatur*; G. C. F. Lisch, *Geschichte der Buchdruckerkunst in Mecklenburg bis zum Jahre 1540*; aus den Jahrbüchern des Vereins für Mecklenburgische Geschichte und Alterthumskunde besonders abgedruckt (Schwerin, Rostock, 1839); Nikolaus Marschalk, *Commencement Address*; delivered at the University of Wittenberg, January 18, 1503 *(Oratio habita albiori academia . . .)*, transl. Edgar C. Reinke and Gottfried G. Krodel (Valparaiso, Ind. 1967); Schoettgen, *Commentatio de vita N. Marschalci* (Rostock, 1752).
4 Cf. Hase, *Bibliographie*, no. 10; F. R. Goff, *Incunabula in American Libraries* (New York, 1964), P – 1080; *British Museum Catalogue*, vol. 249, col. 463; Bauch, 'Wolfgang Schenck', p. 355; Bauch, 'Die Anfänge des Studiums', p. 50. In both instances Bauch claims that it is the first time that Greek type was used in Germany. However, in *Die Universität Erfurt*, (p. 190), he corrects himself by asserting that Antonius Koberger started in 1497 to use Greek type in Nürnberg. The Reinke-Krodel edition of Marschalk's *Oratio habita* has another correction: they assert (p. 5, note 13) that there is a Nürnberg imprint of 1492 by Koberger containing some sentences printed in Greek.
5 Cf. Panzer, *Annales*, IX, 65, 1; Proctor, *Index*, 11826 Grossmann, *Wittenberger Drucke*, 3.

86

who then have to defend themselves in the Greek language. Marschalk told the graduating students that they had made their life's choice not Aphrodite's nor Hera's, but Athena's way, the *vita theoretica* or *contemplativa*. On the same day that he gave the speech, he printed it on his own printing press. Apparently he expected his audience to follow his interpretation of Greek mythology, if not in the original Greek language, at least in the Latin translation which he added to the printed text. Northern humanism must have been delighted with this first official pronouncement from Wittenberg and the first printed book to come from that city.

In the same year three works by the Italian jurist Petrus of Ravenna came from Marschalk's press.[6] Two are legal treatises, of which Petrus published many during his lifetime. The third, *De potestate pontificis maximi & Romani imperatoris* is especially remarkable for its subject. It was Petrus of Ravenna's inaugural lecture, given at the university before a large and illustrious audience that included the elector, his brother Duke Johann, the Duke of Braunschweig-Lüneburg and the entire university faculty and students. He spoke from memory as usual (because of his phenomenal memory he was sometimes called *Petrus ab memoria*) and, although his subject – the powers of the Pope and the Emperor – seemed dangerous and daring, Petrus treated it in the medieval manner.[7] He considered the supremacy of the Pope over the councils and the church as absolute; the power of the emperor in secular matters is just as absolute as the Pope's in spiritual ones; the emperor is God's representative in the world just as the Pope is God's representative in the spiritual sphere. At the end of his speech Petrus considered the question whether the Pope must participate in the foundation of a university or whether the emperor alone can do it. Petrus asserted that since each of the two powers is absolute within his own sphere, the emperor is just as entitled as the Pope to found a new university. Inasmuch as Frederick the Wise had just founded his university with imperial authority only, it must have been pleasing to him, and to the Wittenberg audience, to hear this in public.

This was a speech by a man who was considered a liberal and devoted advocate of humanistic thought; he was a friend of Marschalk, Trebelius and other humanists. When Petrus fled to Cologne in 1506 because of the outbreak of the plague in Wittenberg, he was persecuted as a heretic by Jacob Hoogstraten; Luther later considered him as one of the men who fought against the Roman church. In *De potestate*, however, Petrus did not give any new content to this traditional subject.

Two other works, without date, which came from Marschalk's press in the year 1503–1504, are controversial treatises of Martin Polich of Mellerstadt against Konrad Wimpina.[8] Marschalk thereby allied himself strongly with the humanist forces in Wittenberg where Mellerstadt represented a more progressive position than his Leipzig opponent who defended astrology and abstruse scholasticism.

Marschalk's stay in Wittenberg was brief, his humanist tendencies having brought him into difficulties with many members of the faculty. Elector

6 Cf. Bauch, "Wolfgang Schenck," p. 374; Grossmann, *Wittenberger Drucke*, nos. 4, 5, 6.
7 Cf. Theodor Muther, *Aus dem Universitäts- und Gelehrtenleben*, pp. 70ff.
8 Cf. Grossmann, *Wittenberger Drucke*, nos. 7, 8.

Frederick stood firmly behind him[9] and forwarded his complaints to the university authorities; but intervention on Marschalk's behalf was of only limited success. Like Hermann von dem Busche, Petrus of Ravenna and other early humanists, he soon left Wittenberg (in 1505) in search of a more congenial atmosphere. After spending some time in Brandenburg and at the newly established university at Frankfurt a.d. Oder (at the invitation of elector Joachim of Brandenburg) he went into the service of the Duke of Mecklenburg in Rostock. There he established a printing press and gave lectures at the university, and there he remained until his death in 1525.

Marschalk, who had been the most prominent member in the early humanist circle in Erfurt, held a similar position in Wittenberg. He introduced the Greek language and the study of antiquity at the university; he showed that in order to break the fetters of medieval scholasticism it was necessary to go back to the Greek language and Greek civilization and to exchange the scholastic *diviniora* for the humanistic *humaniora*. He taught his beliefs and influenced his students, among whom were Spalatin, Trebelius, Johannes Lang, Tileman Conradi. To make his influence a lasting one, he printed works that would be the starting point for his pupils on their way to future studies in the *humaniora*. That he established the first printing press in Wittenberg in an enlightened and humanistic spirit was perhaps his most important contribution to that city's intellectual life. Without him the beginnings of humanism in Wittenberg might have been postponed for some years.

Hermann Trebelius

When Marschalk left Wittenberg, his printing press remained with his co-worker and former pupil, Hermann Trebelius of Eisenach.[10] Trebelius had come to Erfurt in 1500, where he worked and studied with Marschalk, as he continued to do after their move to Wittenberg in 1502. When Marschalk left, Trebelius continued the printing program in his spirit. Although most of the works which then came from the press are undated, they are done with Marschalk's types and can be dated from internal evidence.

One of his early dated publications is a *Judicium Paridi*,[11] which suggests that Marschalk's earlier printed work on the same subject aroused a strong interest in

9 Cf. Friedensburg, *Geschichte*, p. 75. Unfortunately Marschalk's letter of complaint about conditions at the university is lost; neither can one establish the persons with whom he had differences. There are two notes, one asking Marschalk to continue his lectures, in spite of his difficulties; the other asking the university to clear up matters for Marschalk
10 Gustav Bauch, *Die Anfänge der Universität Frankfurt a. O. und die Entwicklung des wissenschaftlichen Lebens an der Hochschule, 1506–1540* (Berlin, 1900: Texte und Forschungen, 3); Bauch, 'Biographische Beiträge zur Schulgeschichte des XVI. Jahrhunderts' *MGDESG* 5 (1895), 1–26; Bauch, 'Drucke von Frankfurt a. O., Erweiterungen zu Panzer, *Annales typographici* VII, 54 and IX, 464', *CB* 15 (1898), 241–260. See also Josef Benzing, 'Hermann Trebelius, Dichter und Drucker zu Wittenberg und Eisenach', *Das Antiquariat 9*, nos. 13/14 (July 10, 1953), 203–204; Edmondo Coccia, *Le Edizioni delle opere del Mantovano* (Rome, 1960); Walter Maushake, *Frankfurt an der Oder als Druckerstadt* (Frankfurt a.d. Oder, 1936)
11 Cf. Panzer, *Annales*, IX, 66, 3; Grossmann, *Wittenberger Drucke*, no. 9.

Wittenberg. Another book from his press is a collection of lectures by Petrus of Ravenna,[12] in which Petrus discussed with a new spirit and élan the traditional theological and moral subjects: God, immortality, Anti-Christ, the Last Judgment, death and resurrection, grace and wrath of God, the Jews, family life. Like a good humanist, he not only dedicated his work to his princely masters, but also flattered his benefactors and praised their reign.

The most important of the undated works is the *Eisagoge*,[13] a Greek grammar. It was based on earlier works of the same title, printed by Aldus Manutius, and by Schenck and Marschalk in Erfurt, and was intended to be used by teachers and students of the Greek language in Wittenberg. It soon found wide distribution and was reprinted in 1511 by Rhau-Grunenberg.

Another work from the press of Trebelius is Johann von Kitzscher's *Dialogus de Sacri Romani Imperii rebus*,[14] which he had orginally written in Bologna in 1498. When Kitzscher came to Wittenberg he did not hesitate to have it printed, as a token of admiration for Frederick the Wise. In dedicating this work to the elector in honor of his university at Wittenberg, Kitzscher emphasized the special importance of the foundation of the university, which had grown so rapidly, and he expressed the hope that the students would benefit from his work. He wrote it, he says, in his best possible style and sketched some important events from Roman history and histories of other peoples, gleaned with great care from various sources. If the *Dialogus* finds the favor of the elector, he promises further works of this kind. This is actually the most significant document that had come from the Wittenberg presses since Marschalk's inaugural address. It is written in renaissance literary style — rich in classical symbolism and filled with German pride — and is fearlessly critical of papal, imperial and territorial malpractices. That Kitzscher chose it as the first of his works to be printed on his arrival in Wittenberg in honor of its ruler, suggests that he had found an audience ready for new forms and new ideas.

In the introduction to the *Dialogus* proper, in the form of a letter to his teacher in Bologna, Philippus Beroaldus Senior, Kitzscher speaks of a sojourn to the Bagni della Poretta. He describes how the delights there had turned his mind away from serious studies; now, ready to pursue and continue his philosophical and historical inquiries, he was determined to find an answer to the question which had haunted him for many years: is it true that in the life hereafter the good are separated from the bad, who are condemned to places of unthinkable tortures? The answer to this proposed question Kitzscher presents in an allegoric dream. As Dante finds in Virgil a guide to the world beyond, so Kitzscher is guided to these same places by the Florentine humanist Pico della Mirandola. Any doubts that Kitzscher entertained concerning the fate of sinners are dispersed by his journey through the underworld, where he sees indescribable suffering and torture. From there Pico leads his visitor to the fields of the blessed, where the sages and the great men of

12 Cf. Grossmann, *Wittenberger Drucke*, no. 24.
13 *Ibid.*, no. 17.
14 Cf. Proctor, *Index*, 11827; Grossmann, *Wittenberger Drucke*, no. 22. For an interesting discussion of this work, cf. Brandis, 'Italienische Humanisten', pp. 277–296; Brandis emphasizes Kitzscher's dependence on Dante. For this edition from the press of Trebelius Kitzscher added an index with explanatory notes, in view of the great number of names cited.

virtue live in the splendid cities, Thebes and Athens, Babylon and Alexandria, Constantinople and Syracuse. They meet the heroes of the medieval epics, Lancelot, Tristan, Parzival and other heroes of King Arthur's Round Table.

At Pico's and Kitzscher's arrival in celestial Rome the death of Emperor Frederick III of the Holy Roman Empire is announced, and Octavian Augustus and the Great Caesar with their courtiers hasten to receive him. Caesar welcomes Frederick III and inquires whom he left as his successor on the imperial throne. Frederick, after expressing his satisfaction at being removed from earthly turmoil and being joined to the company of such illustrious men, reveals that this successor to the imperial throne is his son Maximilian. Augustus and Caesar both praise the young emperor, but also admit their anxiety for such a young man having to face such times of crisis for the empire. This gives Kitzscher an opening for his frank and radical criticism of the state of affairs in the empire, and he does not spare either the secular or the ecclesiastical princes. He accuses them of being occupied only in the pursuit of material gains of wealth and power, of luxuries and pleasures. Augustus and Caesar recall the martial deeds, the fearless spirit and the great qualities of the minds of their German adversaries, and they affirm their belief that these qualities still exist among the contemporary Germans if led by a firm and vigilant ruler.

Augustus then recalls that at his recent meeting with Ernst, Elector of Saxony (who had died in 1486), he had been told of the shameful treacheries of German princes who sold out to the French emperor, to the Hungarians and to the Polish king. Augustus expresses his hope that the relations between the sovereign emperor and his princes will improve and that both will be led by a spirit of trust and mutual understanding for the best of the empire and its subjects. Frederick III warmly agrees and recalls how much cooperation and support he had received from trustworthy princes. With a note of confidence the dialogue ends. The participants find themselves in the presence of the throne of the highest and greatest God, surrounded by the Apostles and the martyrs and host of angels. Charlemagne, Saint Louis, and others receive Frederick III and lead him away from the envious pagan emperors to eternal bliss.

This dialogue is purely Renaissance in character. The concern with German problems, the frank criticism of the political and social conditions and the strong condemnation of the Italian papacy bear witness to the spirit of a new national humanism now emanating from Wittenberg.

Three works by Henricus Aquilonipolensis, the Erfurt poet and humanist, can be traced to Trebelius' press. Of these, the *Sophologia*[15] is an encyclopedic work. The author discusses the arts, the invention of the alphabet and of language, logic, geometry, music, astrology, poetry, drama, philosophy, medicine. He commends Polich von Mellerstadt for his views on poetry, as opposing those of Wimpina in the famous Leipzig controversy, and takes this as a starting point for a discussion of the origins of poetry, comedy and tragedy. He also condemns the *Doctrinale* of Alexander Gallus, a courageous stand at such an early date. The work ends with a prayer and blessing for Elector Frederick and his university.

The works that Trebelius printed in Wittenberg show that he continued

15 Grossmann, *Wittenberger Drucke*, no. 21.

Marschalk's interest in the *humaniora* and in Greek studies. Because of the outbreak of the plague in Wittenberg and difficulties with some of his colleagues at the university, in 1506 Trebelius moved to Eisenach where he printed his own work, *Hecastichon Elegiacum de Peste Isenachensi.*[16] The type he gave to Wolf Sturmer of Erfurt, who used it in 1506–1507; a year later it was brought back to Wittenberg where it became the property of Johannes Rhau-Grunenberg. Thus the type that had first come from Erfurt to Wittenberg returned there, this time permanently.

The first printing ventures, the presses of Marschalk and Trebelius, helped to introduce early humanism to Wittenberg, where as the years went by, the art became more and more the tool of the progressive forces.

Wolfgang Stöckel

While the private presses of Marschalk and Trebelius were printing works which reflected new humanistic ideas and tendencies, the conservative forces at the university expressed the desire to have an official printing press established to serve the university and the elector. In the fall of 1503 the first dean of the faculty of arts, Sigismund Epp, on their behalf asked Frederick to provide for having books printed in the *via Scoti*, to be used as official texts, Frederick welcomed the suggestion and wrote to Frederick von Kitzscher (provost of the Castle Church) and to Martin Polich von Mellerstadt (vice-chancellor of the university), asking them to form a committee with two other members of the faculty to consider the matter; they also were to call upon other colleagues for advice. Frederick recommended the project, although he suggested that not only books in the *via Scoti* should be printed, but other books needed by other faculties in the university. Thus the elector modified, according to his own insight, the plan for what he called a 'gemeine truckerei', probably meaning a 'public' or 'common' printing establishment in contrast to the two private printing presses. Frederick further demanded that each faculty should appropriate 500 gulden for the purpose and expressed his willingness to contribute some money towards it himself.[17]

Wolfgang Stöckel was designated the first official printer to the university in 1504, shortly after he moved to Wittenberg from Leipzig.[18] For his first book Stöckel printed a legal treatise by Petrus of Ravenna, the *Compendium pulcherrimum juriscanonici*, part 1.[19] He turned next to the printing of some texts in the *via Scoti*, in accordance with Epp's wish — the task for which he had actually been called to Wittenberg. He printed the *Summula* of Petrus Hispanus, the *Isagoge* of Porphyrius; the *Organon*, the *Natural Philosophy* and the *Metaphysics* of Aristotle

16 Cf. Bauch, "Wolfgang Schenck," pp. 379–380.
17 Cf. Friedensburg, *Urkundenbuch*, I, p. 6.
18 Cf. Bauch, 'Wolfgang Schenck und Nikolaus Marschalk', *passim*; J. Braun, 'Wolfgang Stöckel: ein Beitrag zur Geschichte der Buchdruckerkunst', *Börsenblatt für den deutschen Buchhandel*, No. 301 (1884), 6129–6131; Alfred Götze, *Die hochdeutschen Drucker der Reformationszeit* (Strassburg, 1905); Hans Lülfing, *Leipziger Frühdrucker* (Leipzig, 1959).
19 Cf. Panzer, *Annales*, IX, 65–66, 2; Muther, *Aus dem Universitäts- und Gelehrtenleben*, pp. 378–379; parts 2 and 3 were printed later by Stöckel, after his return to Leipzig.

with the commentaries of Petrus Tartaretus and additions by Scotus – all edited by Sigismund Epp.[20]

The *Metaphysics* of Aristotle carried a dedication to elector Frederick by Polich von Mellerstadt, praising him for his love of philosophy and his help to those engaged in the pursuit of this discipline and alluding to the elector's knowledge of Plato and Homer. Mellerstadt dwells on the excellence of Tartaretus' dialectics as a basis for any future study of philosophy and logic. In vivid imagery he predicts that these works will train as many students as there were soldiers who came out of the Trojan horse. All three books, beautifully adorned with woodcuts and seals of the University of Wittenberg and its patron saint Augustine, are markedly in the spirit of scholasticism. They were used as textbooks by the Scotist professors until 1519 when the university abandoned this school of philosophy.

In the same period Stöckel also printed the work of the Italian Carmelite Baptista Mantuanus on the Virgin Mary.[21]

It may well have been that Scotism, promulgated by Stöckel and his press, was no longer popular among the student body and among some of the professors at Wittenberg, while at Leipzig the old traditional studies were still deeply entrenched. The little success with which Stöckel met at Wittenberg probably accounts for his early return to Leipzig. On account of financial difficulties there, Stöckel moved on to Dresden in 1524 and became the printer to the famous opponents of the Reformation, among them Emser and Cochläus.

Wittenberg was without a printer for some time during 1506–1507. When the professors wanted either their own works or other textbooks printed, they usually commissioned Martin Landsberg in Leipzig, who also maintained a bookstore in Wittenberg. The plague that drove the University of Wittenberg temporarily to the small town of Herzberg in 1506 may have prevented any further printing activities for the moment. When the university returned to Wittenberg, Johannes Rhau-Grunenberg, who was to become the first great Reformation printer there, set up his printing press.

Before turning to Grunenberg, another printer, Symphorian Reinhart and the fine work he did at Wittenberg should be discussed.

Symphorian Reinhart

Symphorian Reinhart[22] was important in the history of printing and woodcutting in Wittenberg, but he has been neglected by historians of printing, perhaps because very little is known about him. He came from Strassburg to Wittenberg and was

---

20 Cf. Grossmann, *Wittenberger Drucke*, nos. 31, 32, 33.
21 Cf. Coccia, *Mantovano*, no. 51; Grossmann, *Wittenberger Drucke*, no. 29.
22 Cf. Gustav Bauch, 'Zur Cranachforschung', *RK*, 17 (1894), 421–435; Otto Clemen, 'Der Wittenberger Holzschneider und Buchdrucker Symphorian Reinhardt', *ZB*, 44 (1927), 523–525; Josef Benzing, *Die Buchdrucker des 16. und 17. Jahrhunderts im deutschen Sprachgebiet* (Wiesbaden, 1963: Beiträge zun Buch- und Bibliothekswesen, 12), pp. 465–466; F.W.H. Hollstein, *German engravings, etchings and woodcuts, ca. 1400–1700*, vol. VI, ed. K.G. Boon and R.W. Scheller (Amsterdam, 1960); Harold Joachim, 'A rare illustrated book by Cranach', *Bulletin of the Art Institute of Chicago*, 43 (1949), 8–11; Hermann Roemer, 'Hans Grueninger und die Buchdruckerfamilie Reinhard aus Markgroeningen', *Mark-*

probably related to the Strassburg printer and woodcutter Johannes Reinhart or Grüninger.

His outstanding achievement is the *Wittenberg Heiligtumsbuch* of 1509, one of the most important works of early printing in Wittenberg. Gustav Bauch was the first to point out that Symphorian Reinhart participated in the printing of this magnificent catalog of the collection of relics accumulated by Frederick the Wise, with woodcuts from the workshop of Lucas Cranach;[23] he pointed to the identicalness of the type between the *Heiligtumsbuch* and the *Ein ser andechtig Buchlein* which Reinhart printed in 1512. He concluded that it was printed by Reinhart, even though he is not cited in the colophon.[24]

Three later imprints of Reinhart are known from the years 1525 and 1527.[25]

Reinhart seems to have had his printing press in the castle in Wittenberg and to have employed several printers in his workshop.[26] Also his collaboration with Lucas Cranach is definitely established. So far as is known, he is only twice mentioned in contemporary literature: Otto Beckmann added to Christoph Scheurl's famous *Oratio attingens literarum prestantiam* a laudatory poem to Cranach in which he mentions Symphorian Reinhart in glowing terms.[27] He calls him a sculptor and woodcutter; thus he may have been not only a printer but also an artisan or artist. The other reference to Reinhart is in a letter from Scheurl to Amsdorff,[28] where he speaks of him in connection with Cranach, 'et quibuscumque nominis mei studiosis, etiam Simphoriano, Luce, in commune omnibus pictoribus, me commendabis diligenter'.

In 1512 Reinhart printed Adam von Fulda's *Ein ser andechtig christenlich*

---

groeningen im Rahmen der Landesgeschichte, I (Markgroeningen, 1933), 277–331; Ernst Schulte–Strathaus, 'Die Wittenberger Heiligtumsbücher vom Jahre 1509 mit Holzschnitten von Lucas Cranach', *Gutenberg Jahrbuch,* 1930, pp. 175–186; Hildegard Zimmermann, *Lucas Cranach d. Ä. Folgen der Wittenberger Heiligtümer und die Illustrationen des Rhau'schen Hortulus animae* (Halle, 1929), and 'Die Titeleinfassungen des Symphorian Reinhart in Wittenberg', *ZB* 45 (1928), 70–71.

23 Bauch, 'Zur Cranachforschung', *passim.*
24 Cf. Schulte-Strathaus, 'Die Wittenberger Heiligtumsbücher', p. 178; Josef Benzing, *Buchdruckerlexikon des 16. Jahrhunderts (deutsches Sprachgebiet)* (Frankfurt a.M., 1952), p. 182; Hollstein, *German engravings* VI, 76; Eduard Flechsig, *Cranachstudien,* erster Teil (Leipzig, 1900), 65-66; Johannes Jahn, *Lucas Cranach als Graphiker* (Leipzig, 1955), p. 52.
25 Hans Volz, 'Bibliographie der im 16. Jahrhundert erschienenen Schriften Georg Spalatins', *Zeitschrift für Bibliothekswesen und Bibliographie,* 5(1958), no. 26; Borchling-Clausen, I, 823; Josef Benzing, *Lutherbibliographie; Verzeichnis der gedruckten Schriften Martin Luthers bis zu dessen Tod* (Baden-Baden, 1966), no. 2457; Kuczynski, no. 36; Luther, WA 30², pp. 64ff; *Supplementa Melanchthoniana. Werke Philipp Melanchthons die im Corpus Reformatorum vermisst wurden* (5 vols., Leipzig, 1910-29; reprint, Frankfurt, 1968), V, 1, cxxix and 61-73; Grossmann, *Wittenberger Drucke,* nos. 37, 38, 39.
26 Cf. Georg Buchwald, 'Allerlei Wittenbergisches aus der Reformationszeit', *Luther,* 10 (1928), 108–109.
27 The poem is reprinted by Bauch, 'Wolfgang Schenck', p; 388.
28 Cf. Bauch, 'Zu Christoph Scheurls Briefbuch', p. 432, no. 70b.

Buchlein.[29] The editor was Wolff Cyclop of Zwickau,[30] a Silesian humanist who had matriculated in Wittenberg in 1502 and remained there until the 1520's. He dedicated the work to Duke Johann of Saxony, the brother of elector Frederick. Adam von Fulda, who had died in Wittenberg in 1506, was a composer and musician and one of the representatives of the German late Gothic style in music; his best known work is *De Musica*, a work on the invention, explanation and praise of music.

The volume is interesting from several points of view: eight woodcuts of Lucas Cranach adorn it and it was printed in the German language – one of the few publications prior to the Reformation in which the people are told in their own native tongue about the dogmas of Christianity, the life and sufferings of Jesus and the last Judgment Day. Reinhart's cooperation with Cranach lent his printing enterprise additional significance in the art history of Wittenberg at that time.

Johannes Rhau-Grunenberg

Johannes Rhau-Grunenberg,[31] who was printing in Wittenberg as early as 1508, was probably born in Gronenberg or Grunenberg in Thuringia. There is little doubt that he was the 'Joh. Ru.' who printed in Erfurt in 1507 with Wolf Sturmer, and was likewise the 'Johannes Decker Viridimontanus' who matriculated in Wittenberg on his arrival there in 1508.

Grunenberg arrived in Wittenberg the same year that Martin Luther was transferred there for the first time, – in 1508. It may have been at the initiative of Johann von Staupitz, who had Luther transferred to Wittenberg in that same year, that Grunenberg also was asked to provide a printing press for the university that lacked any such facility. It was in the same memorable year that new statutes for the university were drawn up by Christoph Scheurl and every effort was being made to make the university more attractive as a center of learning. The fact that Grunenberg's press was, at least for some time after 1512, located in the Augustinian convent where Luther was living also points to contact between Grunenberg, Luther and Staupitz.

Grunenberg inaugurated his printing program, which was to minister to the

29 Cf. E. Weller, *Repertorium typographicum* (Nördlingen, 1864; supplement, 1874), p. 79, no. 680. A facsimile edition was reproduced in 1914, ed. Eduard Flechsig (Berlin, 1914; Graphische Gesellschaft, XIX. Veröffentlichung).
30 Cf. Bauch, 'Beiträge', I, 219–221; Otto Clemen, "Ein Brief des Wolfgang Cyclopius von Zwickau', *NASGA* 23 (1902), 134–137.
31 Cf. G. F. Barwick, "The Lutheran Press at Wittenberg', *Transactions of the Bibliographical Society*, 3 (1895–1896), 9–25; Otto Clemen, "Beiträge zur Geschichte des Wittenberger Buchdrucks in der Reformationszeit I. Bilder trojanischer Helden bei Joh. Grunenberg', *Gutenberg Jahrbuch*, 16 (1941), 174ff; Johannes Joachim, "Die Drucker Johannes Grunenberg und Georg Rhau in Wittenberg', *ZB*, 21 (1904), 433–439; Johannes Luther, "Die Schnellarbeit der Wittenberger Buchdruckerpressen in der Reformationszeit', *ZB*, 31 (1914), 244–264; Johannes Luther, "Der Wittenberger Buckdruck in seinem Uebergang zur Reformationspresse', in *Lutherstudien zur 4. Jahrhundertfeier der Reformation*. Veröffentlicht von den Mitarbeitern der Weimarer Lutherausgabe (Weimar, 1917), pp. 261–282; Wilhelm Velke, 'Der erste Lutherdrucker stammt aus Gruenberg in Oberhessen', *Mitteilungen des oberhessischen Geschichtsvereins*, n.s. 24 (1922), 19–27.

university's need for textbooks, with great vigor and speed. One of the first works to come from his press in 1508 was the *Praecepta Isocratis*,[32] in the Latin translation of the foremost early German humanist, Rudolf Agricola. In the same year Grunenberg also printed a laudatory poem by Georgius Sibutus[33] who had been crowned *poet laureate* by emperor Maximilian. Since 1506 he had been lecturing on the *humaniora* in Wittenberg.

Grunenberg printed in 1511 another and more important work by Sibutus, the *Torniamenta*.[34] This long poem in hexameter described a tournament that took place in 1508 with great festivities in the presence of many princes, dukes and knights. Lucas Cranach decorated this work with several woodcuts, one of which was a portrait of Sibutus himself.

An important publication from Grunenberg's press in 1508 was the Thomist Andreas Bodenstein von Carlstadt's *Distinctiones Thomistarum*[35] − the first work printed in Wittenberg in which Hebrew type was used. It shows Carlstadt's knowledge of Greek and Hebrew and in the choice of subject anticipates his later polemic and controversial tendencies. Ludwig Henning, a Franciscan and Scotist professor at Wittenberg, edited the *Formalitates* of the Paris Scotist professor Antonius Sirecti in 1505 and had it printed in Leipzig so that he could use it as a textbook for his students in Wittenberg. Carlstadt's aim was to present a similar subject from the Thomistic point of view. At the end of his *Distinctiones Thomistarum* Carlstadt claimed that no one before had treated "formalism" in a similar way. In his boastful way he was right, since up to this time no Thomist had ever approached this particular Scotist subject. He had, however, to modify his Thomistic interpretation and came to the conclusion that the differences between these two philosophies were not as great as most people thought. Carlstadt dedicated the *Distinctiones* to Frederick the Wise with a sapphic-verse poem in hexameter. The humanist-poet Sbrulius wrote an accompanying poem, commending the author of the treatise. Even though the work was in content scholastic, in its framework it is of Renaissance character.

How much Carlstadt became attracted to humanism is evident from the friendships he formed. Christoph Scheurl, in an oration on November 16, 1508, called him: *virum latine, graece et hebraice vehementer eruditum, magnum philosophum, maiorem theologum maximum Thomistam . . . Quod si multos Carolstadios haberemus, facile, puto, nos cum Parisiensibus manum posse consere atque pedem conferre.* This is great praise from an outspoken humanist for a man who

---

32 This is a Latin translation of Isocrates' *To Demonicus*, a treatise on practical ethics. The authenticity of the discourse has been challenged, but no definite judgment has been passed. Cf. *Isocrates*, with an English translation by George Norlin, (London, 1928: Loeb Classical Library), pp. 2−38; Grossmann, *Wittenberger Drucke*, no. 44.

We often find in Grunenberg's imprints the following variations of the place of printing: *apud Augustinianos, bei den Augustinern, Apud Aurelianos, apud collegium novum, in aedibus Iohannis Grunenbergii apud Augustinianos.*

33 Cf. Grossmann, *Wittenberger Drucke*, no. 46.

34 Cf. Panzer, *Annales*, IX, 68, 16; Proctor, *Index*, no. 11830; Grossmann, *Wittenberger Drucke*, no. 72.

35 About this scholastic phase of Carlstadt, cf. Bauch, 'Andreas Carlstadt als Scholastiker', *ZK*, 18 (1898), 37−57.

was still in the Thomist camp. Lucas Cranach and Georgius Sibutus also belonged to the circle of friends around Carlstadt.

Between 1508 and 1517 Grunenberg printed many works of humanistic character, only a few of which will be discussed here. In the years 1509 and 1510 he printed three orations by Otto Beckmann, the close friend of Christoph Scheurl, as we know from their rich and warm correspondence.[36] Between the time of Scheurl's departure from Wittenberg and Melanchthon's arrival, Beckmann was the most outstanding representative of humanism in Wittenberg, and to him Melanchthon dedicated his inaugural address in 1518.[37]

In 1509 Grunenberg published Aristotle's *De Anima*,[38] as was mentioned before. Another interesting book from Grunenberg's press was the *Historia Daretis Phrygij de Excidio Troie*.[39] The author purports to be Dares, the priest of Hephaistos in Troy (*Iliad* V, 9ff). The Latin translator, under the name of Cornelius Nepos, had dedicated his work to Sallustius Crispus and claims to have found the Greek original in Athens and to have translated it word for word into Latin. The story starts with the voyage of the Argonauts and ends with the destruction of Troy. Actually it seems to be the work of an author of the fifth or sixth century A. D. It thus shows the continuing interest in Troy and its epic battles towards the end of antiquity. Next to Diktys, Dares exerted most influence upon the medieval works dealing with Troy and its sagas. Eleven beautiful woodcuts decorate the work, the subjects all taken from the Trojan war.

In the next few years Grunenberg printed several works by the controversial Erfurt and Wittenberg poet, Tileman Conradi,[40] who had arrived in 1502 in Erfurt, where he learned the rudiments of Greek. He already wrote Latin poetry and incurred strong criticism from Mutian for his bombastic and flowery language.[41] He left Erfurt for a short study-trip to Venice, Padua and Bologna, where he continued to study Greek. In 1509 he came to Wittenberg and stayed with interruptions, until 1519 or 1520. Later we find him in Worms where he took his stand for reformed religion. His important contribution to humanism in Wittenberg was the private tutoring of Greek, not yet officially part of the university curriculum. After 1516 Conradi also gave private instruction in Hebrew, thus becoming the first teacher of Hebrew in Wittenberg.[42]

The first of Conradi's works printed by Grunenberg was the *Teratologia*.[43] Though the comedy in the form of a dialogue was dedicated, like so many other Wittenberg publications, to Polich von Mellerstadt, this fact did not prevent Conradi from attacking scholastic teaching. Poems by Chilian Reuter and

---

36 Cf. Grossmann, *Wittenberger Drucke*, nos. 50, 57, 58.
37 *CR* XI, cols. 15–25; printed by Grunenberg in 1518.
38 Panzer, *Annales*, IX, 67, 11; Grossmann, *Wittenberger Drucke*, no. 48.
39 Cf. Panzer, *Annales*, IX, 69, 18; here a 1512 edition is described; we must therefore assume that 1513 was a new edition. Cf. Grossmann, *Wittenberger Drucke*, 86.
40 Also known as Thiloninus Cunradus Philymnus Syasticanus. Cf. Hans Volz, 'Der Humanist Tileman Conradi aus Göttingen. Ein Beitrag zum Thema: Humanismus und Reformation', *Jahrbuch der Gesellschaft für Niedersächsische Kirchengeschichte*, 64 (1966), 76–116.
41 *Mutians Briefwechsel*, no. 59.
42 Cf. Bauch, 'Die Einführung des Hebräischen in Wittenberg', *Monatsschrift für Geschichte und Wissenschaft des Judentums* 48 (1904), 147ff.
43 Cf. Grossmann, *Wittenberger Drucke*, 52.

Christian Beyer were added and Greek and Hebrew quotations included to show off Conradi's knowledge of these languages and to strengthen his attacks. In an accompanying poem, moreover, he attacked Euricius Cordus and thus began his poetic controversy with this representative of early Erfurt humanism.[44] In spite of Conradi's attack on the immorality of the times he narrated his own love affair with a married lady; and his *Triumphus Bacchi* appeared in 1511 – a collection of erotic poems, calling for orgiastic enjoyment of life and telling of his amorous adventures in Wittenberg.[45] The same year he edited a new and enlarged edition of Trebelius' *Eisagoge*, though there is no mention of his name. In the introduction, however, Conradi says that he is teaching Greek like Trebelius and at the end he makes several cynical remarks which led Bauch and others to the definite conclusion that Conradi was the editor. The Greek reading exercises were increased in number compared with Trebelius' *Eisagoge* and all were furnished with Latin interlinear translations. The Greek types show no improvement over the Marschalk and Trebelius editions. Conradi probably used this work as a textbook for his students of Greek.

In 1513 Grunenberg published the first Greek text edition in Wittenberg, the *Batrachomiomachia* of Homer,[46] also edited by Conradi, This comic heroic poem, falsely ascribed to Homer, is a parody of the *Iliad* and describes the battle of the frogs and the mice. Conradi had seen a manuscript of this work some years before[47] and was asked by his students to edit it; in so doing he improved the text according to his best knowledge and translated the poem into Latin hexameters. The verses were good enough to evoke from Mutian an accusation of plagiarism which he did not substantiate.[48] A poem by Sibutus again commended this work to readers and it is dedicated to the Erfurt professors of theology Johann Werlich and Maternus Pistoris. The appended *Eulogia Funebris* contains many Latin epitaphs and awkward Greek verses. One epitaph is "Nobilis parasiti Oulenspiegel"; this reference antedates the first German edition of *Till Eulenspiegel* printed in Strassburg in 1513.[49]

Soon after this publication Conradi returned to Erfurt where he became involved in a literary feud with Johannes Femilius, and again provoked Mutian's disagreement. Angry and tired, Conradi returned to Wittenberg in 1515, where he published a bitter pamphlet against Femilius and Cordus, *Choleamynterius in Fellifluum.*[50] The interesting dispute seems to have found an echo in the *Epistolae Obscurorum Virorum.*[51]

---

44 Cf. Bauch, *Die Universität Erfurt*, pp. 163–169.
45 Cf. Grossmann, *Wittenberger Drucke* no. 68.
46 Cf. Panzer, *Annales*, IX, 69, 19; Proctor, *Index*, 11831; Grossmann, *Wittenberger Drucke*, no. 82. – This work has been ascribed to Pigres of Halicarnassos of the fifth century B. C. Cf. Pauly-Wissowa, *Real-Encyclopaedie*, XX, cols. 113–116.
47 His preface indicates that he had seen this in Prague in the hands of Hieronymus Balbus, who was there between 1499 and 1501. Cf. Bauch, *Die Universität Erfurt*, p. 163.
48 *Mutians Briefwechsel*, nos. 245, 294, 330.
49 Cf. W. Krogmann, 'Zwei Grabschriften auf Ulenspegel aus dem Jahre 1513', *Jahrbuch des Vereins für niederdeutsche Sprachforschung*, 69/70 (1943/47), 164–175.
50 Cf. Grossmann, *Wittenberger Drucke*, 95.
51 Cf. *Epistolae Obscurorum Virorum*, ed. F. G. Stokes, (London, 1909), 38.

At this time Conradi turned to religion, and in 1516 his *Triumphus Christi*[52] came from Grunenberg's press. The work dealt with the suffering, death and resurrection of Jesus. He added an *Ode theologica* in which he denounced the collecting of relics. The real relics, he argues, are the books of the Bible, whose reading is neglected and he pleads that man should be concerned above all with the Gospels. Those are interesting statements coming from the town where Frederick the Wise still collected relics intensely and spent money lavishly on the castle church. The *Ode theologica* anticipates the Reformation's stand against relics. It is therefore not surprising that in 1522 Conradi published a work on the Pauline epistles from the Lutheran point of view.

Grunenberg printed a Latin edition of the Psalms in 1513[53] with wide margins for interlinear and marginal notes. It seems certain that this edition was to be used as a textbook in the lecture course on the Psalms which Luther gave in 1513–1515; it is clear that he had used it in these lectures, for the copy at Wolfenbüttel has interlinear and marginal glossae in Luther's own handwriting.[54]

To students of the Reformation Grunenberg is known as Luther's first printer. Before 1517 only two items by Luther had been printed in Wittenberg: the introduction to an incomplete edition of the *Theologia Deutsch*, and *Die sieben Busspsalmen*, written in German.[55] Although they are not, as has been claimed, the first works in the German language printed in Wittenberg, Luther's choice of the vernacular over the customary Latin shows his early concern for a broad audience. Their significance for pre-Reformation printing in Wittenberg lies in the fact that Grunenberg was the first printer of Luther and thereby helped to launch the religious movement.

In 1516 Luther found at Johann Lang's house in Erfurt a copy of Tauler's sermons which he took with him to Wittenberg. In the same year he came into the possession of parts of the work which later became known as *Theologia Deutsch*; these parts (about one-fourth of the actual work, chapters 7–24) made such a deep impression on Luther that he had them published by Grunenberg's press, with a short introduction. Neither the author nor the title of the work was given in Luther's copy and he called this 1516 edition *Eyn geystlich edles Buchleynn*. In the introduction he wrote that the work seemed to be written in the spirit of Tauler, and to Spalatin he emphasized the spiritual relationship of this work to Tauler's sermons, but does not attribute them to him.[56] In 1518 Luther found a complete manuscript of the work and published it together with a new and longer introduction, again in Wittenberg by Grunenberg, now under the title *Eyn deutsch Theologia*. The book was soon reprinted in Leipzig, Augsburg,[57] Strassburg and later again in Wittenberg.

52 Cf. Grossmann, *Wittenberger Drucke*, 102.
53 Luther, *WA* III, p. 2; Benzing, *Lutherbibliographie*, p. 439, no. 68a; Grossmann, *Wittenberger Drucke*, 90.
54 Cf. *WA*, III, introduction.
55 Cf. *WA* I, 152–153; Proctor, *Index*, 11833; Benzing, *Lutherbibliographie*, 69; Grossmann, *Wittenberger Drucke*, 105; *WA*, I, 154–200; Benzing, *Lutherbibliographie*, 74, 75; Grossmann, *Wittenberger Drucke*, nos. 113, 114.
56 *WAB*, I, 79, no. 30.
57 The title of this edition is *Theologia Teütsch*, under which name the book was known from then on.

Luther's *Die sieben Busspsalmen* – his own German translation of each of the penitential Psalms, followed by textual explanations – came from Grunenberg's press in 1517. He had intended this publication for the widest possible public and not for scholars and students, as he explained it in a letter to Christoph Scheurl:[58] 'Non enim Nurinbergensibus, id est, delicatissimis et emunctissimis animabus, sed rudibus, ut nostri, Saxonibus, quibus nulla verbositate satis mandi et praemandi potest eruditio christiana, editae sunt'. He did not encourage his friends to buy the work and regretted that it had found such wide distribution in learned circles. Yet it had also had a wide circulation, and before Grunenberg had finished his first printing, he had to reprint the first part in a larger edition. The *Busspsalmen* were reprinted in Leipzig and in Strassburg and later editions were published in Erfurt and again in Leipzig. In 1525 Luther made a new revised edition which reflects the changes in his religious thinking of this period.

The works from Grunenberg's press prior to Luther's publications, all in Greek or Latin, were intended for educated and academic circles. Luther's concern, however, was to address himself to the people in their own language. A new and gigantic task was set for the Grunenberg press: to supply the printed word for the Reformation.

An examination of printing at Wittenberg between 1502 and 1517 makes it evident that, with the exception of Wolfgang Stöckel, the men promoting these enterprises were in the humanist camp. They were intent upon stimulating interest in classical languages and studies. Marschalk and Trebelius rendered pioneer service in a town not yet ready to support fully their humanistic printing program, and they left after a short stay. However, the changes in the cultural climate of the town were rapid in these years and Grunenberg's printing press devoted to the new learning was soon successful. His early contact with Luther led easily to the transition from the printing of works exclusively used by scholars, to religious material accessible to the people. Wolfgang Stöckel, who had come to Wittenberg as official printer to the university, brought out scholastic material. But the cultural climate was such that there was actually no further demand for the books he offered and for that reason he returned to Leipzig to resume his work along the old conservative lines. The impact of humanism and the new learning is vividly reflected by the books published in Wittenberg, which in their turn helped to promote the new movement.

58 *WAB*, I, 93, no. 38.

CHAPTER VII

THE GROWTH OF A HUMANISTIC LIBRARY

In 1512 Frederick the Wise established a university library, thus putting his splendid collection of books and manuscripts at the disposal of the scholars and students of Wittenberg.[1] As far as we can ascertain, the first purchases of books were made in the year 1493 when Frederick journeyed to the Holy Land.[2] That a growing university would soon be in need of an adequate library could easily be foreseen; and it may well be supposed that the elector, some years before making his library available to the university community, had intended such a course. Many of the acquisitions of the years between 1502 and 1512 point to such a plan This discussion of the library will therefore first take into account the material secured previous to the formal opening of the library in 1512, and then describe its growth in the years between 1512 and 1517. The rich records of the Wittenberg library holdings provide us with one of the most vital sources for understanding the cultural climate and orientation of Frederick the Wise's entourage.

The Wittenberg library was in existence for only thirty-five years. For the early period through the year 1517, information concerning acquisitions can be gathered only from the most disparate sources. In 1536 Spalatin made two catalogues of the collection, one alphabetically by author and the other loosely by subject. The occasion for this project was the reorganization of the library which in turn was part of the general reorganization of the whole university by elector Johann Friedrich. Because some of its books are still extant, it is of interest to know the later fate of the library. After their defeat at the battle of Mühlberg in 1547, the Ernestine line lost the electorate and the electoral lands, including Wittenberg, to Albertine Saxony. The university library, however, was preserved for the Ernestine line and after being packed up and brought to Weimar, it finally landed in Jena where it formed the nucleus of the library of the University of Jena, which was established to take the place of the Wittenberg university.

Probably the majority of the books in Frederick's possession before 1512 had been dedicated to him in accordance with Renaissance custom, by humanists and scholars in acknowledgment of benefits or in the hope of gaining favors. Many such books dedicated to Frederick were in the Wittenberg library; others were found in the libraries of Gotha and Coburg, which suggests that not all of Frederick's private books were given to the university library. He probably kept a small private library of his own, which, after his death, remained in his successor's

---

1 It was again Mutian who encouraged the elector to establish a library and open it up to the public.
2 In his financial accounts of this journey Hans Hundt in the *Rechnungsbuch* says that Frederick spent "1 fl fur zehen gedruckt cronika;" cf. R. Röhricht and H. Meisner, "Hans Hundts Rechnungsbuch', p. 82.

possession and was later distributed to various places. All trace has been lost of some works known to have been in the elector's library.

Several of the books dedicated to Fredrick, which inform us of his interest in humanistic studies, have been discussed earlier in this study: Petrus of Ravenna's *Clypeus contra doctorem Gaium*, his *Compendium pulcherrimum juriscanonici* and his *Sermones extraordinarii*; Christoph Scheurl's famous *Libellus de laudibus Germaniae et Ducum Saxoniae*, Johann Kitzscher's *Dialogus*, Sbrulius' *Cleomachia*, Carlstadt's *Distinctiones Thomistarum* and Mellerstadt's *Cursus Physici*. When Johann von Paltz, the famous Augustinian monk in Erfurt, had preached before Frederick the Wise and Duke Johann in Torgau, they were so impressed with him that Frederick encouraged Johann von Paltz to publish some of his sermons. Thus his two famous works, *Die himmlische Fundgrube* (1490) and *De septem foribus seu festis Beate Marie Virginis* (1491) were published under Frederick's aegis. Celtis' edition of the *Ligurinus* was a gift from Conrad Peutinger to Frederick the Wise — testimony to Frederick's interests and friendships with the humanists. Conrad Celtis, the German 'Arch-Humanist', dedicated his earliest work, the *Ars Versificandi*, to Frederick. Of this work Lewis Spitz has written:

> The *Ars versificandi* was formally in the medieval tradition and comparable to the medieval poesy of a Galfred of Vinosalvo. The leonine mnemonic verses in the first part are in the medieval tradition. Indeed, without naming Alexander Gallus, so despised by the progressive humanists, he used him directly. The humanists maintained the medieval custom of presenting purely grammatical portions in verse form. But with all its conformity to the standard pattern, some of Celtis' new verve emerges, as in his definition of the poet.[3]

The work carries two dedications to Frederick the Wise — one in verse and one in prose. In the poetic dedication Celtis describes how he received the book from Apollo with the instruction to offer it to Frederick. He also added a laudatory poem for elector Ernst of Saxony (who died in 1486) and his sons, elector Frederick, Johann, Ernst and Albrecht. The book ends with a prayer to the Virgin Mary and an ode to Apollo. Frederick received Celtis' dedication favorably, and was responsible for having Celtis crowned *poet laureate* by emperor Frederick III in 1487.

One of the best known dedicatory letters and one which later became a model of its type, is the preface to Celtis' edition of Roswitha's works.[4] It so delighted Frederick the Wise that he paid all the printing costs.[5] This manuscript, which Celtis had discovered at the Benedictine monastery of St. Emmeram, was published by the Rhenish Sodality of which he was a prominent member. In the dedication Celtis emphasizes the educational ideals of humanism and points out the importance of searching for manuscripts and editing them. He also expresses

3 L. Spitz, *Conrad Celtis, the German Arch-Humanist* (Cambridge, Mass., 1957), p. 5.
4 Cf. Panzer, *Annales*, VII, 439 5; also K. Schottenloher, *Die Widmungsvorrede im Buch des 16. Jahrhunderts* (Münster, 1953), pp. 3ff; and Celtis, *Briefwechsel*, no. 267, where the text of the dedication is given.
5 Cf. Bauch, *Die Reception des Humanismus in Wien*, p. 80; Newald, *Probleme*, p. 216; Celtis, *Briefwechsel*, no. 267.

nationalistic feelings when he says that this should be done by the Germans who invented the art of printing, and not by Italians, who in the past had carried away valuable manuscripts which they then published. Celtis deplores the general neglect of scholarship and proclaims a burning desire to acquaint himself with Germany's past. When he found the writings of the medieval Saxon nun Roswitha, he was overjoyed and wanted to present them to the Germans as testimony of their proud spiritual heritage and as an incentive to take up long-neglected inquiries into their history. He considered it his duty to unearth as many of the writings of earlier Germans as possible and to edit whatever he could find. Laudatory poems by other members of the Rhenish Sodality recommending the book are added to Celtis' dedication.

The Roswitha edition was enriched by beautiful woodcuts from the workshop of Albrecht Dürer. One showed Celtis, the *poet laureate*, presenting Roswitha's works to Frederick the Wise. The elector, dressed in an ermine coat, sits on a throne decorated with the Saxon emblem; his right hand reaches for the book and his left holds the sword, the sign of his princely power. The second woodcut, reaching back to an earlier imaginary act of presentation, shows Roswitha handing her work to emperor Otto who takes the scroll with his right hand while his left hand holds scepter and orb. Celtis' dedication and its magnificent adornments link one of the most famous editions by a great German humanist with the name of Frederick the Wise.

An interesting work dedicated to Frederick is Hans von Hermannsgrün's *Somnium*.[6] This Saxon humanist, a friend of Reuchlin, was one of the first scholars in Germany who knew Greek. Hermannsgrün represented Archbishop Ernst of Magdeburg, the brother of Frederick the Wise, at the Diet of Worms in 1495. Just before the members of the diet assembled, he distributed the *Somnium* in the hope of alerting the participants to the perils threatening Germany from the east and west, from the French and from the Turks. In typical humanistic fashion Hermannsgrün presented his ideas in the form of an allegoric dream. At an imperial diet where Charlemagne, Otto I and Frederick Barbarossa are present,[7] Frederick Barbarossa makes a speech in which he warns the Germans of the perils which beleaguer them, especially the dangerous ambitions of Charles VIII of France, who had just demonstrated his strength in the Italian wars. Barbarossa bids the princes come to the diets and preside over the affairs of the empire in order to preserve their inherited greatness and their national freedom and independence. Hermannsgrün clearly considers the princes to be the true wardens of the empire, though he chides them for their egotism and indifference to the public welfare. He thus puts himself squarely into the anti-imperial and pro-princely

6 Cf. H. Ulmann, "Der Traum des Hans von Hermannsgrün. Eine politische Denkschrift aus d. J. 1495," *Forschungen zur deutschen Geschichte*, 20 (1880), 67–92; H. Wiesflecker, *Der Traum des Hans von Hermannsgrün*, eine Reformschrift aus dem Lager des Königs Maximilian, in: *Festschrift Karl Eder zum siebzigsten Geburtstag*, ed. H. J. Mezler-Andelberg (Innsbruck, 1959), pp. 13–32; Friedrich H. Schubert, *Die deutschen Reichstage in der Staatslehre der frühen Neuzeit* (Göttingen, 1966: Schriftenreihe der historischen Kommission bei der Bayerischen Akademie der Wissenschaften, 7) pp.128–133.
7 Hermannsgrün still confuses the figure of Frederick Barbarossa with Frederick II. Cf. p. 81 of Ulmann: "Ego sum Federicus secundus Romanorum imperator Barbarossa cognominatus . . .'

camp. His ideal is no longer the medieval German Empire, but the late medieval *Fürstenrepublik*. He even went so far as to encourage the princes to contemplate dismemberment, and suggested that, in the event Maximilian did not take swift action, the princes ought to make use of their right to elect a *gubernator imperii.*[8] Hermannsgrün's position is in strong contrast to that of most contemporary humanists and writers like Bebel, Wimpheling and Celtis, who saw in Maximilian the only honorable and powerful representative of the empire.

In his long dedication to Frederick, Hermannsgrün called the elector of Saxony the first among the princes of the empire. The treatise, impregnated as it is with political criticism, has been rated as the most important political pamphlet of the era of Maximilian.[9] That Hermannsgrün dared to dedicate it to Frederick indicates that he must have assumed the elector to be sympathetic to his views on the state of the empire and on the need for reforms.

Another work expressing strong patriotic feelings is Jacob Wimpheling's edition of Lupold of Bebenburg's *De Iuribus et translatione imperii.*[10] In his dedication to Frederick Wimpheling praises the elector for his interest in the *humaniora* and his help to scholars. The treatise had been written shortly after the Diet of Frankfurt in 1338, which had issued the *Decretum de iure imperii*, making imperial elections independent of papal approval. Lupold drew his arguments from canon and Roman law to prove the absolute authority of the emperor; he contended that the *Donation* of Constantine was apocryphal and that the electors and princes of the empire are the final and only authority in secular matters.

Two works which demonstrate the emerging nationalism of Saxony are by the Sicilian Priamus Capotius.[11] This poet, who succeeded Celtis at the University of Leipzig, was especially attractive to German humanists because he came from Italy. His poem in praise of the founder of the University of Leipzig, Frederick I, and succeeding Saxon dukes, including Albrecht I, the contemporary ruler of Albertine Saxony, prepared a warm welcome for Capotius. In 1488 he dedicated his *Fredericeis* to Frederick the Wise to endear himself to this Saxon prince too. This is an epic poem, describing in lively verses the victorious battles of Friedericus Admorsus (Friedrich mit der gebissenen Wange) over Adolf of Nassau and his Swabian and Bohemian soldiers. In one passage Capotius introduced Pallas Athena prophesying the destiny of the Saxon lines up to the time of Frederick the Wise. Later in the poem Jupiter sends Mercury to incite Frederick the Wise to resume battle again with Bohemia. Bauch suggests that Capotius had to leave Leipzig because he was suspected of paganism.[12] He soon returned to Italy and died there in a brawl in 1517. Whatever the literary merit of the *Fredericeis*, its theme indicated clearly that glorification of Saxon history was considered a successful method of gaining the elector's good will.

The so-called poet Aquilonipolensis dedicated to Frederick his first published

---

8 *Ibid.*, p. 85.
9 Ulrich Paul, *Studien zur Geschichte des deutschen Nationalbewusstseins im Zeitalter des Humanismus und der Reformation* (Berlin, 1936), pp. 118ff.
10 Cf. Panzer, *Annales*, VI, 42, 134; Proctor, *Index*, 10165.
11 Cf. Bauch, *Leipziger Frühhumanismus*, p. 23; and *Gesamtkatalog der Wiegendrucke*, VI, 123, 6026.
12 Cf. Bauch, *Leipziger Frühhumanismus*, p. 23.

poetic work, the *Dimetromachia*, which was finished before 1494.[13] It is an elegy in hexameter on every conceivable subject: on the invention of the art of writing, on poetry, on the virtues, on mythology. Still in the medieval tradition, it shows the author's knowledge of Greek and Latin, both of which he misuses. The dedication to Frederick reads:

Saxonie illustris dux, Missne marchio, Thurin
Gorum lantgrauius, iure trimembris Atlas.[14]

Aquilonipolensis added an extensive prose commentary in which he cites classical as well as medieval authors, yet he shows greater attachment to the latter than to the writers of antiquity.

Two works published shortly after 1512 — which therefore did not become part of Frederick's library until after the period under consideration — also carry dedications to him and belong to the humanistic and patriotic group of writings.

In 1513 Reuchlin dedicated to Frederick his translation of a life of Constantine the Great;[15] the author of the work, although not identified, is thought to have been a humanist of the fifteenth century. The biography as such is of little value; in the dedicatory preface Reuchlin indulges in the same fantastic speculations on the ancestry of the German people as did many of his contemporaries who sought by such devices to enhance the glory and importance of the German nation. Reuchlin traces the inhabitants of Saxony, Meissen and Thuringia back to the legendary Axenes, Myses and Tyrigetes, and Frederick's princely line back to pre-Homeric times. This genealogical absurdity was wittily ridiculed by Mutian who showered many philological puns on it.[16] Reuchlin had probably finished the translation of the *Constantinus Magnus* before 1513, for he published the work hastily in that year with the dedication intended to swing Frederick's support to his side in his controversy with Pfeffercorn, Jacob Hoogstraten, and the Cologne faculty. In his desire to flatter the elector at that moment, even Reuchlin succumbed to German nationalistic feelings as he tried to prove the superiority of the German nation.

Little attention has been paid to the excerpts from the *Enneades* of Sabellicus which was likewise dedicated to Frederick.[17] The author, an Italian humanist and historian (1436–1506), had been professor of rhetoric and *humaniora* at Udine. Since 1484 he had been director of the library of St. Marco in Venice, which had been given to the Venetian republic by Cardinal Bessarion. Between 1498 and 1504 Sabellicus wrote his *Enneades*, a world history in ninety-two books modelled on Livy's *Ab urbe condita*. Johann Kuschwert edited a compilation of

13 Cf. Bauch, *Erfurt*, pp. 172ff.
14 *Ibid.*, p. 173.
15 Cf. Panzer, *Annales*, VIII, 324, 22; J. Benzing, *Bibliographie der Schriften Johannes Reuchlins im 15. und 16. Jahrhundert* (Bad Boklet, 1955: Bibliotheca Bibliographica, 18), no. 108.
16 *Mutians Briefwechsel*, 321.
17 Cf. Panzer, *Annales*, VI, 194, 145; O. Clemen, "Ein Rektor der Dresdner Kreuzschule, 1511–1514', *NASG*, 30 (1909), 138–140; C. G. Joecher, *Allgemeines Gelehrtenlexikon*, 'Sabellicus'.

excerpts from this work and had it printed in Basel in 1515; he dedicated it to Frederick the Wise. Kuschwert, a native of Weissenstadt in the Fichtelgebirge, had studied at Leipzig and had been appointed rector of the famous *Kreuzschule* in Dresden in 1511. The dedication, dated February 14, 1514, praises the elector for his love and devotion to scholarship, and especially for his daily pursuit of scholarly studies. Although this publication may not be important in itself, it is significant that the *Historia Hebreorum* was dedicated to Frederick just when the Reuchlin controversy was at its height: the author, or editor, Kuschwert must have thought Frederick to be in sympathy with Reuchlin's cause.

Since all the works here discussed were dedicated to Frederick, we may assume that they were in his library. Most of these books were written or edited by humanists; a remarkable number were concerned with the affairs of the empire. That their authors addressed themselves to Frederick implies that they must have felt the elector to be in sympathy with the spirit of both humanism and German patriotism. It can be argued from the contents of these works and their dedications that their authors saw Frederick as the leader of a reform movement which would strengthen the power of the princes over the emperor – a role which Frederick actually played at the imperial diets. Thus a type of book presenting a fusion of German political thinking and humanistic learning is represented in the library of the elector, a type of book which he, as a German political leader and a friend of the humanists, had in his turn encouraged.

Further evidence that books were in Frederick's possession even before 1512 is a passage in Johann Christoph Mylius' *Memorabilia Bibliothecae Academicae Ienensis*. He relates that in 1504 the Meissen canon Thomas Loesser left in his will a number of theological, philosophical and legal works to Frederick,[18] a gift which appreciably increased the already existing collection. The titles of the books are not known; but from the scholastic orientation of the donor, it has been deduced that they were medieval works.[19] Mylius also mentions that the contents of eight monastic libraries were given to the elector: Grünhain, Lenin, Leipzig, Halle, Meissen, Rainhardsbrun and two from Nürnberg.[20]

Several letters point to the fact that Frederick tried to purchase books before 1512. Among them is a letter from Aldus Manutius to Spalatin, dated May 11, 1514,[21] which provides definite evidence that Frederick had been negotiating with Aldus for the purchase of books as early as 1506. In the *post scriptum* Aldus states that he is unable to recall any communication from Frederick or Spalatin since their last letter written in 1506. At that time he had answered Frederick and sent him a catalogue of his printed books. A letter from Christoph Scheurl of Nürnberg, dated December 6, 1512,[22] refers to an earlier attempt of Frederick to secure the library of the great astronomer Regiomontanus.

Even before 1512 Frederick had acquired many books through gifts and

18 J. C. Mylius, *Memorabilia Bibliothecae Academicae Jenensis* (Jena, 1746), pp. 2 and 26.
19 Cf. E. Schwiebert, "Remnants of a Reformation library', *Library Quarterly*, 10 (1940), 518.
20 Mylius, *Memorabilia*, pp. 21–26.
21 Cf. J. Schück, *Aldus Manutius und seine Zeitgenossen in Italien und Deutschland* (Berlin, 1862), pp. 135–137.
22 Scheurl, *Briefbuch*, 67.

purchases; during these years Frederick was much concerned with enhancing the status of the university. He tried to secure outstanding scholars as teachers, and he attached to his personal staff as many educated men as he could persuade to come to Wittenberg. Foremost among these was Spalatin, who had arrived in Wittenberg in 1511. Spalatin was eminently qualified to help the elector transform the major part of his collection of books and manuscripts into a university library. When, in the spring of 1512, Frederick formally established the library for the students and professors of the university, he appointed Spalatin as librarian.

Among Spalatin's entries for the year 1512 in his *Ephemerides* is the following: 'Hoc anno Fridericus III Elector Saxoniae Bibliothecam in Arce Wittembergensi auspicatus, ministro et bibliothecario in hac, me G. Spalatino, usus'.[23] The date which Spalatin gives for the founding of the library is supported by other evidence. We have knowledge, for instance, that books were transported from Torgau to Wittenberg in 1512 and that in the spring of 1512 carpenters, cabinet-makers, masons and other laborers were employed to get space ready for books. Spalatin during this spring traveled back and forth between Wittenberg and Torgau to supervise the work and on each trip transferred some books to Witten-berg.[24]

Between 1505 and 1508 Spalatin had been in charge of the library at the monastery in Georgenthal. There he was assisted by the humanist Urbanus, who was the *oeconomus* of the monastery, and both benefited from the advice of their friend Mutian in near-by Gotha. From their correspondence we learn that as early as 1505 Spalatin intended to purchase books from Aldus Manutius in Venice.[25] Spalatin hunted through the Erfurt bookstores and Mutian informed him of the book treasures offered at the Leipzig Fair in 1506.[26] Thus, when Spalatin started on his new assignment in Wittenberg, he was well experienced, in addition to being a passionate book collector.

The correspondence between Frederick, Spalatin and Aldus Manutius in the year 1512 shows with what great vigor and speed the elector and the new librarian tried to enrich the collection. Already on March 25th, 1512, Spalatin, at the behest of Frederick, wrote to Aldus asking him to send a complete catalogue of his books in print.[27] Spalatin invited Aldus to write directly to the elector recommending him as a generous patron of scholars, and on May 1 Spalatin repeated his request to Aldus, because he had not yet had any answer from him. As there was again no response forthcoming from Venice, Frederick himself wrote to Aldus on

23   Berbig, *Spalatiniana*, pp. 53ff.
24   Georg Buchwald, "Zu Spalatins Reisen, insbesondere nach Wittenberg in Angelegenheiten der Kurfürstlichen Bibliothek', *Archiv für Bibliographie, Buch- und Bibliothekswesen*, 2 (1928), 92–96. Cf. E. Schwiebert, "Remnants of a Reformation Library', 494ff; E. Hilde-brandt, "Die kurfürstliche Schloss- und Universitätsbibliothek zu Wittenberg, 1512–1547', *Zeitschrift für Buchkunde*, 2 (1925). 34ff; in this the author discusses at length the possibility that the library may have been founded in 1514, but also comes to the conclusion that this tradition was in error. It had originated with J. S. Müller, *Des Chur- und Fürstlichen Hauses Sachsen Ernestin- und Albertinischer Linien Annales* (Weimar, 1700) and perpetuated by Mylius, *Memorabilia* and Grohmann, *Annalen*.
25   *Mutians Briefwechsel*, nos. 12, 13, 14, 24, 25, 26, 33, 34.
26   *Ibid.*, no. 43.
27   Cf. Friedensburg, *Urkundenbuch*, p. 68.

December 1, addressing him as follows: "Meditamur bibliothecam, mi Alde, in arce nostra Electoria Wittenbergensi in Saxonia pro communi omnium utilitate, et doctorum et discipulorum nostrae academiae tam posteriorum quam praesentium." Frederick clearly expresses his intention to open his library to the university community and his wish that it might serve not only the present generation of scholars but also future ones. He explains to Manutius the kind of library he wants to establish and describes the books he is eager to find. He repeats the request for catalogues of Aldus' publications as well as of other publishers and booksellers. Frederick compliments Aldus on his books, which enrich the libraries of Europe, and reiterates his own desire to purchase Aldines, although he already owns some – above all, Greek, Latin and Hebrew books printed by Aldus.[28]

On December 13, Spalatin sent another letter to Aldus[29] requesting that the catalogues be given to the office of the Fuggers in Venice, which could speedily dispatch them to Wittenberg. Spalatin asked Aldus specifically to mark the books that were in stock at his *affinis* in Frankfurt a. M., shrewdly calculating that it would be cheaper to buy the books in Frankfurt, because the expensive transportation costs across the Alps would then have to be paid by Aldus and his representative there.

In a letter to Spalatin dated May 11, 1514,[30] Aldus stresses how anxious he is to be of special assistance to him. He deplores accusations that he had neglected to procure the desired catalogues, and claims that the letters in which these requests were made had not reached him. He now encloses a list of the books that he had printed. In concluding the letter, Aldus complains of the very difficult times Venice is going through and the evil consequences for the local trade. Upon receiving this communication from Aldus, Frederick sent his order for books to him.

Spalatin entered in his *Ephemerides* for the year 1515:[31] 'Eodem anno Friederi-

---

28 Cf. G. Buchwald, "Archivalische Mittheilungen über Bücherbezüge der kurfürstlichen Bibliothek und Georg Spalatins in Wittenberg', *Archiv für Geschichte des deutschen Buchhandels* 18 (1896), 10–11. Because of its importance, the complete text is given here:
Dei Gratia Fridericus Princeps Elector, Dux Saxoniae. S. P. Meditamur bibliothecam, mi Alde, in arce nostra Electoria Wittenbergensi in Saxonia pro communi omnium utilitate, et doctorum, et discipulorum nostrae academiae tam posteriorum quam praesentium. Nam ope diuina aedem diuis omnibus sacram et Athenaeum architectati libris quoque studiosos augere constituimus. Itaque ad Kal. Maii ministro nostro Spalatino iniunximus tibi scribendum, quid eam in rem abs te fieri cuperemus, certi onmia facturum, si literae in manus tuas venissent. Neque enim nos latet, eo te promouisse rectis studiis et optimis quibusque autoribus non solum a situ et carie, sed ab ipso interitu vindicandis, vt de bonis literis eruditorum omnium iudicio optime merearis. Sed dum responsum tuum expectamus, renunciator nobis te Venetias reuersum, posteritatis causam, vt antea agere. Quapropter nobis rem feceris gratissimam, si indicem bibliopolii tui et caeterorum insignium istic miseris. Etsi nihil scire malumus quam libros omnes graecos, latinos, hebraeos, tuis hactenus formis excussos. Quibus tum propter tuum genium, tum ob singularem tuam fidem et industriam tantum est autoritatis, vt totius Europae bibliothecas ornent. Reddemus ergo et ipsi nostram bibliothecam libris ex tua officina tabernaque emendis, etiamnum tuis vigiliis non vacuam, refertiorem, illustrioremque. Vale reliquum clientis epistola accepturus ex arce nosta Vinariensi intra Kal. Decemb. M. C. XII. Aldo Manutio Ro. Viro. Doctiss suo.
29 Cf. Friedensburg, *Urkundenbuch*, p. 68.
30 Cf. Schück, *Aldus Manutius*, pp. 135–137.
31 Berbig, *Spalatiniana*, p. 55.

cus III. Saxoniae Elector Aldo Manutio scripsit Venetias pro libris et graecis et latinis ad Bibliothecam Witebergensem, sed Aldo paulo ante defunto, Andreas Asulanus socer Aldi libros misit.' Aldus had died on February 8, 1515, and his father-in-law, the recipient of the letter, forwarded the books to Saxony. We do not know which and how many Aldines came to Wittenberg at that time; but in addition to the ones already in Frederick's possession in 1512 and those which Wolf Fries had secured (which will be described presently) it must have been a substantial collection.

It is not surprising that Spalatin's former associated friends were consulted on the building up of the library. Christoph Scheurl was asked to help in the purchase of books for the Wittenberg library. Scheurl, in a letter of December 6, 1512[32] tells Spalatin of a visit of Degenhart Pfeffinger, one of Frederick's councillors. Pfeffinger had reported to Scheurl how busy Spalatin was with the library, which explained why he had no direct news from him. Pfeffinger also asked Scheurl, at the request of the elector, to secure a catalogue of the library of Regiomontanus. Scheurl urged Spalatin to persuade the elector to purchase this library, however expensive, because in his opinion such a collection was not soon to be found again. Two days later he wrote to Amsdorf and Beckmann that he was able to send Spalatin the catalogues of Regiomontanus' collection.[33] From later letters of Scheurl we learn that Frederick intended only to buy some mathematical books and a few others, but was not interested in acquiring the whole collection. In a letter of May 4[34] Scheurl informs Spalatin that the collection would not be divided; it is the last we hear of it. Frederick was not farsighted enough to realize the importance of this collection. In appraising his decision one must also consider the purchase cost of the collection. Regiomontanus' heir had asked 1000 Hungarian gulden from King Matthias of Hungary who wanted to buy it in 1478. This was a very large sum of money at that time, and, although Scheurl had promised in 1513 to secure the books at a reasonable price for Frederick, this earlier estimated value of the collection indicates that it was not to be obtained cheaply. Frederick who was always in financial difficulties might have thought that he could not commit himself to the purchase of such an expensive collection. That Frederick could not, in fact, have purchased the collection, even had he wanted to do so, we know now from the records of the Nürnberg city council; at this particular time no one in Nürnberg knew the whereabouts of the books and in any event the administrator of Regiomontanus' estate was not to dispose of them.

Important sources for our knowledge of additions to the Wittenberg library for the years 1512–1513 are invoices for books puchased from one Wolf Fries.[35] The

---

32 Scheurl, *Briefbuch*, 67; cf. Bauch, 'Zu Christoph Scheurls Briefbuch', nos. 70c, 73b, 74g, where Bauch adds some documents concerning this desired purchase.
33 Scheurl, *Briefbuch*, no. 68.
34 Bauch, 'Zu Christoph Scheurls Briefbuch', 74g. Concerning the library of Regiomontanus and its disposal, cf. H. Petz, "Urkundliche Nachrichten über den literarischen Nachlass Regiomontans und B. Walters, 1478 bis 1522', *Mitteilungen des Vereins für Geschichte der Stadt Nürnberg*, Heft 7 (1888), pp. 237–262.
35 Cf. Buchwald, "Archivalische Mittheilungen' (including Kirchhoff's comments), pp. 7–10; and Buchwald, 'Zu Spalatins Reisen', p. 94.

invoices are bound with the catalogue Spalatin made in 1536 of his own private library, which is preserved at the Landesbibliothek in Gotha. Who this Wolf Fries was is not known. Alfred Kirchhoff has added to Buchwald's transcript of the Fries invoices a few remarks speculating about the character of Fries's business and his personality. Some of these reflections by a scholar of the booktrade are intriguing, yet no factual basis exists for any of these hypotheses which seek to locate Fries in southern Germany or in Basel. From the invoices we learn that altogether Spalatin purchased 153 volumes at the price of 202 fl. and 5 gr. They are listed on six invoices dated at intervals between July 28, 1512 and the spring of 1513. The books were delivered to Spalatin at the library in the castle, except for those which Spalatin himself transported from the Spring-Fair of 1513 in Leipzig. Not all the payments were made in money; for the value of 140 fl. Fries received "1 vass zinns'. Kirchhoff is of the opinion that Fries provided printers in western and southern Germany or Switzerland with the tin, of which Saxony was at that time almost the sole source of supply.

If one scrutinizes these invoices the following major groups emerge: Bibles, Bible commentaries and sermons, the writings of the Church Fathers, the Greek and Latin classics, the works of humanists, grammars and language manuals, works on church history and secular history, scholastic treatises and books on science and law. Of the 153 books 18 are by classical authors and 23 are writings of humanists. Among the latter almost all of the leading names are found: Ficinus, Aeneas Sylvius, Angelus Politianus, Leo Aretinus, Picus Mirandola, Laurentius Valla, Reuchlin and Erasmus. Law books, histories and scientific works number about 25. Approximately the same number can be allotted to the Bible group. Thirteen entries can be identified as works by the Fathers of the Church. Fourteen books are of a scholastic nature. Not a single work by Aristotle is listed in the invoices. Friedensburg[36] has called these purchases the real humanist basis for the university library. Certainly no other purchases which we know of give such a clear picture of the ambitions of Frederick and Spalatin for their library. This analysis of the purchases, which show such great strength quantitatively as well as qualitatively in the new learning, the revival of ancient languages and humanist writings, confirm Friedensburg's judgment.

In 1516 Frederick and Spalatin renewed their efforts to acquire more of the coveted Aldines. In Burkhard Schenk vom Simau who was well known as a purchaser of relics for Frederick, they found an efficient intermediary who lived in Venice and was expected to represent the interests of the Wittenberg library there.[37] Schenk von Simau lived in the Franciscan monastery in Coburg for some time and we know from his letters that he later was transferred to the Franciscan monastery in Venice, where he lectured in theology. In the first of the extant letters from Venice, dated October 28, 1516, Schenk encloses a catalogue of the house of Aldus Manutius which the elector had requested. This must, in fact, have

36 Friedensburg, *Geschichte*, p. 154.
37 Cf. P. Kalkoff, *Alblass und Reliquienverehrung an der Schlosskirche zu Wittenberg unter Friedrich dem Weisen* (Gotha, 1907), pp. 66ff, 79ff; part of the correspondence has been published in Chr. W. Schneider, ed., "Zehn Briefe Burkhards Schenks von Simau . . . an d. Kurf. zu Sa., Friedrich III und an G. Spalatin . . ." *Bibliothek der Kirschengeschichte*, vol. 2, pt. 1 (Weimar, 1781), pp. 1–90.

been the same catalogue that Frederick had already received from Aldus himself in 1514, for no new catalogues had been published since 1513. The correspondence between Spalatin, Frederick, and Schenk von Simau, which reveals an intensive search for books for the Wittenberg library, continued on after 1517.[38]

Book purchases at the Leipzig Fair of 1514 are mentioned in a letter of Spalatin to Hans von Doltzig, the electoral treasurer and later marshal.[39] Spalatin inquired whether the books and the paper which he had ordered from the Fair through Bernhard von Hirschfeld had been secured. The following year Spalatin himself bought books and paper at the Fair. The receipt for this purchase, dated October 6, 1515, states that the sum of money was spent for the elector's library.[40] Unfortunately Spalatin did not specify the individual items, only the names of the printers from whom they were bought are recorded; "Zwey rayss Papyres" were bought at the same time from Melchior Lotter.

Spalatin and Frederick were fortunate in being able to draw again on their Nürnberg friend, Christoph Scheurl, for assistance in securing books. Nürnberg was a center of the south German book trade and Italian imprints could be found there. We know that Scheurl inquired in a letter of April 23, 1515, if he should purchase a certain lot of books.[41] In a letter of April 1, 1517, Scheurl suggests to Eck that the best way to endear himself to Spalatin and Frederick was to give books to the library at Wittenberg.[42]

In order to assess the humanistic character of a library of the period, it is necessary to determine the relative importance of Erasmus' works in it. According to the invoice of Wolf Fries the *Opera Erasmi Rotterodami* had been purchased as early as July 1512. Spalatin wrote his first letter to Erasmus on December 11, 1516,[43] at the request of Luther. Luther had asked Spalatin to convey to Erasmus the content of his letter concerning the Pauline concepts of justice.[44] He reminded Erasmus of common friends, especially of Mutian, who had been Erasmus' schoolmate at Deventer. Although Spalatin did not mention Luther by name, he said that he was writing at the request of a pious and scholarly Augustinian monk. Certainly in the belief that it would please Erasmus, he informed him that the library of the elector Frederick contained all the books and publications of Erasmus.[45] Frederick was eager to secure any new work of his and his books were among the prince's preferred reading. Even if this letter was written with the intent of impressing Erasmus favorably, the elector's interest in the works of Erasmus seems to have been genuine.

·Complete accounts of the purchases and holdings of the Wittenberg library are lacking but the multitudinous efforts of Spalatin and the elector demonstrate vividly their alert and carefully planned library policy. There was no highly organized book trade as there is today, to supply and handle books; all this was

38 Cf. Hildebrandt, pp. 121–123.
39 P. Drews, 'Spalatiniana', *Zeitschrift für Kirchengeschichte*, 19 (1899), 70.
40 G. Berbig, 'Spalatiniana', *Theologische Studien und Kritiken*, 81 (1908), no. 33.
41 Scheurl, *Briefbuch*, 92.
42 *Ibid.*, 123.
43 Erasmus, *Opus epistolarum*, II, no. 501.
44 *WAB*, I, 27.
45 Erasmus, *Opus epistolarum*, II, no. 501.

left to the individual eager to secure books. If one keeps in mind the small editions of books and the hazards of communications, the accomplishment of those who built up the Wittenberg library can be appreciated. The book purchases of these years reflect clearly Frederick the Wise's paramount interest in the writings of the humanists. He was, above all, avid to collect Aldines, the most cherished books of the Renaissance, works in Greek, Latin and Hebrew, dictionaries, legal, medical, astronomical, and historical works – all to serve the large purpose of a university library. All branches of the faculty were thus considered, even if the *humaniora* held a preferred place.

In a long eulogy, celebrating the second marriage of Frederick's younger brother, Duke Johann, to Margarete of Anhalt, the Wittenberg humanist Philipp Engentinus makes reference to the library.[46] We can well understand the book-loving humanist's praise for this library which so well represented the thoughts and hopes of the new movement.

From 1512 on, at least, the collection was intended to be at the disposal of the teachers and students of Wittenberg; and we are justified in assuming that it was used by them. As to lending procedures, one bit of evidence sheds some light on the general policy. Johann Lang wanted to borrow the *Epitaphium* of Thomas Wolph.[47] Spalatin sent him the book with a letter dated March 3, 1514, begging him to return the work as soon as possible because the elector wished the books to be available for use in the library.

Among the borrowers and users of the Wittenberg library at that time was Martin Luther. In August 1516 he asked Spalatin either to send him on loan the *Epistolae Hieronymi* or to copy for him a passage concerning Saint Bartholomew from Jerome's *De viris illustribus*.[48] This request indicates not only that Luther used the library but that he was intimately familiar with its collection.

It seems probable that some of the book selections made by Luther's friend Spalatin were directly prompted by the new demands made on the library by Luther and his followers.

Considering the character of the book collection which was in the making at Wittenberg, a statement made by Luther a few years later – yet still during Frederick's life time – deserves special attention. In his address of 1524, *An die Ratherren aller Städte deutschen Landes*[49] it is as if Luther were formulating his experiences at the Wittenberg library as a blueprint for a library to serve his reform movement and future library planners as well. Admonishing the city councillors to provide for the right schooling of Christian youth Luther turned to the role of the library in education.

> Am letzten ist auch das wol zu bedencken allen den yenigen, so lieb und lust haben, das solche schulen und sprachen ynn Deutschen landen auffgericht und erhallten werden, das man fleys und koste nicht spare, gutte librareyen odder

46 Cf. Bauch, 'Zur Cranachforschung', pp. 424ff.
47 Hildebrandt, p. 178.
48 *WAB*, I, no. 19.
49 *WA* XV, 9–53.

bücher heuser sonderlich ynn den grossen stedten, die solichs wol vermügen, zuverschaffen.[50]

Luther stresses that the example had been set in Old Testament times for the preservation of the written word and he describes the infinite care which was taken by the Hebrew priests in the housing and safeguarding of their Holy Scriptures. The example was followed in the Middle Ages by the monastic libraries; but unfortunately, Luther complains, they chose to keep the wrong books.

> . . . an stat der heyligen schrifft und gutter bücher den Aristotelem komen mit unzelichen schedlichen büchern, die uns nür ymer weytter von der Byblien fureten.[51]

Yet he condemns as most harmful those works which only corrupt the students' knowledge of Latin. The treasures of the ancient languages have now to be recaptured by painstaking work. Luther then proceeds to outline his own guiding principles for book selection: books should not be bought indiscriminately for the sake of acquiring mere quantity. He first sets out what should *not* be acquired: juridical commentaries, the common scholastic compilations of *sententiae* and *questionae* and the collections of sermons by monks. Not only should such works not be bought; they should not be kept on the shelves of the library and must therefore be discarded.

On the other hand the books which are needed should be chosen with great care and with the advice of the scholars. The Holy Scriptures should be in a library in Latin, Greek, Hebrew and German, and in translations in other languages when available. Furthermore, the best and the oldest commentaries to the Scriptures – again those in Greek, Hebrew or Latin – should be acquired. In the second place, all those books which will help the study of languages – regardless of whether their authors were Christian or pagan – should also be included. All the arts and sciences, also medicine and law, should be represented and the works carefully selected. This remarkable commentary concludes with a special plea to include chronicles and other historical works dealing with the history of the Germans. One cannot fail, in a study of the library purchases at Wittenberg, to notice how the actual policy was congruent with Luther's later advice to the city councillors.

From its beginnings the Wittenberg library was a humanist stronghold. Books by humanists flowed in as gifts to the elector. As the library became more and more a place for students and scholars, the works of the humanists, of the classical writers and of the Church Fathers were collected in increasing numbers. That a library of such a humanistic character could be the best basis for the new movement originating at Wittenberg is borne out by Luther's own testimony.

50 *Ibid.*, p. 49.
51 *Ibid.*, p. 50.

CHAPTER VIII

THE ARTS IN WITTENBERG UNDER FREDERICK THE WISE

From the beginning of his reign Frederick the Wise took an active interest in architecture, painting, book illustration and many other artistic endeavors of his time. At his Lochau castle he had written on the wall of his bedroom: you have inherited a Sparta, it is your task to beautify it.[1] Hardly a year of Frederick's reign went by without large building projects for churches and castles; sculptors and painters were engaged, among them some of the greatest artists of the time. The elector was the only German prince who continuously over a period of thirty years gave Albrecht Dürer large orders. Lucas Cranach became Frederick's court painter and the records show that he ordered and acquired works of Jacopo de' Barbari, Michel Wolgemut, Hans Burgkmair, Tilmann Riemenschneider, Peter Vischer the Elder, Konrad Meit, Adriano Fiorentino and others; he had a genuine understanding of art and was willing to spend great sums of money on it. Invoices, accounts and letters show that he had agents in the art centers of Europe who secured for him excellent pieces of art that he desired for his court and surroundings. Frederick can be called a Maecenas of the Northern Renaissance. Unfortunately much of what he collected has been destroyed through wars, bombings and other misfortunes. But it is possible to reconstruct the scope of these activities from contemporary records.[2] That Frederick's love for art had early roots might be conjectured from the fact that he was accompanied by artists on his travels to the Holy Land in 1493 and to the Netherlands in 1494. These journeys certainly provided a magnificent education for the prince and stimulated his desire to create a center for art in his own state.

I

When Frederick on his accession in 1486 decided to make Wittenberg the capital of his domain it was natural that the embellishment of the town should be uppermost in his mind. Since their appointment as electors of the Holy Roman Empire in 1423, the house of Wettin had not resided in Wittenberg, but rather in Torgau, Altenburg or Weimar. Thus Wittenberg had in general been neglected architecturally and artistically. The German princes of the time did not build magnificent palaces like the Italians; they were more interested in converting their medieval castles into residential castle-palaces with more utilitarian purposes. The

---

1 Cf. J.G. Schadow, *Wittenbergs Denkmäler der Bildnerei, Baukunst und Malerei* (Wittenberg, 1825), p. 48. Cf. also: Richard Muther, 'Sachsens Kunstleben im sechzehnten Jahrhundert', *Die Grenzboten* 43 (1884), pt. 1, pp. 21–22.
2 The aim in this chapter is not to give an interpretation of the art history of Saxony during the years 1486–1517, but rather to see what kind of art Frederick was interested in and how his interest was connected with the contemporary development of humanism.

castle, at that time, was a complex group of connected buildings, each serving a different purpose, with a court in the center. Frederick followed this pattern in his architectural undertakings.[3]

The elector was well aware that the building trade helped many poor people in his realm.[4] Spalatin relates that Frederick built in the towns of Wittenberg, Torgau, Belzig, Lochau, Eilenburg, Altenburg, Neu Lochau, Grimma, Colditz, Weimar, Hirtzberg, Eisenach, Wartburg and Liebenswerd. Just a short time after his accession he started an extensive building program in Wittenberg[5] at a cost for the castle and the castle church[6] of about 200,000 gulden. The old castle of the Ascanians was taken down and the stones from this building were used for the new building which was actually started in 1490.

As architect for Wittenberg Frederick engaged Konrad Pflüger,[7] a former pupil of Arnold von Westfalen.[8] One of the most original architects of the late Gothic period,[9] Arnold von Westfalen had built for Ernst and Albrecht of Saxony the castle at Torgau as well as the cathedral and the Albrechtsburg in Meissen and the Kunigundenkirche in Rochlitz. He was the founder of a whole school of architecture, of which Pflüger was the best known and most talented member. Konrad Pflüger had been working at Görlitz as early as 1488,[10] as well as at Weimar and Annaberg; he also helped build the Kreuzkirche in Dresden for the Albertines. Having called on him to direct Wittenberg's building program, Frederick kept Pflüger in his service for many years, and the architect became one of the leaders among the Upper Saxon single-nave-church builders.

The castle was laid out in a rectangle, with the castle church forming the northern wing, the castle proper the southern wing, and the two buildings connected by the city walls on the west wide. The outside facade of the castle was simple, a *Wehrbau* with corner towers in late Gothic style. The inside decorations, however, were lavish. The castle church was completed by 1499 on the site where the Ascanian Rudolf I had built the *Stiftskirche Allerheiligen* around 1353. The best picture of it is a woodcut by Lucas Cranach in the *Wittenberger Heiligtumsbuch* of 1509; the outside of the church was also simple and in keeping with the

---

3 Cf. Bruck, *Friedrich der Weise, passim.*
4 Spalatin, 41–42.
5 Cf. Hans-Joachim Mrusek, 'Das Stadtbild von Wittenberg zur Zeit der Reformation und der Universität', in *450 Jahre Reformation*, pp. 322–340; Sibylle Harksen, 'Schloss und Schlosskirche in Wittenberg', *ibid.*, pp. 341–365.
6 Spalatin, 28; cf. Köstlin, *Friedrich der Weise*, p. 14, where this is estimated to be about 4 million Marks of that time. Cf. also Bruck, *Friedrich der Weise*, pp. 261ff, for published accounts of Wittenberg invoices for building purposes, and pp. 271ff. for invoices paid to individual architects.
7 Cf. Ulrich Thieme and Felix Becker, *Allgemeines Lexikon der bildenden Künstler von der Antike bis zur Gegenwart* (37 vols., Leipzig, 1907–50), vol. 26. p. 534.
8 *Ibid.*, vol. 2, pp. 134–135.
9 The inadequacy of the term 'late Gothic' for a style that was rather a forerunner of Renaissance architecture than a late phase of Gothic, has been pointed out by A. Schmarsow, 'Zur Beurtheilung der sogenannten Spätgothik', *Repertorium für Kunstwissenschaft*, 23 (1900), 290–298.
10 Cf. E. Wernicke, 'Sächsische Künstler in Görlitzer Geschichtsquellen', *NASG*, 6 (1885), 251ff.
11 Cf. C. Gurlitt, *Kunst und Künstler am Vorabend der Reformation*; ein Bild aus dem Erzgebirge (Halle, 1890: Schriften des Vereins für Reformationsgeschichte, 29)

style of the churches of the Erzgebirge, Annaberg and Schneeberg, Halle and the chapel of the Moritzburg — all works of the school of Arnold von Westfalen.[11] In 1503 the castle church became the university church where all ceremonies of the university took place, and it was on the door of this church that Luther posted his 95 Theses.

The interior of both castle and castle church must have been magnificent.[12] Frederick spared no money to get the services of artists to decorate his church; work was commissioned to the Dutch painter Jan Gossaert (called Mabuse), the Italian Jacopo de' Barbari, sculptors like Conrad Meit and Claus Heffner. Altar pieces were created by Michel Wolgemut, Jakob Elsner and Hans Burgkmair; Albrecht Dürer and Lucas Cranach provided for the interior decoration, and Peter Vischer and other sculptors in Nürnberg supplied Frederick with some of the bronze sculptures. Here Frederick housed his treasured relics in beautiful gold and silver containers, especially made for the purpose, and here indulgences were easily available. Unfortunately today there is very little left of the original building or the artistic works that adorned its interior to give us a real picture of what the castle and its church looked like. We can only piece it together from older descriptions; they certainly bear witness to Frederick's desire to have his surroundings aesthetically beautiful.

Wittenberg's magnificent town church was built in the fourteenth century, on the site of the old Ascanian church of St. Mary; it was expanded in the early fifteenth century and completed in 1470. The church has remained unscathed through all the centuries and stands today with its firm square towers guarding its front entrance. The famous Reformation altar of 1547 by Cranach is still preserved and so is the bronze baptismal font cast in 1457 by Hermann Vischer.[13] This church became the real church of the Reformation, and its history and treasures belong to a period later than the one here under consideration.

When Frederick founded his university in 1502 he immediately realized the need for buildings to house the new institution. Again Konrad Pflüger was entrusted with the plans and the erection of the first college building, the Old Friederici College, was completed in 1503. In 1509 when the university began to expand the New Friederici College was built as another house where the university students and members of the faculty could live and study. Other buildings put up under the supervision of Konrad Pflüger were the new cloister and dormitory of the Augustinian convent. These had been started in 1503 but, because of the shortage of funds, were not finished till 1518. Elector Johann later gave the dormitory to Luther as a wedding gift, to be used to house his family. It was bought back by the university in 1564. Having undergone several changes it is still in the original location, and its famous *Lutherstube* has been turned into a museum.

Frederick wanted the buildings which he commissioned to be useful as well as beautiful. Little "Renaissance" style can be detected in the architecture that had developed in the Upper Saxon school of Arnold von Westfalen and of his best

12 Cf. for a detailed description: Matthaeus Faber, *Kurtzgefasste historische Nachricht von der Schloss- und Academischen Stifftskirche zu Aller-Heiligen in Wittenberg* ... Samt einer Vorrede Herrn D. Gottlieb Wernsdorffs ... (Wittenberg, 1717), pp. 102–200.
13 Cf. W. Lange, *Stadt- und Schlosskirche zu Wittenberg* (Berlin, 1954: Das christliche Denkmal, 10).

students, notably Konrad Pflüger. Although not touched by the great architectural innovations of Italy, these masters transformed and adapted late Gothic forms to more simple and functional designs.

II

Frederick took special joy and pride in the interior of his buildings and as a consequence the decorative arts flourished. He apparently sought out the best wood-carvers, stone-cutters, sculptors in wood and bronze-casters and also engravers, for medals were employed in great numbers. From the accounts of the payments to all these artisans one gets the impression of a whole workshop industry entirely in the service of electoral Saxony. Unfortunately most of the works of art are no longer in existence and we have to be content with the information we can gather from accounts, early descriptions and early pictures. Many wood-carvings of the early sixteenth century fell victim to the iconoclastic controversies during the Reformation; the only major work that survives is the choir chancel of the castle church in Altenburg.

It can be inferred from the accounts that Frederick employed a wood-carver on a permanent basis. The first of these court wood-carvers, Nickel Francke, had fallen while working on the tower of the church at Wittenberg, and though he survived, was no longer able to exercise his art. He was succeeded by Claus Heffner, called Meister Claus[14] whose work can be traced through the year 1510. Heffner owned a house in Wittenberg and was also employed as a stonecarver. In 1492 he went to Magdeburg to buy some stone for coats-of-arms and all through the years the records show that he provided Frederick with carved tables, altarpieces and chandeliers. In 1510 Heffner moved to Pirna where he was engaged in selling stone for coats-of-arms, and his brother 'Hans Bildschnitzer' who had also worked for Schloss Hartenfels in Torgau, took over.

In 1505 Frederick commissioned Tilman Riemenschneider to make a large woodcarving of Christ on the Cross for the castle church in Wittenberg.[15] Riemenschneider, a decade earlier than Dürer and not in touch with the developments in Italy, sought for clearer forms than the intricate ornate late Gothic style provided him. The desire to express directly the inner drama of the believer led to a powerful yet simple presentation.[16] It is splendid evidence of the elector's aesthetic sensitivity that he entrusted to Riemenschneider the crowning piece for his castle church.

Two important works of alabaster-sculpture are still there: the life-sized statues of Frederick and his brother Johann,[17] modeled about 1520. Both princes are ·represented praying, with hands folded. Since it is soft material, alabaster was well suited for chiseling out the fine suits of armor. The unknown artist attempted to make his representation of the princes as life-like as possible: Frederick was already sick and the expression in his face shows his suffering.

Cranach's workshop was used by many artists, among them Conrad Meit of

14 Cf. Thieme-Becker, vol. 16, p. 238.
15 Bruck, *Friedrich der Weise*, pp. 274–275.
16 Cf. J. Bier, *Tilmann Riemenschneider*; ein Gedenkbuch (Vienna, 1948), p. 9.
17 Cf. O. Thulin, *Die Lutherstadt Wittenberg und Torgau* (Berlin, 1932), tables 10 and 11.

Worms.[18] Scheurl referred in his *Libellus de Sacerdotum* to Meit's double presentation of the madonna with forty angels. On the one side Mary the mother is offering grapes to the Jesus child; on the other, as queen of heaven, she holds the scepter amid adoring angels.[19] Meit made the sculpture on commission from Frederick and his brother Johann, and it was placed in the center of the castle church in Wittenberg. He later went into the service of the regent Margaretha of Austria in the Netherlands and became her personal court-sculptor. He probably had already met Dürer in Wittenberg but their close relationship dates from their stay in the Netherlands according to Dürer's records of his journey to the Low Countries.

Bronze-sculpture and bronze-works in general were well known in Saxony at that time and some fine examples of this art are to be seen in its churches. Many of the important orders went to the bronze-casting workshop of the Vischers in Nürnberg,[20] with whom the house of Wettin had long-established connections. Hermann Vischer, the founder of the workshop had cast the splendid bronze baptismal font in 1457; he put his name as well as the year right on his work.[21] Another work which may possibly have come from Vischer's workshop is the bronze tablet for the tomb of Elisabeth of Saxony, wife of elector Ernst and mother of Frederick, now in the Paulinerkirche in Leipzig.

When Hermann Vischer died in 1487, his son Peter (the Elder) took over; he and his son Peter (the Younger) were continuously employed by Frederick. Among the many bronze tablets made by them were one for the tomb of elector Ernst, for which the record of a bill exists; and one for Anna von Habsburg, the wife of Duke Wilhelm of Thuringia, now preserved in the convent of Reinhardsbrunn. In 1504 the Vischers made the bronze tablet for the grave of duchess Sophie, wife of Duke Johann, which may still be seen in the town church in Torgau.[22] The coffin itself is of hewn stone, which a certain Georg Petzsch had sent from Pirna; other work on this grave was done by Claus Heffner and Jacopo de' Barbari. This tombstone, like so many others of the time, represents the duchess, in clothes of the period, against a background of trees. The coat is exquisitely done and the fine quality of the dress is well brought out.

When Peter Vischer the Younger became active in his father's workshop, a new spirit came into it. He was interested in humanism and traveled in Italy in 1507–1508 where he saw Renaissance buildings and decorations of Italy. He did not copy slavishly the Italian masters, but their influence can be seen in all his works. In the Wittenberg castle church is the magnificent bronze epitaph for Frederick the Wise. When the younger Vischer applied for membership in the Nürnberg guild, he cited this work as evidence of his qualifications – one of his few larger pieces attested as genuine. Among other bronze tablets made by Peter

18 Cf. Thieme-Becker, vol. 23, 349ff; W. Bode, 'Die bemalte Thonbüste eines lachenden Kindes im Buckingham Palace und Meister Conrad Meit', *Jahrbuch der Königlich-Preussischen Kunstsammlungen*, 22 (1901), iv–xiv.
19 Cf. H. Michaelson, 'Cranach des Älteren Beziehungen zur Plastik', *Jahrbuch der Königlich-Preussischen Kunstsammlungen*, 21 (1900), 276.
20 Cf. Ludwig Justi, 'Vischerstudien', *Repertorium für Kunstwissenschaft*, 24 (1901), 36ff; Heinrich Weizsäcker, 'Peter Vischer, Vater und Sohn', *ibid.*, 23 (1900), 299ff.
21 Cf. Thulin, *Lutherstadt Wittenberg*, table 27.
22 *Ibid.*, table 72.

the Younger are one for Hans Hundt, the well known knight and bailiff of Frederick, who died in 1509, and an exquisite one for the jurist Henning Göde depicting a coronation of Mary — a work equal to the greatest Renaissance bronze sculptures of its time.[23]

A somewhat later work (1524) of Peter Vischer demonstrates the intellectual changes of a humanist sculptor, closely connected with Wittenberg and Frederick in the first decade of the Reformation. It is a sketch for a bronze plate in which the artist presented an allegory of the Reformation.[24] Luther is shown leading a family out of the crumbling Papal palace inhabited by the vices *superbia, luxuria* and *avaritia*. Pointing to Christ, the good shepherd, Luther shows the way towards salvation. In the corner opposite the destroyed Papal palace, another building is shown with a veiled entrance in front of which a prince is seated, holding sword and imperial globe, ready to pronounce justice. *Justitia*, covering her eyes, whispers to him; her hands point towards three allegorical figures, *fides, spes* and *charitas*, without whose assistance no one can be a Christian judge. The demonstrative action inspired by the Reformation is presented in Renaissance style and symbols, with Luther in the role of a Greek hero, Hope, Faith and Charity represented as Greek Graces, and the house of the prince resembling a Renaissance building.

The seated prince has been interpreted as representing Frederick holding the imperial insignia. Frederick the Wise may have been offered the imperial crown in 1519, and if so, had refused it. At the moment in German history that is here presented, many Germans certainly would have wished the elector of Saxony on the throne rather than the foreigner Charles V, the enemy of Luther. Thus, this sketch presents a wish-image in which the Reformer and the Elector, devoted to the same Christian ideals, establish a better order. Like all the great artists in Frederick's services, Vischer was a humanist who became an adherent of the Reformation.

Peter Mühlich,[25] another member of the Vischer family, worked for Frederick for many years, having been first called to Saxony in 1501 to test whether the soil could be used for baking pottery since this was essential for works of brass. From 1523 on Mühlich was employed in Zwickau as gunsmith; he served the Saxon electors for over thirty years, casting bells, tombstones, fire arms of brass and copper; in 1557 he was pensioned by Johann Friedrich der Mittlere, who also gave him the house in which he lived and some other property. By calling Peter Mühlich to Saxony, Frederick the Wise imported into Saxony a trade that flourished well into the seventeenth century.

At the beginning of the sixteenth century the Italian custom of casting medals had come into vogue in Germany. The bronze medal, a typical expression of Renaissance thirst for honor and glory, would preserve to eternity the image of the individual whom it commemorated. The earliest medals made in Germany came from the house of the Vischers in Nürnberg. A medal of 1507 represents

23 Cf. *ibid.*, table 8.
24 Cf. Georg Seeger, *Peter Vischer der Jüngere. Ein Beitrag zur Geschichte der Erzgiesserfamilie Vischer* (Leipzig, 1897; Beiträge zur Kunstgeschichte, 23), 35–42; Bruck, *Friedrich der Weise*, table 8.
25 Cf. Thieme-Becker, vol. 25, p. 215.

Hermann Vischer and another (1509) his brother Peter,[26] who had returned from a journey to northern Italy in 1507. It is probable that Peter had learned there the use and value of medals. Spalatin mentions twice in his biography of Frederick that the elector had medals made and that he had given many as gifts.[27]

Frederick had the first portrait-medals made in Nürnberg, through the help of Anton Tucher, with whom he carried on a large correspondence about these orders. Between 1508 and 1510 records and correspondence show that one Hans Krug was working in Nürnberg for the elector and between 1510 and 1523 Hans Kraft. In 1510 Frederick tried also to get medals from Holland and in 1512 from Augsburg and Innsbruck.[28] After 1522 medals were made for Frederick in Saxony by Torgau and Wittenberg goldsmiths.[29] It seems quite certain that Cranach's workshop produced the designs for the medals which were then sent to Nürnberg to be cast.[30]

As Frederick put great emphasis on interior decorations, he employed gold and silversmiths in many lands and also glassblowers, chandelier-makers, silk-embroiderers and expert cabinet-makers. Unfortunately few pieces have survived and again we have to obtain our information from records.

One of the major sources of our knowledge of Frederick's collection of works by gold- and silversmiths is the *Wittenberger Heiligtumsbuch* of 1509 with its 116 woodcuts by Lucas Cranach. It contained descriptions of the relics in the castle church and the woodcuts show the splendid containers in which they were kept. This collection was one of the enterprises most dear to the elector and he made every effort to acquire the desired relics. To this end he was in correspondence with King Francis of France, the Cardinal of Mantua, the Bishop of Paris, the Bishop of Utrecht and others, and in Venice he employed Burkhard Schenk von Simau as agent. At the Diet of Constance in 1507 Frederick secured from Pope Julius II a letter to all archbishops, bishops, abbots and prelates of the Holy Roman Empire asking them to send to Frederick any relics they were willing to dispose of. The visitation of these relics at the castle church bought for the penitent individual a great many indulgences, the number of which was increased as late as 1516 by Pope Leo X. Frederick's interest, however, slackened and in 1522 the relics were still displayed but no indulgences given; the following year he gave up altogether the showing of the relics.[31]

Considering the importance attached to the relics it is understandable that Frederick desired to secure for them containers such as Cranach's woodcuts represent. Many were actually made from Cranach's sketches, others date from earlier periods. Some pen and ink drawings, preserved in the Weimar archives,[32] served as sketches and it is likely that they were sent first to elector Frederick for approval. These drawings were originally kept by Brother Berthold, the confessor of the

26 Cf. Georg Habich, *Die deutschen Medailleure des XVI. Jahrhunderts* (Halle, 1916), p. 3ff.
27 Spalatin, pp. 22, 32.
28 Cf. Bruck, *Friedrich der Weise*, pp. 328–9.
29 *Ibid.*, 318.
30 Cf. *Lucas Cranach der Aeltere*: Der Künstler und seine Zeit; ed. H. Lüdecke (Berlin, 1953: Veröffentlichung der Deutschen Akademie der Künste), pp. 157–158.
31 Bruck, *Friedrich der Weise*, p. 304.
32 *Ibid.*, tables 34–41.

elector, who attached a note to each sketch stating for which relic the container was to serve and the amount of indulgences that could be derived from it.[33]

The goldsmiths used enamel, in addition to silver, gold and precious stones, in executing the containers. The best known goldsmith in Frederick's employ was Paul Müllner or Möller of Nürnberg.[34] In 1502 he became court-goldsmith to Frederick and the invoices recording the payments made to him still exist. He visited Frederick in Torgau in 1502 and bought some items for him in Erfurt. An amazing number of pieces came from his workshop in Nürnberg, where he must have employed several craftsmen. He must also have produced jewelry there since mention is made of diamonds, emeralds, rubies and other valuable stones. We have records for silver bowls, rings, crucifixes, chains and pendants. If Frederick wanted to give an especially fine gift, he had it ordered from Müllner, as for instance the wedding presents for Duke Johann and for the King of Denmark. From Müllner's workshop came the chandeliers for the castle church and other interior decorations. Gold- and silversmiths from Nürnberg and Augsburg are mentioned in the accounts,[35] along with artists from Leipzig, Torgau, Coburg, Weimar, Zwickau and Dresden. It is evident that a local artisanry had developed in Saxony to a considerable degree with the support of Frederick.

Frederick enjoyed tournaments and knightly performances and was therefore interested in exquisite armor. A whole industry of making implements for armor-plating and laminating arose around Frederick's court and some makers of armor always accompanied him on his journeys.[36] From 1488 to 1523 he maintained an armory in Torgau in charge of one Ewalt Heseler. The armor was used during tournaments; it was often lent out and sometimes given away to other princes and knights. Frederick made such gifts to a prince of Denmark in 1505 and to Markgrave Casimir of Brandenburg in 1514.[37] The measurements for the armor were taken and sent to the men who did the plating and laminating. The decorations were planned and executed with great skill, using gold, silver, and other fine metals. In connection with the making of armor, even painters are mentioned, among them Jacopo de' Barbari who must have been well acquainted with the decoration of armor in Italy.[38] The armorer's trade flourished especially in Austria where emperor Maximilian commissioned much work; Innsbruck was the most important trade center[39] and Frederick had made contact with the armorer Lucas Gassner there on his way to the Holy Land in 1493.[40] In 1496 payments were made to emperor Maximilian's armorer Meister Albrecht. Frederick also employed armorers in Landshut, Nürnberg, Munich and Wittenberg and bought materials at the Leipzig Fairs. The names of many local armorers of Wittenberg, Weimar and other Saxon towns are known to us.

33 *Ibid.*, p. 303.
34 Cf. Thieme-Becker, vol. 24, p. 250.
35 Bruck, *Friedrich der Weise*, pp. 307ff.
36 Cf. Spalatin, p. 52; also Cornelius Gurlitt, *Deutsche Turniere, Rüstungen und Plattner des XVI. Jahrhunderts* (Dresden, 1889; Archivalische Forschungen, 8).
37 Bruck, *Friedrich der Weise*, pp. 320, 324.
38 *Ibid.*, 324.
39 Cf. Wendelin Böheim, *Meister der Waffenschmiedekunst vom XIV. bis ins XVIII. Jahrhundert* (Berlin, 1897).
40 Bruck, *Friedrich der Weise*, p. 320.

Frederick purchased textiles wherever he could find beautiful pieces. At the Leipzig Fair of 1505 Frederick bought some Dutch cloth;[41] on his journey to Holland, carpets and rugs, later used to decorate walls; large sums were spent for carpets to be woven on order for his own household and for gifts. None of the textiles have been preserved, but according to an inventory taken at Weimar in 1496[42] many such items existed, embellished with scenes of religious and mythological content.

As a lover of books and manuscripts Frederick paid careful attention to book illustrations, coats-of-arms and vignettes and other types of book decorations. He was anxious to find the best book illustrators and also craftsmen who could furnish artistic bindings for his books. The two best known book illustrators at that time were Georg Glockendon and Jakob Elsner.[43] Glockendon came from a well-known Nürnberg artist family and he and his sons were famous book illuminators, engravers and goldsmiths. However, only the records remain of the works that he did for Frederick. Jakob Elsner is known as the illuminator of the famous *Gänsebuch*,[44] signed by him and dated 1513. It was done on order for Dr. Anton Kress, the provost of the St. Lorenz Church in Nürnberg where it was kept in the vestry. Its renown rests on the charming and extremely beautiful illustrations. In the records in Weimar, we find that Elsner illuminated two books for elector Frederick in the years 1507 and 1509.[45] These books, pericopes from the Gospels and the Epistles, are now in the library of the University of Jena. The corners of the books and their locks are of gold-plated silver and enamel; Elsner's illuminations of these two works show the strong influence of Schongauer and Dürer.

In the university library at Jena are three other books which belonged to Frederick and are illuminated by Dutch hands.[46] Bruck reproduces several of these miniatures, among them one of Frederick praying, behind him an angel who puts his hands on the elector's shoulders.[47] Another picture of Frederick represents him with St. Catherine at a window looking out into a beautiful landscape with a pond in which trees and birds in flight are mirrored. The portraits of Frederick seem to be based on some by Cranach. Yet, these miniatures are typical works of Dutch art with their style of presenting landscapes, portraits, flowers and still-life.

III

Frederick was attracted to the new humanistically-oriented Renaissance style in painting. He loved painting and, as a patron and collector of works of art, he showed excellent taste in his selections. The Weimar archives record names of many painters and works of art; though not many of the canvases have survived, a

---

41 *Ibid.*, 320.
42 *Ibid.*, p. 235.
43 Cf. Thieme-Becker, vol. 14, pp. 259–260; and vol. 10, pp. 488–489.
44 Cf. Robert Bruck, 'Der Illuminist Jakob Elsner', *Jahrbuch der Königlich-Preussischen Kunstsammlungen*, 24 (1903), 302–317; also Henry Thode, *Die Malerschule von Nürnberg im XIV. und XV. Jahrhundert in ihrer Entwicklung bis auf Dürer* (Frankfurt, 1891), pp. 194–195.
45 Bruck, *Friedrich der Weise*, p. 303.
46 *Ibid.*, pp. 205–206.
47 Plate III.

full account can be reconstructed of all the activities that Frederick encouraged, sponsored, and financed.

At the beginning of Frederick's reign Meister Kunz was the court painter.[48] He drew some decorations for elector Ernst's gravestone in 1486 and in 1487 he painted on armor to be used at tournaments. He is also mentioned frequently in the archives as book-illustrator and painter of crucifixes and altarpieces. He was apparently among those who accompanied Frederick on his journey to the Holy Land[49] and must, on this occasion, have become acquainted with the splendors of Venice and the Holy Land. Another painter of the period was Meister Ludwig of Leipzig,[50] who, according to the records, painted cloth and textiles. Other painters, including Friedrich der Maler, Stefan Maler, Benedictus Maler and Jacob Coch der Maler, are mentioned. Michel Wolgemut of Nürnberg, the teacher of Albrecht Dürer, is mentioned once in the archival entries of 1503, when he made for the elector a wood-panel which was probably an altarpiece.[51] The work may have been done by one of his pupils since Wolgemut was then in his old age.

In 1506 Hans Burgkmair of Augsburg, who had done work for emperor Maximilian and Conrad Celtis, was commissioned by Frederick to make an altarpiece representing St. Sebastian and other martyrs.[52] Coming from the workshop of Martin Schongauer, Burgkmair became acquainted with the work of the Renaissance artists in Italy when he went there about 1490. Bruck found in the Weimar archives an illustrated chronicle written by Spalatin, entitled *Auszug Nahmhaffter Mann und Weibes Personen, . . .*[53] On the basis of comparisons with Burgkmair's illustrations to Maximilian's *Weiskunig* and *Theurdank* he concludes that the illustrations, several of which he reproduces, must have been made either by Burgkmair himself or at least by his workshop.

From Nürnberg came Hans von Speier who worked for Frederick after 1491 in Wittenberg, and also in Weimar and in Leipzig, where he made murals for the Paulskirche and designed a tombstone for Frederick's mother, Elizabeth of Bavaria.

A Dutch painter was imported by Frederick and Bruck concludes that it was Jan Gossaert (called Mabuse, 1478–1533) who had been in the employ of Philip of Burgundy as painter, woodcutter and etcher.[54] The artist went with Frederick to the Holy Land in 1493 and in 1494 accompagnied him on his journey to the Netherlands. He traveled for Frederick to Cracow and to Venice and when he returned to the Netherlands sometime in 1505 or 1506 he was still doing work for

48   Bruck, *Friedrich der Weise*, pp. 282ff.
49   Spalatin, p. 90.
50   Bruck, *Friedrich der Weise*, pp. 281ff.
51   Thode, *Malerschule*, pp. 124ff.
52   Bruck, *Friedrich der Weise*, p. 296.
53   Auszug nahmhaffter Mann und Weibes Personen, geist- und weltlicher in das edle Hauss der Herzog in Thüringen, und Markgrafen zu Meissen gehörig. Durch Georg Spalatinum zusammen getragen, 1513. MS., in Weimar Archiv. Cf. Willy Flach. 'Georg Spalatin als Geschichtsschreiber' in: *Zur Geschichte und Kultur des Elb-Saale-Raumes*. Festschrift für Walter Möllenberg, ed. Otto Korn (Burg, 1939), pp. 211–230.
54   Cf. Thieme-Becker, vol. 14, pp. 410–412; for doubts concerning this painter, cf. Georg Dehio, *Geschichte der deutschen Kunst*, III: Texte (Berlin, 1926), 22; and F. Becker's review of Bruck's book in *NASG*, 28 (1907), 146–148.

the elector. Apparently only one of the works done for him has survived, the *Gefangennahme Christi* of 1494, a part of an altarpiece, now in Dresden.

A lifelong and mutually fruitful relationship between Frederick the Wise and Albrecht Dürer began during the elector's visit to Nürnberg in April 1496. Deeply impressed by the genius of the artist, Frederick was the first to commission paintings from Dürer: an altarpiece for the castle church in Wittenberg and a portrait. These are from the most creative phase in the artist's career in which Dürer, established as an independent master, reaped the harvest of his varied experience. Of the two paintings Panofsky writes: 'The iconography of the Dresden alterpiece can thus be understood as a synthesis of Bellinesque invention with the tradition of the Low Countries and Germany . . . The general effect [of the portrait of Frederick the Wise] is strongly Mantegnesque, a characteristic apparent not only in the style and in the treatment of such details as the hair, but in the psychological interpretation as well.'[55] Evidence of the next contact between Frederick and Dürer appears in the account books of 1501, which mention a work of art that was transported to Torgau. They also show that during the years 1501–1503 Frederick paid the tuition and board for a boy whom he apprenticed to Dürer.[56]

In 1503 the interior of the Wittenberg castle underwent major changes and was greatly improved; many rooms were newly painted, the walls as well as the ceilings. From Meinhardi's *Dialogus* we have a detailed description of the castle: the *aestuarium commune*, the *aestuarium maius*, the living room of Frederick and his bedroom and Duke Johann's bedroom, also the *consistorium* and other lesser rooms. Invoices of the year show that Dürer painted in Frederick's rooms in Wittenberg in which were kept most of the portraits of the dukes and electors of Saxony.[57] There is no way to trace any specific work of art that Dürer undertook there, but there is evidence that Dürer worked on decorating the castle church on one of his two stays in Wittenberg, in 1494–1495 and in 1503. It was on the latter occasion that he met, among others, Jacopo de' Barbari.

Several of the works that Dürer made for Frederick are extant today. In addition to the two already discussed, the *Mater Dolorosa* polyptych, designed by Dürer,[58] was probably executed by an assistant and was ordered by Frederick as a composite canvas for the castle church. There are several other works of Dürer that were made after 1500 at the request of Frederick the Wise. An altarpiece drawing, a study for the Ober St. Veit altarpiece, signed 'Albertus Dürer, 1502'[59] is extant, but its genuineness has recently been doubted by Panofsky. Several altarpieces were ordered by Frederick, as for instance the fragments of a triptych, known as the Jabach Altarpiece,[60] for the castle church in Wittenberg and the Adoration of the Magi of 1504, now at the Uffizi in Florence,[61] its original place

55 Cf. Erwin Panofsky, *Albrecht Dürer*, 3rd ed. (2 vols., Princeton, 1948), I, 39–40.
56 Bruck, *Friedrich der Weise*, p. 289.
57 *Ibid.*
58 Cf. Panofsky, *Dürer*, II: handlist of works, no. 3; cf. E. Buchner, 'Die sieben Schmerzen Mariae', *Münchner Jahrbuch der bildenden Kunst*, n.s. 11 (1934/6), 250ff.
59 Panofsky, *Dürer*, II, no. 476.
60 *Ibid.*, no. 6.
61 *Ibid.*, no. 11, table 113.

having been in the castle church. Kaufmann suggested that Frederick had a direct part in the selection of the story of Job as depicted on what probably were the exterior wings of the altarpiece.[62] Job, smitten with painful boils yet cured in the end, was worshiped and invoked by those who suffered from what all ancient medicine called 'melancholy' or from such diseases as leprosy, ulcers, or scabies. Panofsky, following Kaufmann's thesis concludes: 'It was in this capacity of a healer that Job was honored by Frederick the Wise. A typical valetudinarian, the elector was more than normally afraid of those epidemics which had haunted Germany since 1503, and there is little doubt that this preoccupation with the plague and other contagious diseases accounts for the choice of the subject.'[63]

Shortly after Dürer's return from Italy in 1507 Frederick ordered a picture, the Martyrdrom of the Ten Thousand.[64] In a letter to Jakob Heller, a Frankfurt merchant, Dürer discussed this picture with which he was rather pleased; he finished the work in 1508. As on other occasions, Dürer painted himself in this picture, and next to him Conrad Celtis[65] who had died a few months before the work was finished and whom Dürer, like the elector, had loved and admired.

From that time until 1520 the sources fail to record any contact between Dürer and Frederick. In a letter to Spalatin of January or February 1520 Dürer announced that he had dispatched three prints of his recently completed engraving of Albrecht of Mainz;[66] he also asked Spalatin to thank Frederick for the gift of a volume of Luther's writings and begged him to recommend Luther to the elector for the sake of Christian truth. When Frederick visited Nürnberg in 1524 Dürer once more made a portrait of the prince who had been his loyal patron.

Among the painters whom Frederick succeeded in drawing to Wittenberg was Jacopo de' Barbari.[67] This artist, born probably around the middle of the fifteenth century in Venice, stayed in his native town until 1500. Then he left Italy for good and went to Nürnberg, where he stayed for three years. He may have realized that he was not a great enough artist to compete with his contemporaries on native soil, but that in Germany his art would be more appreciated. In Nürnberg the influence of the humanists was strong and he could therefore expect that his Renaissance style of painting would be appreciated. In Germany and later in the Netherlands he became known as Jakob Walch (*Jakob der Welsche*).

In 1502 Jacopo de' Barbari wrote a letter to Frederick[68] in which he praised the elector as a renowned patron of the arts. In 1503, with Dürer, he came to

62 Cf. Hans Kaufmann, 'Albrecht Dürers Dreikönigsaltar', *Westdeutsches Jahrbuch für Kunstgeschichte, Wallraf-Richartz-Jahrbuch*, 10 (1938), 166–178.
63 Panofsky, *Dürer*, I, 93.
64 *Ibid.*, II, no. 47, table 166.
65 Cf. E. Panofsky, 'Conrad Celtes and Kunz von der Rosen: two problems in portrait-identification', *Art Bulletin*, 24 (1942), 39ff; cf. also A. Gümbel, *Der kursächsische Kämmerer Degenhart von Pfeffinger, der Begleiter Dürers in der 'Marter der Zehntausend Christen'* (Strassburg, 1926: Studien zur deutschen Kunstgeschichte, 238); cf. also Bruck, *Friedrich der Weise*, p. 126, who identified the man next to Dürer as Pirkheimer.
66 This is the portrait known as the 'Small Cardinal', dated 1519; cf. Panofsky, *Dürer*, II, no. 209, table 248.
67 Cf. P. Kirn, 'Friedrich der Weise und Jacopo de' Barbari', *Jahrbuch der königlich preussischen Kunstsammlungen* 46 (1925), 130–134; also Heinrich Wölfflin, *Die Kunst Albrecht Dürers*, Munich, 1905, pp. 313–316.
68 Cf. Kirn, 'Friedrich der Weise', pp. 133–34.

Wittenberg and stayed for the following two years as court painter, working in Wittenberg, Torgau and Lochau. One may surmise that the early humanists at the university were delighted to have an Italian artist in their midst. He entertained professors, among them Marschalk, Petrus of Ravenna and Vincentius of Ravenna, who mentions Jacopo as working with Frederick the Wise in his oration in praise of Wittenberg in 1505. Dürer, whom he had known in Nürnberg and with whom he worked in Wittenberg, also came to his house. Later on Jacopo went to Frankfurt a. d. Oder and then to the Netherlands as court painter to Margareta of Austria; he probably died around 1516. Little is preserved of what Jacopo de' Barbari painted during his years in Wittenberg, with the exception of three pictures. His major assignment may have been in connection with the decorations of the electoral castle, but since the whole interior has been destroyed, no trace of his work is left. It is probable that some of the scenes from Roman history on the interior walls that Meinhardi described were from the hand of Jacopo, especially as these murals reflected an intimate knowledge of Rome and its buildings. The influence of Jacopo on Dürer has been much discussed but no definitive conclusions have been reached. It seems certain that, through Jacopo, Dürer came into close contact with Venetian art and also became acquainted with the theories concerning proportion that Jacopo mentioned in his letter to Frederick. That Frederick availed himself of the opportunity to attract an Italian Renaissance artist to his court indicates what style in contemporary art he favored.

Lucas Cranach was the one great artist whom Frederick was able to attract and hold at his court. After the elector's death in 1525 Cranach remained in Saxon service under the princes Johann and Johann Friedrich until his death in 1553. Today Cranach is known as the artist of the Reformation; in his paintings he has conveyed to us the likeness of Luther and many of his contemporaries; many of his portraits of the humanists are still preserved, among them the paintings representing Christoph Scheurl, Georg Spalatin and Philip Melanchthon. Cranach was not an innovator who developed new artistic concepts like his Italian contemporaries and Albrecht Dürer, but he was deeply interested in Renaissance art and humanism; he became a staunch supporter of the Reformation and a friend to many reformers; he was one of Wittenberg's most solid and active citizens and his life and work are permeated with the new bourgeois spirit. It may have been that a similarity in personal qualities and general outlook drew Frederick and Cranach close to each other; neither was a radical in his thinking but both were open to the new ideas of their times.

Cranach, the son of a painter, was born in 1472 in the Franconian town of Cranach;[69] of his early years little is known except that between 1495 and 1500 he worked for elector Frederick in Coburg and Gotha.[70] After 1500 he wandered

69 There is much literature, old as well as new, on Cranach. Of the earlier works there are two basic ones: Christian Schuchardt, *Lucas Cranach des Älteren Leben und Werke*, 3 vols., Leipzig, 1851–1871: and Joseph Heller, *Lucas Cranachs Leben und Werke*, 2nd. rev. ed. (Nürnberg 1854). Of later studies the following should be mentioned: Hans Posse, *Lucas Cranach d. Ae.* (Vienna, 1942); *Lucas Cranach der Ältere. Der Künstler und seine Zeit*, ed. Heinz Lüdecke (Berlin, 1953); *Lucas Cranach der Ältere im Spiegel seiner Zeit*, ed. H. Lüdecke (Berlin, 1953: Veröffentlichung der Deutschen Akademie der Künste); Oscar Thulin, *Cranach-Altäre der Reformation* (Berlin, 1955).
70 Bruck, *Friedrich der Weise*, pp. 300ff. Cf. also Heller, pp. 279ff; and Schuchardt, pp. 17ff.

down the Danube towards Vienna. That this was his storm-and-stress period can be seen from the works of this time. He was in contact with the members of the Danubian sodality to which he may actually have belonged; in Vienna he met Celtis and Cuspinian who, like Cranach himself, were natives of Franconia and who drew the talented artist into their circle. This early contact with the Viennese humanists became decisive for Cranach's future development; their battle for the renewal of the humanities and against the preponderance of scholasticism prepared him for his future role in Wittenberg. Well-known pictures by Cranach of this period are the portraits of Dr. Johannes Cuspinian and his wife Anna, and of Dr. Stephan Reuss and his wife. The Crucifixion from the Wiener Schottenstift is usually considered to be Cranach's earliest work of this period.[71] Two other crucifixions from this period are preserved: a woodcut of 1502 and the so-called Schleissheimer crucifixion of 1503. It is apparent that Cranach's favorite theme of this time was the crucifixion, but his paintings differ from the conventional ones. Instead of a well balanced, rather quiet representation of the scene of grief, he portrays passionate and violent sorrow.

Of the other works preserved from this time, the finest is the *Ruhe auf der Flucht nach Aegypten*,[72] which illustrates the familiar passage from Matthew II, 13–14. Cranach transformed the biblical story: Joseph, Mary and the Jesus child form a simple yet serene bourgeois family resting in the shade of the tree on a pleasant summer day. For the first time the signature of the master, LC, is to be found, next to the date, 1504. This, one of the best known works of Cranach, concludes his early period.

In 1505, at the invitation of Frederick, Cranach came to Wittenberg. Frederick naturally searched for a brilliant artist to be attracted to his court and Cranach followed his call, possibly because he believed the elector to be a real patron of the arts. The invitation was backed up by a substantial annual salary of 100 gulden (the same that Dürer received from the city of Nürnberg). That year, Cranach married Barbara Brengbier, daughter of the wealthy mayor of Gotha, and thus established his own household in Wittenberg, where he remained for the next forty-five years. Cranach's presence certainly strengthened the then still small circle of humanists in Wittenberg and we know how in later years the humanists there honored him more than any other artist of the time.

Cranach's work in his early Wittenberg years encompassed a great variety of artistic enterprises. The most important project on hand was the execution of altarpieces, the first of which was the so-called *Katharinenaltar* of 1506.[73] The subject probably was chosen because it offered an excellent opportunity for combining several ideas. An appropriate subject for an altarpiece, St. Catharine, the erudite and valiant saint, would well be revered as a patron of all learning. At least one humanist (Hans von Schwarzenberg)[74] was portrayed in this populated canvas, and in the far left corner the elector Frederick and duke Johann mounted on horses are seen. The Veste Coburg appears in the background. Noteworthy are the delicately presented pages, one of them in garments displaying the Meissen and

71 Posse, tables 6–9.
72 Posse, table 10.
73 Posse, tables 11–20.
74 *Lucas Cranach der Aeltere*, p. 35.

Thuringian colors. This picture, so different in its loose composition from Cranach's previous work, shows an unmistakable kinship to similar Italian Renaissance paintings, inspired by princely patrons and reflecting courtly splendor.

There is extant yet another altarpiece of this period, though not comparable in beauty: the *Sippenalter* (or *Torgauer Fürstenaltar*) of 1509.[75] Cranach executed this after returning from his trip to the Netherlands in 1508–1509, where he painted a portrait of the future emperor Charles V, then only eight years old. Cranach had come in contact with the Dutch painters who at that time had close connections with the Italian school. Unlike Dürer, Cranach had never been to Italy and his acquaintance with Renaissance painting came through the works of other painters and of the Italian Jacopo de' Barbari whom he had met in Wittenberg. On the *Sippenaltar* Cranach gracefully arranged the various figures in the framework of a balcony-like structure in Renaissance architectural style. Again Frederick and Johann are portrayed, and Cranach posed emperor Maximilian and himself looking down from the balcony on the charming family scene. On one of the columns a little poster is affixed with the Latin inscription: *'Lucas Chronus faciebat anno 1509.'* In the following year, another altarpiece, the *Dessauer Fürstenaltar*, was finished,[76] so named because on its two wings the two dukes of electoral Saxony are represented, this time with their patron saints, Frederick with St. Bartholomew and Johann with St. James the Elder.

From these early years in Wittenberg we possess several woodcuts by Cranach, depicting secular and religious scenes. He signed each one 'LC' and added the Saxon coat-of-arms to most pictures. Many show saints and martyrs as well as tournaments, hunting scenes and men and women on horseback.[77] One of the tournament paintings has been described by the humanist-poet Sibutus in his *Torniamenta*; it is interesting to note that the background is always a peaceful Saxon landscape, however violent an action appears in the picture.

In the year 1508 honors were showered on Cranach in Wittenberg, and from this time on he became a major figure in public life. He received a patent *(Wappenbrief)* as a special distinction; this was also the year when Christoph Scheurl delivered his *Oratio attingens*, in which he praised Wittenberg, elector Frederick and Dürer. When it was printed in 1509, it included poems by Sbrulius, Beckmann, Christian Beyer and Carlstadt in praise of Cranach, and Scheurl prefaced it with a dedicatory letter to Cranach.

The letter is typically elaborate and grandiose humanistic oratory, eulogizing Cranach above all German painters with the exception of Dürer, Scheurl's fellow townsman from Nürnberg. Cranach is considered by the Italians as their equal and by the French their master; his paintings in the castle church of Wittenberg are so famous that people come from all over Europe just to see them. Scheurl praises Cranach's tremendous ability to portray objects, animals and individuals, and he relates anecdotes like the one about the birds which attempted to fly right into the antlers of a painted deer, only to fall down on impact; of grapes painted on a table so realistically that birds came to eat them and thus destroyed the master's work. In Coburg Cranach had painted a stag so true to life that the dogs barked at

75 Posse, tables 21, 233; plate V.
76 *Ibid.*, table 26.
77 Cf. Bauch, 'Zur Cranachforschung', pp. 432ff.

it. His portrait of Duke Johann was so accurate that when people saw the picture, they lifted their hats and bent their knees. Scheurl finds many more examples of Cranach's striking realism and praises him for his devotion to his work. No day passes without Cranach working from dawn to sunset; whenever he accompanies his princely masters on hunting expeditions, he draws many pictures of animals and landscapes. Cranach is friendly, talkative, generous and helpful and therefore loved by elector Frederick as Apelles was loved by Alexander, by Duke Johann as Protogenes was by King Demetrius. The princes visit him often in his workshop and talk about art with him. The letter ends with a long dedicatory phrase and Scheurl finally mentions Cranach's portrait of himself. Even taking its mannerisms into account, this letter gives an idea of how highly Cranach was esteemed in Wittenberg even in his early years there.

A poem by Carlstadt, dating from the year 1509 and dedicated to both Cranach and Scheurl, has been preserved. Carlstadt makes reference to Scheurl's dedicatory letter. He praises Cranach in typically humanist fashion with many references to classical personalities, Pliny, Androcydes, Ajax, Apelles. Carlstadt stresses especially the artist's skilful use of perspective, one of the most important gains of Renaissance art.

Cranach was now at the height of his productivity. From this period date a great number of woodcuts: the *Judgment of Paris*, where an armed knight asleep under a tree in a south German setting is being awakened; the fourteen Passion woodcuts, which were republished as a book in 1509;[78] and finally the *Wittenberger Heiligtumsbuch* with 117 woodcuts. As title page Cranach used an engraving of Frederick and Johann. This book also contains the famous woodcut of the castle church which conveys an idea what this building was like at that time, even though the steep hill behind it with the woods and small buildings did not correspond to reality. Cranach evidently did not reproduce exactly what he saw in the woodcuts, but gave his imagination and phantasy free range.

There is another interesting series of eight woodcuts by Cranach, the last one showing the Saxon coats-of-arms; they were drawn for Adam von Fulda's *Ein ser andechtig Cristenlich Buchlein.*

When she married Duke Johann in 1513, Margareta of Anhalt received a bridal bed, decorated by Cranach, that seemed a little marvel to humanistic eyes. Philipp Engelbrecht of Engen, called Engentinus, who belonged to the Wittenberg humanistic circle around Scheurl, Beckmann and Sibutus, celebrated the event in a long poem and gave an enthusiastic description of Cranach's decorations. These were all illustrations of classical themes; the judgment of Paris, Apollo's tending the sheep of King Admetus, Hercules and Hippolytus. Like Scheurl in his dedication, Engentinus concludes the description, comparing Cranach with Apelles, Aristides and Protogenes.

Cranach used many other classical themes and it is evident that in these years he was a friend of the humanists, interpreting their works while at the same time continuing his studies of Biblical and Christian subjects. The theme of Mary and Child, of which Cranach portrayed many variations and interpretations, particularly attracted him.

78 This work was later used by Georg Rhaw and Johann Kraft in several of the works they printed, e.g. the *Passion Book* of 1540. It was reprinted in 1543 and 1561.

If Cranach did any portraits before 1509 in Wittenberg they have not been preserved. The first dated portrait is the one of Christoph Scheurl from 1509. One depicting the mayor of Weissenfels dates from 1512 and there is a still later one of Frederick. Landscapes no longer form the background for these studies; the artist employs a neutral background, against which the person emerges sharply and with dignity. Cranach's life-sized portraits of Duke Heinrich der Fromme and his wife Katharina (1514) are magnificent examples of courtly representation of the German Renaissance.

In 1515 Cranach contributed several drawings as decorations for the prayerbook of emperor Maximilian,[79] as did Dürer, Cranach, Baldung and Burgkmair. Cranach provided eight pages, two of which he surrounded with Christian themes; the rest, without any relation to the text, contain his beloved masterly drawings of animals, stags, deer, foxes and monkeys.

Under the impact of Luther's appearance in Wittenberg and the events of 1517 there Cranach's interests and outlook changed; from the beginning he openly stood by Luther and his reforming work: from the early years of Cranach's contact with the Viennese humanist circle, to the humanist circle in Wittenberg, and then to Protestantism. Very few of the humanists left the Roman Catholic camp to join the Protestant forces, but for Cranach there never seems to have been any question at all about the course he was to take. Until his death in 1553 he was a staunch supporter of Lutheranism and the names of Wittenberg, Protestantism and Cranach were always linked together. Our image of Luther is based on the many portraits Cranach made of him. A letter from Luther is evidence of how close this friendship between the religious leader and the painter was. He reveals to Cranach, and to him alone, his whereabouts at the Wartburg, where he was taken by Frederick's 'secret agents' — after the Diet of Worms in 1521.[80] When Protestant iconoclasts tried to eliminate all artistic expression of religious subjects, Luther definitely took the side of the Protestant artist when he stated that the adoration of pictures is not permitted, but that the making of and looking at them certainly is permissible.[81] And in 1525 Luther in his treatise *Wider die himmlischen Propheten* again upholds Christian art as an expression of beauty and a worthy vehicle for commemorating great and beloved persons.[82] Cranach is known today as the painter of the German Reformation, and his friendship with Luther certainly bears witness to the fact that Luther approved of his art.

In reflecting upon the activities in all the visual arts — building, stone-carving, illustrating, and above all, painting — one cannot fail to admire Frederick's tireless efforts and excellent taste in bringing some of the foremost artists to Wittenberg. In hardly any other sphere of cultural life was the impact of humanism so strong. By 1500 the great German artists were decisively under the influence of the Italian Renaissance. Dürer, Barbari and Cranach found a warm welcome among the Wittenberg humanists whose language delights in the same images of antiquity that the artists portrayed in the paintings. Traditional Christian themes also found worthy expression in the new style. When the Reformation conquered the Witten-

79 Cf. Ludwig Baldass, *Der Künstlerkreis Kaiser Maximilians* (Vienna, 1923), tables 42–53.
80 *WAB* 2, no. 400.
81 *WA* 10, 3, p. 11.
82 *Ibid.*, 18, p. 80.

berg scene and made humanism its handmaiden, it also began to dominate the theme and iconography of painting.

IV

Among the paintings, engravings and stone-carvings that have conveyed to us the image of Frederick the Wise, probably the oldest representation still extant is on a painting of a madonna by an artist of the Nürnberg school of the late fifteenth century.[83] Several kneeling personalities are adoring Mary, among them the youthful *'Friedericus dux Saxoniae Elector'*, as he can be identified from the inscription on the waving ribbon. The lower corners of the painting show the Saxon coat-of-arms, and Frederick himself holds the electoral sword in his hand. From his youthful appearance one would conclude that this was done shortly after the beginning of his reign in 1486, probably in the workshop of either Michel Wolgemut or Hans von Speier. The schematic treatment of the robes and hands suggest that only the head, with its large open eyes, was sketched from nature.

The first well-known portrait of the elector was made by Albrecht Dürer, probably in 1496.[84] In this picture the elector is dressed in black with some gold decorations against a light background. It is a dramatic picture, of somewhat heroic quality, sombre and commanding. It is very different from the later portraits of Frederick that show him as a much mellower and milder personality.

From the hand of Adriano Fiorentino we have a bronze bust of Frederick, probably done in 1498. Cornelius v. Fabriczy is of the opinion that Adriano made the bust in Italy and that it was cast in Saxony.[85] This representation of Frederick is very different from the Germanic ones; he is idealized, appears as a beautiful man, with long, flowing locks; the hair style is Italian rather than German and the lower portion of his face, mainly the chin which is protruding in all other pictures, is set forward to make his features more symmetrical. The bust is not recognizable as a representation of Frederick; it is rather that of a Roman soldier.

Lucas Cranach has left us several portraits of Frederick the Wise which, in view of the intimate relations between the prince and the artist and of the realistic style of Cranach, may be regarded as the most authoritative. One of these portraits serves as titlepage for the *Wittenberger Heiligtumsbuch* of 1509. It is a powerful and realistic copper engraving of the brothers Johann and Frederick with the Saxon coat-of-arms in the upper two corners and Cranach's own famous coat-of-arms in the lower corner. Frederick carries a chain around his neck and wears a coat with a fur collar. In his hands he holds a rosary. His beard is shorter than it appears in later portraits and he looks thoughtful and kind.

Another portrait by Cranach, from the year 1515, shows Frederick in a similar pose, with a heavy coat; his hands, adorned with many rings, are resting on a table; his eyes gaze thoughtfully into space. Here we have a dark background

---

83 Cf. Max Lossnitzer, 'Die frühen Bildnisse Kurfürst Friedrichs des Weisen', *Mitteilungen aus den sächsischen Kunstsammlungen*, 4 (1913), 8–18.
84 Cf. Panofsky, Dürer, II, table 65.
85 Cornelius von Fabriczy, 'Adriano Fiorentino', *Jahrbuch der königlich-preussischen Kunstsammlungen*, 24 (1903), 71–98.

showing a Saxon landscape.[86] Also from the year 1515 is a woodcut showing Frederick adoring Mary with the child. Schuchardt[87] calls this one of the most beautiful pictures by Cranach in expression and composition. The Christ-child is on Mary's lap looking towards the elector, who adores it with folded hands; in the window a contemporary German landscape can be seen. Another representation of Frederick that has already been discussed is in the socalled *Fürstenaltar*, on the left wing.

Another of the portraits by Cranach is a later picture of Frederick.[88] He is very large, with big beard, big hat, big coat, looking alert and kind, with a great deal of expression; again a Saxon landscape serves as a background. Cranach's image of Frederick suggests a benevolent ruler, thoughtful and pious, somewhat aloof, looking dreamily into nowhere.

This last known picture by Cranach bears resemblance to Dürer's engraving of 1524, executed one year before Frederick's death.[89] This shows a tragic old man, sickness written in his face. It is done in great detail, one can feel the heaviness and awkwardness of the ailing prince; it can be surmised that Frederick could no longer sit for the engraver for any length of time and it thus testifies to Dürer's excellent memory. It is a picture of an old man, tired of life, and one might almost say prepared to die.

After Frederick's death Peter Vischer the Younger made the bronze tablet for Frederick's grave.[90] It is signed *'opus M. Petri. Fischer. Norimbergensis, 1527'*. It is a magnificent work of art: both the face and the life-sized figure of Frederick are chiseled out to the very finest detail; it can only be compared in its concept and understanding to Dürer's last picture of the elector. The prince is clothed in electoral hat and coat with ermine collar, and his hands hold firmly on to the electoral sword. In the center over his head is his coat-of-arms and over it two angels, holding a laurel wreath with Frederick's favorite motto: *'Verbum domini manet in Aeternum'*. On the sides of the figure are two pillars, decorated with many different designs. The foundation is decorated like the rest with Renaissance motifs; simplicity and grandeur, dress and expression give the whole work a truly princely and imperial quality. Next to the bronze tablet Melanchthon put two Latin epitaphs for Frederick, praising him for his love of peace, his perceptive mind, his love of scholarship and his piety. The bronze tablet and Melanchthon's epitaphs were a fitting end to a great prince's life.

86 Posse, table 34; plate VII.
87 Schuchardt, I, 234–235.
88 Cf. Schwiebert, *Luther*, plate IX.
89 Cf. Panofsky, *Dürer*, II, table 302.
90 Cf. Schadow, table B; plate IX.

CONCLUSION

The problem of German humanism has always provoked stimulating and controversial discussion. Some of the major points of the debates arising from the problems will be recapitulated here in order to show how these issues are related to the particular situation in Wittenberg. Certain trends of the cultural development in Wittenberg, which have emerged in the course of this study, may perhaps shed light on some of the larger questions concerning humanism.

The religious factors which played a dominant part in the origins of humanism in Germany were also largely responsible for the particular shape the movement took in that country. Yet, scholars have taken different positions in accounting for this phenomenon. Hermelink and Hyma sought the roots of German humanism in the intellectual developments peculiar to Germany: not in Italy, but in the North. Hermelink strongly advocated the acknowledgment of the *via antiqua* as a major force that prepared an atmosphere receptive to German humanism. He went even further, ascribing to the impact of the *via antiqua* the desire to return to the early sources of Christianity and the ensuing movement for church reform. Hyma believed that in the *Devotio Moderna* he had discovered the beginnings of German humanism.

Ritter, who devoted special attention to trends and developments in late scholastic thinking, rejected the theses of both Hermelink and Hyma. Although recognizing that the inner-scholastic reaction against Occamism eased the way for humanism at the universities, he could not find in the *via antiqua* a force powerful enough to initiate a movement labeled German humanism. In this evaluation Joachimsen and Baron concurred, and like Ritter, they rejected the paramount role Hyma ascribed to the *Devotio Moderna* in the religious life of Germany. The transformation from the late medieval world to the world of humanism, according to Ritter and Joachimsen, was not due to peculiar theological movements in the North, but was achieved under the impact of Italian humanism.

Ritter and Mestwerdt also pointed out that German humanists, following the example of their Italian colleagues, had discovered through the study of antiquity a new world, independent of Christian concepts and dogmas. The possibilities of this new intellectual orientation were, however, limited by the contact of humanism with the new and powerful Reformation movement. Therefore most studies have been concerned not directly with humanism in Germany but with the religious transition from the world of scholasticism to the Reformation.

The theme has been taken up in recent years by several scholars. Lewis W. Spitz, in the conclusion to his book, has given a variety of reasons 'why German humanism failed to develop into a major historical force'.[1] Was it because it was an aristocratic movement? Was it a lack of an economic or social base for humanism? Was it because the religious renaissance of the humanists 'failed to develop or to rediscover the theological principle which could serve as a weapon in assaulting the work-righteousness which lay at the root of many, if not most, of the worst abuses in need of reform'. Or was it because German humanism 'failed to satisfy the deepest longing of the people for a religious renewal coming from

1 Spitz, *Religious Renaissance*, pp. 290–291.

132

the heart of Christianity. Really deepening the religious dimension was left to Luther, a prophetic type'.

Hans Rupprich[2] finds that even though Italian humanism influenced German humanism it was an autochthonous movement, especially since it produced scientific contributions of a Cusanus, Regiomontanus and Copernicus. Before German humanism reached its maturity, it encountered Martin Luther and it reached its height in the controversy between Luther and Erasmus. Rupprich points to the three major areas in which German humanism has influenced German intellectual and cultural life: science, literature and art. It brought a new *'Welt- und Kunstanschauung'*, new educational ideas and a changed life-style.

In his essay 'The German humanists and the Reformation', Bernd Moeller says: 'It seems obvious that the common opinion that humanism had no significance for the Reformation is false when expressed simplistically. The humanists were the first to accept Luther and to give him a lasting following. It was they who first made his cause into a far-reaching movement. Without them he would have failed as did many before him who had tried to stand up against the old church. One can state this pointedly: no humanism, no Reformation.'[3]

The problem of German humanism and its relationship to other movements contemporary with it will continue to be a 'historical problem' which will be discussed over and over again. It is the elusive character of the movement which makes it so attractive to muse upon. We can not expect any 'solutions'; we can only hope for clarification.

The prerequisite materials for any interpretation, valid in scope and penetrating in depth, are the studies of the individual cities, territories, universities and personalities. Those studies which exist are concerned, for the most part, with the well-known personalities and centers of the humanistic movements in western and southern Germany. In the East contacts with Italy were not as close and long-standing as in the West. A different cultural climate prevailed in Rostock, Greifswald, Leipzig and Wittenberg than in the country on the Rhine. Since the studies of Gustav Bauch, to which I have referred so frequently, almost no efforts have been made to explore humanism in the eastern part of Germany. In view of the fact that discussions about German humanism have linked the movement with the Reformation, it is even more surprising that the area in which Luther lived and taught did not receive the expected attention. Such considerations naturally led to this study of Wittenberg. In its own peculiar way, Wittenberg dealt with the humanism of Italy and with what there was of indigenous humanism. But just as it was ready to embrace its own kind of humanism, Luther, the *homo religiosus*, appeared in its midst.

Rediscovery of early Christianity as conceived by Luther became the major preoccupation at Wittenberg. In this process, however, humanism became an important force in preparing the soil for the reception of Luther's reform. But the freedom of the Christian man as Luther preached it had little relation to the

---

2 Hans Rupprich, *Die deutsche Literatur vom späten Mittelalter bis zum Barock*, part 1: Das ausgehende Mittelalter, Humanismus und Renaissance, 1370–1520, (Munich, 1970: Geschichte der deutschen Literatur von den Anfängen bis zur Gegenwart, IV/1) pp. 452–460.
3 Bernd Moeller, *Imperial cities and the Reformation*; three essays; ed. and transl. by H.C. Erik Midelfort and Mark U. Edwards, Jr. (Philadelphia, 1972), p. 36.

humanists' concept of man, and it is a dubious supposition to regard humanism as a natural ally of Protestantism. Nevertheless, by undermining scholasticism, humanism helped to bring about the transition to Protestantism.

The cultural policy of Frederick the Wise, which this study has tried to clarify, was largely responsible for the place that humanism assumed in the life of Wittenberg. In his epitaph for Frederick, a fitting tribute to this great elector,[4] Melanchthon praised him for using as his weapons reason, understanding and wisdom, while other princes resorted to the sword. It was Frederick who did more than any other ruler to make the *humaniora* and the muses again respectable and who rewarded men engaged in scholarly and artistic pursuits. He had founded the university to promote the search for truth and the true Christian religion, and when the true teachings of the Gospel emanated from his town, Wittenberg, he protected them against all attacks. Melanchthon, who was himself reared in humanism, attempted to unite humanism and Christianity into a new philosophy of life. According to him, Frederick had tried to do the same and had succeeded.

The beginning of the Reformation in Wittenberg overshadowed the humanistic interlude which preceded it; yet this earlier phase in the town's history which has been examined here was likewise in itself vigorous, colorful and interesting.

---

4 Cf. Eberhard Winkler, 'Melanchthons lateinische Leichenrede auf Kurfürst Friedrich den Weisen', *Zeitschrift für Religions- und Geistesgeschichte*, 18 (1966), 33–42.

BIBLIOGRAPHY

PRIMARY SOURCES

Adam von Fulda. *Ein ser andechtig Cristenlich Buchlein aus hailigen schrifften und Lerern von Adam von Fulda in teutsch reymenn gesetzt* . . . [Wittenberg, 1512]; facsimile, ed. Eduard Flechsig [Berlin, 1914].

Acten der Erfurter Universitaet. Ed. J.C. Hermann Weissenborn. 3 vols. Halle, 1881–1899 (Geschichtsquellen der Provinz Sachsen und der angrenzenden Gebiete, 8).

Album Academiae Vitebergensis. Ed. Carl. Eduard Foerstemann. 3 vols. Leipzig, 1894–1906.

Aquilonipolensis, Henricus. *Carmen de arte metrica Magistri Henrici Aquilonipolensis.* [Wittenberg, 1505]

Aquilonipolensis, Henricus. *Dimetromachia de virtutum et viciorum conflictu* . . . [without place or date of publication, probably Leipzig].

Aquilonipolensis, Henricus. *Epitaphiale Magistri Hinrici Aquilonipolensis Poetae una cum testamento suo.* [Wittenberg, 1505].

Aquilonipolensis, Henricus. *Sophologia M. Henrici Aquilonipolensis Poetae de originibus arcium & quattuor facultatibus Achademiae.* [Wittenberg, 1505].

Aristotle. *Liber de Anima Aristotelis nuper per Joannem Argiropilum de Greco in Romanum sermonem elegantissime traductus cum commentariolis diui Thome Aquinatis* . . . [Wittenberg, 1509].

Baptista Mantuanus. *Celebradi patris Baptiste Mantuan. Carmelite theologi Parthenices* . . . [Wittenberg, 1504].

Batrachomiomachia Homeri Philymno interprete et evlogia funebria. [Wittenberg, 1513].

Beckmann, Otto. *Oracio magistri Othonis Beckman Uartbergij ad patres conscriptos et pubem Academie Vuittenbergensis in laudes sanctissime Parthenices Catharine tocius rei litterarie de Tutelaris* . . . [Wittenberg, 1510].

Beckmann, Otto. *Oratio Othonis Beckman Vuartbergii artius ac philosophiae doctoris in laudem philosophiae ac humaniorum litterarum ad patres conscriptos et pubem famigeratissimae Academiae Wittenbergensis habita.* [Wittenberg, 1510].

Beckmann, Otto. *Panegyricus Othonis Beckman Vuartbergii Artius* . . . [Wittenberg, 1509].

Brant, Sebastian. *Varia Sebastiani Brant Carmina.* [Basel, 1498].

Buder, Christian Gottlieb. *De Friderico III, Saxoniae electore,* . . . Jena, 1731.

Burkhardt, Carl August Hugo, ed. *Ernestinische Landtagsakten*, vol. 1: Die Landtage von 1487–1532. Jena, 1902 (Thüringische Geschichtsquellen, Neue Folge, V).

Busche, Hermann von dem. *In hoc libello hec continentur: Hermanni Cesaris Stolbergij Epistola ad Buschium* . . . [appended] *Hermanni Buschij Pasiphilio Oratio exhortatoria ad Eloquentie et philosophie studium: habita Albiori: in plectione Metamor. Ovidiana.* [1505].

Cammermeister, Hartung. *Die Chronik Hartung Cammermeisters.* Ed. R. Reiche. Halle, 1896. (Geschichtsquellen der Provinz Sachsen, 35).

Capella, Martianus Felix. . . . *De arte grammatica liber incipit* . . . [Erfurt, 1505].

Capotius, Priamus, . . . *lilibite fredericeis liber incipis* . . . [Leipzig, 1488].

Capotius, Priamus. *Oratio metrica Priami Capoty lilybite in alma lipsensi universitate habita.* [without place or date of publication; probably Leipzig, Maur. Brandis].

Carlstadt, Andreas Bodenstein von. *Distinctiones Thomistarum* . . . [Wittenberg, 1508; i.e. 1507].

Celtis, Conrad. *Ars versificandi et carminum conradus celtis protucius* . . . [Leipzig, ca. 1486].

Celtis, Conrad. *Briefwechsel.* Ed. Hans Rupprich. Munich, 1934. (Veröffentlichungen der Kommission zur Erforschung der Geschichte der Reformation und Gegenreformation, Humanistenbriefe, III).

Conradi, Tileman . . . *Choleamynterius in Fellifluum Philymnomastigam Hercinefurdensem, laes den hunt schlaffen, es beyst dych.* [Wittenberg, 1515].
Conradi, Tileman. *Comoedia Philymni Syasticani cul nomen Teratologia* . . . [Wittenberg, 1509].
Conradi, Tileman. *Triumphus Bacchi. Cupido. Xenia.* [Wittenberg, 1511].
Conradi, Tileman. *Triumphus Christi.* [Wittenberg, 1516].
Crappus, Andreas. *Modus vitandi peccata* . . . [Wittenberg, 1513].
Dares of Phrygia. *Historia Daretis Phrygij de Excidio Troie* . . . [Wittenberg, 1513].
Deutsche Reichstagsakte. Jüngere Reihe. 7 vols. Gotha, 1893–1935.
Eisagoge pros ton grammaton hellenon. [Wittenberg, 1511].
Eisagoge pros ton grammaton hellenon. [Wittenberg, 1515].
Engelbrecht, Philip. . . . *Epothalamium* . . . [Wittenberg, 1513].
Epistolae Obscurorum Virorum. The Latin text with an English rendering, notes and an historical introduction by Francis Griffin Stokes. London, 1909.
Erasmus, Desiderius. *In Latinam Novi Testamenti Interpretationem ex Collatione Graecorum Exemplarius Adnotationes.* [Paris, 1505].
Erasmus, Desiderius. *Opus Epistolarum Des. Erasmi Roterodami.* Ed. P.S. Allen and H.M. Allen and H.W. Garrod. 12 vols. Oxford, 1906–1958.
Erler, Georg, ed. *Die Matrikel der Universität Leipzig.* 3 vols. Leipzig, 1895–1902. (Codex diplomaticus Saxoniae Regiae II, vols. 16–18).
Faber, Matthaeus. *Kurtzgefasste historische Nachricht von der Schloss- und Academischen Stifftskirche zu Aller-Heiligen in Wittenberg.* . . . Samt einer Vorrede Herrn D. Gottlieb Wernsdorffs . . . Wittenberg, 1717.
Faber Stapulensis. *Quincuplex Psalterium Gallicum, Romanum, Hebraicum* . . . [Paris, 1509].
Faber Stapulensis. *S. Pauli Epistolae XIV ex Vulgata editione* . . . *cum commentariis* Jacobi Fabri Stapulensis . . . [Paris, 1512].
Friedensburg, Walter, ed. *Urkundenbuch der Universität Wittenberg.* Vol. 1: 1502–1611. Magdeburg, 1926 (Geschichtsquellen der Provinz Sachsen und des Freistaates Anhalt, Neue Reihe, vol. 3)
Garzoni, Giovanni. *De rebus Saxoniae, Thuringiae, Libonotriae, Misniae et Lusatiae et de bellis Friederici Magni libri duo.* [Basel, 1518].
Gersdorf, E.G., ed. *Urkundenbuch des Hochstifts Meissen.* 3 vols. Leipzig, 1864–1867. (Codex Diplomaticus Saxoniae Regiae, II, 1–3)
Goerlitz, Woldemar, ed. *Staat und Stände unter den Herzögen Albrecht und Georg, 1485–1539.* Leipzig, 1928. (Sächsische Landtagsakte I).
Grohmann, J.C.A., ed. *Annalen der Universität Wittenberg.* 2 vols. Meissen, 1801.
Hammelmann, Hermann. *Geschichtliche Werke.* Ed. Heinrich Detmer. 3 vols. Münster, 1908–1940. (Veröffentlichungen der Historischen Kommission der Provinz Westfalen).
Hutten, Ulrich von. *Opera Ulrichi Hutteni equitis Germani.* Ed. Eduard Böcking. 7 vols. Leipzig, 1859–1870.
Isocrates; with an English translation by George Norlin. London, 1928 (Loeb Classical Library)
Isocrates. *Praecepta Isocratis per eruditissimum virum Rudolphum Agricolam Graeco sermone in latinu traducta* . . . [Wittenberg, 1508].
Judicium Paradis Troiani de tribus deab. Veneri, Junone & Pallade per Catalycium . . . [Wittenberg, 1504].
Kitzscher, Johann von. *Dialogus de Sacri Romani Imperii rebus perquam utilis* . . . [Wittenberg, 1505].
Kitzscher, Johann von. *Oracio Funebris (de obitu Annae* . . . *ducis Pomeraniae conjugis).* [Wittenberg, 1503].
Kitzscher, Johann von. *Oratio ad serenissimum Polonorum Regem habita Petrocoui.* [Leipzig, 1513].
Kitzscher, Johann von. *Tragicomedia de iherisolomitana profesione illustrissimi principis pomeriani* . . . [Leipzig, 1501].
Kitzscher, Johann von. *Virtutis et fortune dissidentium certamen.* [Leipzig, 1505].
Lang, Johann. *Enchiridion Sexti Philosophi Pythagorici* . . . [Wittenberg], 1514.
Lang, Johann. *Quae hoc libello habentur: Divi Hieronymi epistola ad magnum vrbis oratorem*

136

elegantiss. Eiusdem ad Athletam de filiae educatione. [Wittenberg, 1514].

Leoniceno, Nicolo. *Libellus de Epidimia, quam vulga morbum gallicum vocant siue brossulas.* [Venice, 1497].

Liber Decanorum: das Dekanatsbuch der theologischen Fakultät zu Wittenberg; im Lichtdruck nachgebildet. Ed. Johannes Ficker. 2 vols. Halle, 1918-1923.

Liber Decanorum Facultatis Theologicae Academiae Vitebergensis. Ed. Carl Eduard Foerstemann. Leipzig, 1838.

Lindner, Johann. *Onomasticon.* In: Mencken, Jo. Burch. *Scriptores rerum Germanicarum praecipue Saxonicarum* : . . vol. 2, cols. 1447–1632.

Lupold of Bebenburg. . . *de iuribus et translatione imperii* . . . [Strassburg, 1508].

Luther, Martin. *Luther's Vorlesung über den Galaterbrief, 1516/1517.* Ed. Hans von Schubert. Heidelberg, 1918 (Abhandlungen der Heidelberger Akademie der Wissenschaften, Philosophisch-Historische Klasse, 1918, 5. Abhandlung).

Luther, Martin. *Vorlesung über den Römerbrief, 1515–1516.* Ed. Johannes Ficker. Leipzig, 1908 (Anfänge Reformatorischer Bibelauslegung, I).

Marschalk, Nicolaus. *Commencement Address. Delivered at the University of Wittenberg, January 18, 1503.* Translated into English with introduction and notes by Edgar C. Reinke and Gottfried G. Krodel. Valparaiso, Ind., Valparaiso University Association, 1967.

Marschalk, Nicolaus. *Enchiridion poetarum clarissimorum.* [Erfurt, 1502].

Marschalk, Nicolaus. *Grammatica exegetica* . . . [Erfurt, 1501].

Marschalk, Nicolaus. . . . *introductio ad litteras hebraicas* . . . (without date or place of publication).

Marschalk, Nicolaus. *Laus musarum ex Hesiodi Ascraei Theogonia* . . . [Erfurt, 1501].

Marschalk, Nicolaus. *Oratio habita albiori academia* . . . See his *Commencement Address,* above.

Marschalk, Nicolaus. *Orthographia NMT* . . . [Erfurt, 1501].

Mathesius, Johann. *Ausgewählte Werke.* Ed. Georg Loesche. 4 vols. Prague, 1897–1908 (Bibliothek deutscher Schriftsteller aus Böhmen, 4, 6, 9, 14).

Meinhardi, Andreas. *Dialogus illustrate ac Augustissime urbis Albiorenae vulgo Vittenberg dicte* . . . [Leipzig, 1508].

Meisner, Johannes. *Descriptio ecclesiae collegiatae omnium sanctorum Wittebergensis.* Wittenberg, 1668.

Mela, Pomponius. . . . *Cosmosgraphia de situ orbis* . . . (Ed. Bartholomeus Stenus Brigensis) [Wittenberg, 1509].

Melanchthon, Philipp. *Supplementa Melanchthoniana. Werke Philipp Melanchthons die im Corpus Reformatorum vermisst werden.* 5 vols. Leipzig, 1910–29; reprint, Frankfurt, 1968.

Mellerstadt, Martin Polich von. . . . *Cursus physici. Collectanea. Cursus philosophie naturalis.* [Leipzig, 1514].

Mellerstadt, Martin Polich von. *In Wimpiniamas offensiones & denigrationes Sacre-Theologie.* [Wittenberg, 1504].

Mellerstadt, Martin Polich von. *Laconismos* . . . [without year or date of publication; probably Leipzig, J. Thanner, 1502].

Mellerstadt, Martin Polich von. *Theoremata aurea pro studiosis philosophie & theologie.* [Wittenberg, 1504].

Mencken, Joh. Burch. *Scriptores rerum Germanicarum, praecipue Saxonicarum, in quibus scripta et monumenta illustria, pleraque hactenus inedita, tum ad historiam Germaniae generatim,* . . . 3 vols. Leipzig, 1718–1730.

Müller, Johann Joachim. *Des heil. römischen Reichs teutscher Nation Reichs Tags-Staat, von anno MD bis MDXII so wohl unter Kaysers Maximiliani I* . . . *als ChurFuerst Friedrich III zu Sachsen ReichsStadthalterschafften* . . . Jena, 1708.

Müller, Johann Joachim. *Des heil. Reichs* . . . *Reichstagstheatrum, wie selbiges unter Keyser Friedrichs V* . . . *Regierung* . . . *gestanden.* 2 vols. Jena, 1713.

Müller, Johann Joachim. *Des heil. röm. Reichs* . . . *Reichstagstheatrum, wie selbiges unter Keyser Maximilians I* . . . *Regierung* . . . *gestanden.* 2 vols. Jena, 1718–1719.

Müller, Johann Sebastian. *Des Chur- und Fürstlichen Hauses Sachsen, Ernestin- und Albertinischer Linien Annales von Anno 1400 bis 1700.* Weimar, 1700.

Mutian, Conrad. *Briefwechsel.* Ed. K. Gillert. Halle, 1890 (Geschichtsquellen der Provinz Sachsen, 18)

Myconius, Friedrich. *Historia Reformationis vom Jahr Christi 1517 bis 1542.* Ed. Ernest Salomon Cyprian. Gotha, 1715.

Mylius, Johann Christoph. *Memorabilia Bibliothecae Academicae Ienensis.* Jena, 1746.

Neues Urkundenbuch zur Geschichte der evangelischen Kirchenreformation. Ed. Carl Eduard Foerstemann, Hamburg, 1842.

Nicolai de Bibera. *Carmen Satiricum.* Ed. Theobald Fischer. Halle, 1870 (Geschichtsquellen der Provinz Sachsen, 1)

Pistoris, Simon. *Positio de morbo Franco . . .* [Leipzig, 1498].

Ravenna, Petrus. *Aurea opuscula . . .* [Leipzig, 1502].

Ravenna, Petrus. *Clypeus doctoris Petri Rauennati contra doctorem Caium . . .* [Wittenberg, 1503].

Ravenna, Petrus. *Compendium iuris ciuilis . . .* [Wittenberg, 1503].

Ravenna, Petrus. *Compendium pulcherrimum juriscanonici . . .* part 1 [Wittenberg, 1504].

Ravenna, Petrus. *Lectio pulcherrima de potestate pontificis maximi & romani imperatoris . . .* [Wittenberg, 1503].

Ravenna, Petrus. *Sermones extraordinarii & pulcherrimi . . .* [Wittenberg, 1505].

Ravenna, Vincentius . . . *Oracio publice habita ad felicissimum gloriosissimumque . . .* [Wittenberg, 1505].

Reuchlin, Johannes. *Briefwechsel.* Ed. Ludwig Geiger. Stuttgart, 1875. (Bibliothek des Literarischen Vereins in Stuttgart, 126).

Reuchlin, Johannes. *Constantinus magnus romanorum imperator . . .* [Tübingen, 1513].

Reuchlin, Johannes. *De Rudimentis hebraicis . . .* [Pforzheim, 1506].

Reuchlin, Johannes. *In septem Psalmos poenitentiales . . .* [Tübingen, 1512].

Roswitha von Gandersheim. *Opera . . .* nuper a Conrado Celte inventa . . . [Nürnberg, 1501].

Sabellicus, Marcus Antonius. *Historia Hebreorum . . .* per Johannem Kusthvert . . . [Basel, 1515].

Sagittarius, C. *Oratio de bibliotheca Jenensi.* In: *De bibliothecis nova accessio Collectioni Maderianae* adiuncta a Joh. Andr. Schmidt. Helmstedt, 1703.

Sbrulius, Ricardus . . . *Cleomachia.* [Wittenberg, 1510].

Scheurl, Christoph. *Briefbuch.* Ein Beitrag zur Geschichte der Reformation und ihrer Zeit. Ed. F. v. Soden and J.K.F. Knaake. 2 vols. Potsdam, 1867–1872; reprint, Aalen, 1962.

Scheurl, Christoph. *De sacerdotum et rerum ecclesiasticarum praestatia . . .* . [Leipzig, 1511].

Scheurl, Christoph. *Libellus de laudibus Germaniae et Ducum Saxoniae . . .* [Bologna, 1506].

Scheurl, Christoph. *Libellus de laudibus Germaniae et Ducum Saxoniae . . .* [Leipzig, 1508].

Scheurl, Christoph. *Oratio doctoris Scheurli attingens laudes virtutis M. Fortes Fortuna Formidate . . .* [Leipzig, 1508].

Scheurl, Christoph. *Oratio doctoris Scheurli attingens litterarum prestantiam* [Leipzig, 1509].

Scheurl, Christoph. *Orationes . . . habite in gymnasio Vittenburgensi . . .* [no place; 1507].

Schoettgen, Christian. *Commentatio de vita N. Marschalci Thurii.* Rostock, 1752.

Seckendorf, Veit Ludwig von. *Commentarius historicus et apologeticus de Lutheranismo sive de reformatione religionis ductu M. Lutheri stabilita.* [Frankfurt, 1692].

Sibutus, Georgius . . . *astipulatur puelle, que hesterna luce summam felicitatem in matrimonio dixit . . .* [Leipzig, 1507].

Sibutus, Georgius. . . . *Carmen . . .* [Wittenberg, 1508].

Sibutus, Georgius. *Carmen de Musica Chiliana et alia eiusdem carmina . . .* [Leipzig, 1507].

Sibutus, Georgius. *De diui Maximiliani Cesaris aduentu in Coloniam . . .* [Cologne, 1505].

Sibutus, Georgius. . . . *Silvula in Albiorim illustratam . . .* [Leipzig, 1507].

Sibutus, Georgius . . . *Torniamenta . . .* [Wittenberg, 1511].

Sirecti, Antonius. *Formalitates . . .* [Leipzig, 1505].

Spalatin, Georg, *Annales Reformationis oder Jahr-Buecher von der Reformation Lutheri,* aus dessen autographo ans Licht gestellt von Ernst Salomon Cyprian. Leipzig, 1718. In: W.E. Tentzel, *Historischer Bericht vom Anfang und ersten Fortgang der Reformation Lutheri.* Leipzig, 1918.

Spalatin, Georg. *Chronica und Herkomen der Churfürsten und Fürsten des löblichen Haus zu Sachsen, . . .* [Wittenberg, 1541].

138

Spalatin, Georg. *Spalatins Chronik für die Jahre 1513 bis 1520*. Ed. Alfred Kleeberg. Leipzig, 1919.

Spalatin, Georg. *Friedrichs des Weisen Leben und Zeitgeschichte*. Ed. Chr. Gotth. Neudecker and Ludw. Preller. Jena, 1851 (Georg Spalatins historischer Nachlass und Briefe, 1).

Spalatiniana. Ed. Georg Berbig. Leipzig, 1908 (Quellen und Darstellungen aus der Geschichte des Reformationshunderts, V).

'Spalatiniana'. Ed. Georg Berbig. *Theologische Studien und Kritiken*, 80 (1907), 513–534; 81 (1908), 27–61.

'Spalatiniana'. Ed. Peter Drews. *Zeitschrift für Kirchengeschichte*, 19 (1899). 69–98.

Staupitz, Johann von. *Decisio questionis de audientia misse . . .* [Tübingen, 1500].

Stier, G., ed. *Inscriptiones Vitebergae Latinae*. 2nd ed. Wittenberg, 1856.

Stolle, Konrad. *Memoriale Thüringisch-Erfurtische Chronik*. Ed. R. Thiele. Halle, 1900 (Geschichtsquellen der Provinz Sachsen, 39)

Struvius, B.G. *Historia et memorabilia bibliothecae Jenensis*. In: *De bibliothecis accessio altera Collectioni Maderianae adjuncta a Joh. Andr. Schmidt*. Helmstedt, 1703.

Stübel, Bruno, ed. *Urkundenbuch der Universität Leipzig von 1409 bis 1555*. Leipzig, 1879.

Tartaretus, Petrus. *Clarissima singularisque totius philosophie necnon metaphysice Aristotelis*. [Wittenberg, 1504].

Tartaretus, Petrus. *Expositio magistri Petri Tartareti sup summulas Petri hispani . . .* [Wittenberg, 1504].

Tartaretus, Petrus. *Expositio magistri Petri Tartareti sup textu logices Aristotelis . . .* [Wittenberg, 1504].

Toepke, Gustav, ed. *Die Matrikel der Universität Heidelberg*. vol 1: 1386–1553. Heidelberg, 1884.

Trebelius, Hermann. *Hecastichon Elegiacum de peste Isenachensi*. [Eisenach, 1506].

Trithemius, Johannes. *Opera Historica*, 2 vols. [Frankfurt, 1601].

Trutfetter, Jodocus. *Epitome seu breuiarium logice . . .* [Erfurt, 1507].

Valla, Laurentius. *In Latinam Novi Testamenti . . .* [Paris, 1505].

Verulanus, Johannes Sulpitius. *Posterior editio Sulpitiana in partes tres diuisa que com pectuntur . . .* [Without date or place of publication].

Wimpina, Konrad. *Apologeticus in sacretheologie defensionem . . .* [Without date or place of publication, probably Leipzig, 1500].

Wimpina, Konrad. *Palollogia de theologico fastigio . . .* [Without date or place of publication, probably Leipzig, 1500].

Wimpina, Konrad. *Responsio et apologia Conradi Wimpine de Fagis ad Mellerstatinas offensiones et denigrationes sacretheologie*. [Without date or place of publication, probably Leipzig, 1503].

Wittenberger Heiligtumsbuch. [Wittenberg, 1509].

SECONDARY WORKS

Abe, Horst Rudolf. *Der Erfurter Humanismus und seine Zeit*; die Geschichte des Erfurter Humanismus bis zum Jahre 1516. Jena, 1953.

Abe, Horst Rudolf. 'Die Universität Erfurt in ihren berühmtesten Persönlichkeiten. I. Mittelalter (1391–1521)', In: *Beiträge zur Geschichte der Universität Erfurt* (1392–1816). Hrsg. vom Rektor der Medizinischen Akademie Erfurt, Heft 4/1958, pp. 17–138.

Adams, H.M. *Catalogue of books printed on the continent of Europe, 1501–1600 in Cambridge libraries*. Cambridge, 1967.

Adelung, Johann Christoph. *Directorium, d.i. chronologisches Verzeichnis der Quellen der süd-sächsischen Geschichte, sofern selbige aus Geschichtsschreibern aller Art und Denkmälern bestehen*. Meissen, 1802.

Bake, Werner. *Die Frühzeit des pommerschen Buchdrucks im Lichte neuerer Forschung*. Ein Beitrag zur deutschen Buchdruckergeschichte mit Wiedergabe zweier pommerscher Drucke vom Jahre 1537. Pyritz, 1934.

Baldass, Ludwig. *Der Künstlerkreis Kaiser Maximilians*. Vienna, 1923.

Baltin, E. *Friedrich der Weise, Kurfürst zu Sachsen*. Torgau, 1896.

Barge, Hermann. *Andreas Bodenstein von Karlstadt.* 2 vols. Leipzig, 1905.

Baron, Hans. 'Zur Frage des Ursprungs des deutschen Humanismus und seiner religiösen Reformbestrebungen', *Historische Zeitschrift* 132 (1925), 413–446.

Barwick, G.F. 'The Lutheran Press at Wittenberg', *Transactions of the Bibliographical Society*, 3 (1895–6), 9–25.

Bauch, Gustav. 'Andreas Carlstadt als Scholastiker', *Zeitschrift für Kirchengeschichte*, 18 (1898), 37–57.

Bauch, Gustav. *Die Anfänge der Universität Frankfurt a. O. und die Entwicklung des wissenschaftlichen Lebens an der Hochschule (1506–1540).* Berlin, 1900 (Texte und Forschungen zur Geschichte der Erziehung und des Unterrichts in den Ländern deutscher Zunge, 3).

Bauch, Gustav. *Die Anfänge des Humanismus in Ingolstadt.* Munich, 1901 (Historische Bibliothek, 13).

Bauch, Gustav. 'Die Anfänge des Studiums der griechischen Sprache und Litteratur in Norddeutschland', *Mitteilungen der Gesellschaft für deutsche Erziehungs- und Schulgeschichte,* 6 (1896), 47–98, 163–193.

Bauch, Gustav. 'Aus der Geschichte des Mainzer Humanismus', *Archiv für hessische Geschichte und Altertumskunde,* N.F. 5 (1907), 3–86.

Bauch, Gustav. 'Beiträge zur Litteraturgeschichte des schlesischen Humanismus I', *Zeitschrift des Vereins für Geschichte und Alterthum Schlesiens,* 26 (1892), 213–248.

Bauch, Gustav. 'Beiträge zur Litteraturgeschichte des schlesischen Humanismus II', *Zeitschrift des Vereins für Geschichte und Alterthum Schlesiens,* 30 (1896), 128–164.

Bauch, Gustav. 'Biographische Beiträge zur Schulgeschichte des XVI. Jahrhunderts', *Mitteilungen der Gesellschaft für deutsche Erziehungs- und Schulgeschichte,* 5 (1895), 1–26.

Bauch, Gustav. 'Christoph Scheurl in Wittenberg', *Neue Mitteilungen aus dem Gebiet historisch-antiquarischer Forschungen,* 21 (1903), 33–42.

Bauch, Gustav. 'Dr. Johann von Kitzscher. Ein meissnischer Edelmann der Renaissance', *Neues Archiv für Sächsische Geschichte,* 20 (1899), 286–321.

Bauch, Gustav. 'Drucke von Frankfurt a. O. Erweiterungen zu Panzer, *Annales typographici* VII, 54 und IX, 464', *Centralblatt für Bibliothekswesen,* 15 (1898), 241–260.

Bauch, Gustav. 'Die Einführung des Hebraeischen in Wittenberg, mit Berücksichtigung der Vorgeschichte des Studiums der Sprache in Deutschland', *Monatsschrift für Geschichte und Wissenschaft des Judentums,* 48 (1904), 22–32, 77–86, 145–160, 214–223, 283–299, 328–340, 461–490.

Bauch, Gustav. *Geschichte des Leipziger Frühhumanismus,* mit besonderer Rücksicht auf die Streitigkeiten zwischen Konrad Wimpina und Martin Mellerstadt. Leipzig, 1899 (Centralblatt für Bibliothekswesen, Beiheft 22).

Bauch, Gustav. 'Melanchthonia', *Zeitschrift für Kirchengeschichte,* 18 (1898), 76–89.

Bauch, Gustav. *Die Reception des Humanismus in Wien;* eine litterarische Studie zur deutschen Universitätsgeschichte. Breslau, 1903.

Bauch, Gustav. 'Der sächsische Rat und Humanist Heinrich von Bünau, Herr in Teuchern', *Neues Archiv für Sächsische Geschichte,* 26 (1905), 41–62.

Bauch, Gustav. *Die Universität Erfurt im Zeitalter des Frühhumanismus.* Breslau, 1904.

Bauch, Gustav. 'Wittenberg und die Scholastik', *Neues Archiv für Sächsische Geschichte,* 18 (1897), 285–339.

Bauch, Gustav. 'Wolfgang Schenck und Nikolaus Marschalk', *Centralblatt für Bibliothekswesen,* 12 (1895), 354–409.

Bauch, Gustav. 'Zu Christoph Scheurls Briefbuch', *Neue Mitteilungen aus dem Gebiet historisch-antiquarischer Forschungen,* 19 (1898), 400–456.

Bauch, Gustav. 'Zur Cranachforschung', *Repertorium für Kunstwissenschaft,* 17 (1894), 421–435.

Bauer, Karl. *Die Wittenberger Universitätstheologie und die Anfänge der deutschen Reformation.* Tübingen, 1928.

Bauer, Karl. 'Das Wort bei den Reformatoren in seinem Verhältnis zum Humanismus', *Reformierte Kirchenzeitung,* 77 (1927), 385–387, 393–395, 401–404, 409–412.

Bebb, Philip Norton, 'The Lawyers, Dr. Christoph Scheurl and the Reformation in Nürnberg', In: *The social history of the Reformation,* eds. L.P. Buck and J.W. Zophy. Columbus, Ohio, 1972, pp. 52–72.

Becker, Felix. [Review of] Robert Bruck. *Friedrich der Weise als Förderer der Kunst, Neues Archiv für Sächsische Geschichte*, 28 (1907), 146–148.

Below, Georg von. *Die Ursachen der Reformation*. Munich, 1917 (Historische Bibliothek, 38).

Bemmann, Rudolf. *Bibliographie der Sächsischen Geschichte*. 3 vols. Leipzig, 1918–1932. (Schriften der Königl. Sächsischen Kommission für Geschichte).

Benary, Friedrich. *Via antiqua und via moderna auf den deutschen Hochschulen des Mittelalters mit besonderer Berücksichtigung der Universität Erfurt*. Erfurt, 1919.

Benary, Friedrich. *Zur Geschichte der Stadt und der Universität Erfurt am Ausgang des Mittelalters*. Ed. A. Overmann. Gotha, 1919.

Benesch, Otto. *The Art of the Renaissance in Northern Europe*; its relation to the contemporary spiritual and intellectual movements. Cambridge, Mass., 1945.

Benz, Ernst. 'Der Traum Kurfürst Friedrich des Weisen', In: *Humanitas-Christianitas*. Walter v. Loewenich zum 65. Geburtstag. Hrsg. Karlmann Beyschlag, Gottfried Maron and Eberhard Wölfel. Witten, 1968, pp. 134–149.

Benzing, Josef. *Bibliographie der Schriften Johannes Reuchlins im 15. und 16. Jahrhundert*. Bad Bocklet, 1955 (Bibliotheca Bibliographica, 18).

Benzing, Josef. *Der Buchdruck des 16. Jahrhunderts im deutschen Sprachgebiet*. Leipzig, 1936. (Beiheft zum *Zentralblatt für Bibliothekswesen*, 68).

Benzing, Josef. *Die Buckdrucker des 16. und 17. Jahrhunderts im deutschen Sprachgebiet*. Wiesbaden, 1963 (Beiträge zum Buch- und Bibliothekswesen, 12).

Benzing, Josef. *Buchdruckerlexikon des 16. Jahrhunderts (deutsches Sprachgebiet)*. Frankfurt a. M. 1952.

Benzing, Josef. 'Hermann Trebelius, Dichter und Drucker zu Wittenberg und Eisenach', *Das Antiquariat*, IX, Nr. 13/14, 10. Juli, 1953, 203–204.

Benzing, Josef. *Lutherbibliographie*; Verzeichnis der gedruckten Schriften Martin Luthers bis zu dessen Tod. Baden-Baden, 1966.

Berbig, Georg. *Georg Spalatin und sein Verhältnis zu Martin Luther auf Grund ihres Briefwechsels bis zum Jahre 1525*. Halle, 1906. (Quellen und Darstellungen aus der Geschichte des Reformationsjahrhunderts, 1).

Beschorner, Hans. 'Die Chemnitzer Teilung der Wettinischen Lande von 1382 im Kartenbilde', *Neues Archiv für Sächsische Geschichte*, 54 (1933), 135–142.

Bezold, Friedrich von. 'Konrad Celtis, der deutsche Erzhumanist', *Historische Zeitschrift*, 49 (1883), 1–46, 193–229.

Bier, Justus. *Tilmann Riemenschneider*; ein Gedenkbuch. Vienna, 1948.

Blanke, Fritz. 'Ikonographie der Reformationszeit. Fragen um ein Cranachbild', *Theologische Zeitschrift*, 7 (1951), 467–471.

Blaschka, Anton. 'Von den Gründungsurkunden der Wittenberger Universität', *Wissenschaftliche Zeitschrift der Martin-Luther-Universität Halle-Wittenberg*, gesellschaft- und sprachwissenschaftliche Reihe, I, 1951/2, pp. 53–65.

Bode, Wilhelm. 'Albrecht Dürers Bildnis des Kurfürsten Friedrich von Sachsen, genannt der Weise', *Jahrbuch der Königlich-Preussischen Kunstsammlungen*, 5 (1884), 57–62.

Bode, Wilhelm. 'Die bemalte Thonbüste eines lachenden Kindes im Buckingham Palace und Meister Conrad Meit', *Jahrbuch der Königlich-Preussischen Kunstsammlungen*, 22 (1901), iv–xvi.

Böheim, Wendelin. *Meister der Waffenschmiedekunst vom XIV. bis ins XVIII. Jahrhundert*. Berlin, 1897.

Boehmer, Heinrich. *Der junge Luther*, 4th ed. Ed. H. Bornkamm, Stuttgart, 1951.

Boettiger, Karl Wilhelm. *Geschichte des Kurstaates und Königreiches Sachsen*. 2 vols. Gotha, 1830–1831. (Geschichte der europäischen Staaten, ed. A.H.L. Heeren und F.A. Ukert).

Borchardt, Frank L. *German antiquity in Renaissance myth*. Baltimore, Md., 1971.

Borchling, Conrad and Bruno Clausen. *Niederdeutsche Bibliographie*. 3 vols. Neumünster, 1931–1957.

Borkowsky, Ernst. *Das Leben Friedrichs des Weisen, Kurfürsten zu Sachsen*. Jena, 1929.

Bornkamm, Heinrich. 'Kurfürst Friedrich der Weise (1463–1525)', *Archiv für Reformationsgeschichte*, 64 (1973), 79–85.

Brandi, Karl. *Mittelalterliche Weltanschauung, Humanismus und nationale Bildung*. Berlin, 1925.

Brandi, Karl. 'Renaissance und Reformation, Wertungen und Umwertungen', *Preussische Jahrbücher*, 200 (1925), 120–135.

Brandis, Carl Georg. *Beiträge aus der Universitätsbibliothek zu Jena zur Geschichte des Reformationsjahrhunderts.* Jena, 1917. (Zeitschrift des Vereins für Thüringische Geschichte und Altertumskunde, N.F., Beiheft 8).

Brandis, Carl Georg. 'Italienische Humanisten in Sächsisch-Thüringischen Landen', *Zentralblatt für Bibliothekswesen*, 46 (1929), 277–296

Brandis, Carl Georg. 'Luther und Melanchthon als Benützer der Wittenberger Bibliothek', *Theologische Studien und Kritiken*, 90 (1917), 206–221.

Braun, J. 'Wolfgang Stöckel; ein Beitrag zur Geschichte der Buchdruckerkunst', *Börsenblatt für den deutschen Buchhandel*, no. 301 (1884), 6129–6131.

Bruck, Robert. *Friedrich der Weise als Förderer der Kunst.* Strassburg, 1903 (Studien zur deutschen Kunstgeschichte, 45).

Bruck, Robert. 'Der Illuminist Jacob Elsner', *Jahrbuch der Königlich-Preussischen Kunstsammlungen*, 24 (1903), 302–317.

Buchner, Ernst. 'Die sieben Schmerzen Mariae', *Münchner Jahrbuch der bildenden Kunst*, 11 (1934), 250–270.

Buchwald, Georg. 'Allerlei Wittenbergisches aus der Reformationszeit', *Luther*, 10 (1928), 107–112.

Buchwald, Georg. 'Allerlei Wittenbergisches aus der Reformationszeit, VI', *Luther*, 12 (1930), 56–61.

Buchwald, Georg. 'Archivalische Mittheilungen über Bücherbezüge der kurfürstlichen Bibliothek und Georg Spalatins in Wittenberg', *Archiv für Geschichte des Deutschen Buchhandels*, 18 (1896), 7–15.

Buchwald, Georg. 'Zu Spalatins Reisen, insbesondere nach Wittenberg, in Angelegenheiten der Kurfürstlichen Bibliothek (Aus Akten des Thüringischen Staatsarchivs in Weimar)', *Archiv für Bibliographie, Buch- und Bibliothekswesen*, 2 (1928), 92–96.

Burchdorf, Martin. *Der Einfluss der Erfurter Humanisten auf die Entwicklung Luthers bis 1510*, Leipzig, 1928.

Burchdorf, Martin. *Johann Lang, der Reformator Erfurts.* Kassel, 1911.

Burdach, Konrad. *Reformation, Renaissance, Humanismus*; zwei Abhandlungen über die Grundlage moderner Bildung und Sprachkunst, 2nd ed. Berlin, 1926.

Burger, Heinz Otto. *Renaissance, Humanismus, Reformation*. Bad Homburg, Berlin, 1969. (Frankfurter Beiträge zur Germanistik, 7).

Burkhardt, Carl August Hugo. 'Abriss der Geschichte des Ernestinischen Gesamtarchivs in Weimar', *Archivalische Zeitschrift*, 3 (1878), 80–109.

Burkhardt, Carl August Hugo. 'Das tolle Jahr zu Erfurt und seine Folgen, 1509–1523', *Archiv für Sächsische Geschichte*, 12 (1874), 337–426.

Burkhardt, Carl August Hugo. 'Die Vermählung des Herzogs Johann von Sachsen, 1. bis 5. März, 1500,' *NASG*, 15 (1894), 288ff.

Campenhausen, Hans Frhr. v. 'Die Bilderfrage in der Reformation', *Zeitschrift für Kirchengeschichte*, 68 (1957), 96–128.

Clemen, Otto. 'Aus den Anfängen der Universität Wittenberg', *Neue Jahrbücher für Pädagogik*, 9 (1906), 132–135.

Clemen, Otto. 'Beiträge zur Geschichte des Wittenberger Buchdrucks in der Reformationszeit I: Bilder trojanischer Helden bei Joh. Grunenberg', *Gutenberg Jahrbuch*, 16 (1941), 174–185.

Clemen, Otto. 'Ein Brief des Wolfgang Cyclopius von Zwickau', *Neues Archiv für Sächsische Geschichte und Altertumskunde*, 23 (1902), 134–137.

Clemen, Otto. 'Kleine Beiträge zur sächsischen Gelehrtengeschichte', *Neues Archiv für Sächsische Geschichte*, 30 (1909), 133–140.

Clemen, Otto. 'Kleine Beiträge zur sächsischen Gelehrtengeschichte im 15. und 16. Jahrhundert', *Neues Archiv für Sächsische Geschichte*, 25 (1904), 296–305; 28 (1907), 122–134.

Clemen, Otto. *Luthers Lob der Buchdruckerkunst*; zur 500-Jahrfeier der Erfindung der Buchdruckerkunst. Zwickau, 1939.

Clemen, Otto. 'Ein Rektor der Dresdner Kreuzschule, 1511–1514', *Neues Archiv für Sächsische Geschichte*, 30 (1909), 138–140.

142

Clemen, Otto. 'Weitere Beiträge zur Geschichte des Buchdrucks und des Buchgewerbes in Wittenberg in der Reformationszeit', *Gutenberg Jahrbuch*, 1942/3, pp. 114–126.

Clemen, Otto. 'Der Wittenberger Holzschneider und Buchdrucker Symphorian Reinhardt', *Zentralblatt für Bibliothekswesen* 44 (1927), 523–525.

Coccia, Edmondo. *Le Edizioni delle opere del Mantovano*. Rome, 1960.

Dehio, Georg. *Geschichte der deutschen Kunst*. 4 vols. Berlin, 1919–1934.

Demmer, Dorothea. 'Beobachtungen an Luthers Auslegung von Psalm 5 in seiner ersten Vorlesung', In: *Reformation und Humanismus*; Robert Stupperich zum 65. Geburtstag. Ed. Martin Greschat and J.F.G. Goeters. Witten, 1969, pp. 44–57.

Devrient, Ernst. *Die älteren Ernestiner*. Berlin, 1897.

Dobenecker, Otto. 'Ein Kaisertraum des Hauses Wettin', *Festschrift Armin Tille zum 60. Geburtstag*. Weimar, 1930, pp. 17–38.

Doenges, Willy. 'Kunst und Kultur unter den sächsischen Kurfürsten', *Westermanns Monatshefte*, 104 (1908), 837–856.

Dommer, A. von. *Lutherdrucke auf der Hamburger Stadtbibliothek, 1516–1523*. Leipzig, 1888.

Ebeling, Gerhard. 'Luthers Psalterdruck vom Jahre 1513', *Zeitschrift für Theologie und Kirche*, 50 (1953), 43–99.

Ebeling, Gerhard. 'The new hermeneutics and the early Luther', *Theology Today*, 21 (1964–5), 34–46.

Eberhardt, Hans, ed. *Übersicht über die Bestände des Thüringischen Landeshauptarchivs Weimar*. Weimar, 1959 (Veröffentlichungen des Thüringischen Landeshauptarchivs Weimar, 2)

Ehrenberg, R. 'Nachrichten über Nürnberger Münz- und Medaillen-Prägungen im Auftrag Friedrichs des Weisen von Sachsen', *Mittheilungen der Bayerischen Numismatischen Gesellschaft*, 8 (1889), 97–111.

Ehwald, R. 'Drei Stücke aus dem Briefwechsel Friedrichs des Weisen', In: *Aus den Coburg-Gothaischen Landen, Heimatblätter*, Heft I. Ed. R. Ehwald, Gotha, 1903.

Eichsfeld, Ephraim Gottlob. *Relation vom Wittenbergischen Buchdrucker-Jubilaeo 1740*. Nebst einer historischen Nachricht von allen Wittenbergischen Buchdruckern; Wittenberg, 1740.

Ellinger, Georg. *Geschichte der neulateinischen Literatur Deutschlands im sechzehnten Jahrhundert*. 3 vols., Berlin, 1929–1933.

Engel, James E. *Renaissance, Humanismus, Reformation*. Bern, 1969. (Handbuch der deutschen Literaturgeschichte 2. Abt. Bibliographien, 4)

Engelhardt, Eduard. *Georg Spalatins Leben*; für christliche Leser insgemein erzählt. Leipzig, 1863. (Das Leben der Altväter der lutherischen Kirche, 3)

Entner, Heinz. 'Der Begriff "Humanismus" als Problem der deutschen Literaturgeschichtsschreibung', *Klio*, 40 (1962), 260–270.

Entner, Heinz. 'Probleme der Forschung zum deutschen Frühhumanismus, 1450–1500', *Wissenschaftliche Zeitschrift der Ernst-Moritz-Arndt-Universität Greifswald*, 15 (1966), gesellschaft- und sprachwissenschaftliche Reihe, no. 5/6, pp. 587–590.

Eschenhagen, Edith. *Beiträge zur Sozial- und Wirtschaftsgeschichte der Stadt Wittenberg in der Reformationszeit*. Wittenberg, 1927.

Fabian, Ekkehart. 'Zum Wittenberger Reformatorenbild Cranachs: Brück und Bugenhagen', *Theologische Zeitschrift*, 8 (1952), 232–236.

Fabriczy, Cornelius von. 'Adriano Fiorentino', *Jahrbuch der Königlich-Preussischen Kunstsammlungen*, 24 (1903), 71–98.

Falke, Johannes. 'Beitrag zur sächsischen Münzgeschichte, 1444–1461', *Mittheilungen des Königlich-Sächsischen Vereins für Erforschung und Erhaltung vaterländischer Geschichts- und Kunstdenkmäler*, 16 (1866), 77–106.

Falke, Johannes. 'Beitrag zur sächsischen Münzgeschichte, 1461–1470', *Mittheilungen des Königlich-Sächsischen Vereins für Erforschung und Erhaltung vaterländischer Geschichts- und Kunstdenkmäler*, 17 (1867), 78–103.

Falke, Johannes. 'Beitrag zur sächsischen Münzgeschichte, 1474–1486', *Mittheilungen des Königlich-Sächsischen Vereins für Erforschung und Erhaltung vaterländischer Geschichts- und Kunstdenkmäler*, 18 (1868), 93–119.

Falke, Johannes. 'Die Steuerbewilligungen der Landstände im Kurfürstenthum Sachsen bis zu Anfang des 17. Jahrhunderts', *Zeitschrift für die gesammte Staatswissenschaft*, 30 (1874), 395–448.

Falke, Johannes. 'Zur Geschichte der hohen Landstrasse in Sachsen', *Archiv für Sächsische Geschichte*, 7 (1869), 113–143.

Ficker, Johannes. *Luther als Professor*. Halle, 1928 (Hallische Universitätsreden, 34).

Flach, Willy. 'Georg Spalatin als Geschichtsschreiber. Beiträge aus Spalatins Nachlass im Thüringischen Staatsarchiv Weimar', In: *Zur Geschichte und Kultur des Elb-Saale-Raumes*, Festschrift für Walter Möllenberg, ed. Otto Korn. Burg, 1939, pp. 211–230.

Flechsig, Eduard. *Cranachstudien*; erster Teil. Leipzig, 1900.

Flemming, Paul. 'Zur Geschichte der Reliquiensammlung der Wittenberger Schlosskirche unter Friedrich dem Weisen', *Zeitschrift des Vereins für Kirchengeschichte der Provinz Sachsen* 14 (1917), 87–92.

Forschungen aus Mitteldeutschen Archiven; Zum 60. Geburtstag von Hellmut Kretzschmar. Hrsg. von der staatlichen Archivverwaltung im Staatssekretariat für innere Angelegenheiten. Berlin, 1953.

Four Hundred Years; commemorative essays on the Reformation of Dr. Martin Luther and its blessed results. In the year of the four-hundredth anniversary of the Reformation. Ed. W.H.T. Dau. 3rd ed. St. Louis, Mo., 1917.

Freytag, Hermann. 'Dr. Johann von Kitzscher im Dienste des Deutschen Ordens', *Neues Archiv für Sächsische Geschichte*, 28 (1907), 117–122.

Friedberg, Emil Albert. *Die Universität Leipzig in Vergangenheit und Gegenwart*. Leipzig, 1898.

Friedensburg, Walter. *Geschichte der Universität Wittenberg*. Halle, 1917.

Friedensburg, Walter. 'Wittenberg, Stadt und Universität zur Zeit der Reformation', *Luther*, 10 (1928), 1–13.

Fuchs, C.H. *Die ältesten Schriftsteller über die Lustseuche in Deutschland von 1495 bis 1510*. Göttingen, 1843.

Geiger, Ludwig. *Johann Reuchlin*, sein Leben und seine Werke. Leipzig, 1871.

Geiger, Ludwig. *Renaissance und Humanismus in Italien und Deutschland*. Berlin, 1882 (Allgemeine Geschichte in Einzeldarstellungen, II, 8).

Geiger, Ludwig. *Das Studium der hebräischen Sprache in Deutschland*. Breslau, 1870.

Gesamtkatalog der Wiegendrucke; ed. Kommission für den Gesamtkatalog der Wiegendrucke. Leipzig, 1925–1940, 8 vols.

Glagau, Hans. *Eine Vorkämpferin landesherrlicher Macht, Anna von Hessen, die Mutter Philipps des Grossmütigen, 1485–1525*. Marburg, 1899.

Goetze, Alfred. *Die hochdeutschen Drucker der Reformationszeit*. Strassburg, 1905.

Goff, Frederick Richmond. *Incunabula in American Libraries; A third Census*. New York, 1964.

Goldfriedrich, Rolf. *Die Geschäftsbücher der kursächsischen Kanzlei im 15. Jahrhundert*. Leipzig, 1930.

Graf, Wilhelm. *Doktor Christoph Scheurl von Nürnberg*. Leipzig, 1930. (Beiträge zur Kulturgeschichte des Mittelalters und der Renaissance, 43).

Green, Lowell C. 'The Bible in sixteenth-century humanist education', *Studies in the Renaissance*, 19 (1972), 112–134.

Gretschel, C. *Geschichte des Sächsischen Volkes und Staates*. 3 vols. Leipzig, 1843–1853.

Grossmann, Maria. 'Bibliographie der Werke Christoph Scheurls', *Archiv für Geschichte des Buchwesens*, 10 (1969), 373–395.

Grossmann, Maria. *Wittenberger Drucke 1502 bis 1517*; ein bibliographischer Beitrag zur Geschichte des Humanismus in Deutschland. Wien-Bad Boklet, 1971.

Grotemeyer, Paul. "Die Statthaltermedaillen des Kurfürsten Friedrich des Weisen von Sachsen," *Münchner Jahrbuch der bildenden Kunst*, ser. 3, 21 (1970), 143–166.

Gümbel, Albert. *Der Kursächsische Kämmerer Degenhart von Pfeffinger, der Begleiter Dürers in der 'Marter der Zehntausend Christen'*, Strassburg, 1926 (Studien zur deutschen Kunstgeschichte, 238).

Gurlitt, Cornelius. *Deutsche Turniere, Rüstungen und Plattner des XVI. Jahrhunderts*. Dresden, 1889 (Archivalische Forschungen, 8).

Gurlitt, Cornelius. *Kunst und Künstler am Vorabend der Reformation*; ein Bild aus dem Erzgebirge. Halle, 1890 (Schriften des Vereins für Reformationsgeschichte, 29).

Habich, Georg. *Die deutschen Medailleure des XVI. Jahrhunderts*. Halle, 1916.

Hänsch, Ernst. *Die wettinische Hauptteilung von 1485 und die aus ihr folgenden Streitigkeiten bis 1491*. Leipzig, 1909.

Hartfelder, Karl. 'Friedrich der Weise von Sachsen und Desiderius Erasmus von Rotterdam', *Zeitschrift für vergleichende Litteraturgeschichte und Renaissance-Litteratur* 4 (1891), 203—214.

Hase, Martin von. *Bibliographie der Erfurter Drucke von 1501—1550*. 3. erweiterte Auflage. Nieuwkoop, 1968.

Hashagen, Justus. *Staat und Kirche vor der Reformation*; eine Untersuchung der Vorreformatorischen Bedeutung des Laieneinflusses in der Kirche. Essen, 1931.

Haussleiter, Johannes. *Die Universität Wittenberg vor dem Eintritt Luthers*; nach der Schilderung des Magisters Andreas Meinhardi vom Jahre 1507. Leipzig, 1903.

Helbig, Herbert. *Der Wettinische Ständestaat*; Untersuchungen zur Geschichte des Ständewesens und der landständischen Verfassung in Mitteldeutschland bis 1485. Münster, 1955.

Heller, Joseph. *Lucas Cranachs Leben und Werke*. 2nd rev. and enl. ed. Nürnberg, 1854.

Herding, Otto. 'Probleme des frühen Humanismus in Deutschland', *Archiv für Kulturgeschichte*, 38 (1956), 344—389.

Hermann, Rudolf. *Thüringische Kirchengeschichte*. 3 vols. Jena, 1936—1947.

Hermelink, Heinrich. *Die religiösen Reformbestrebungen des deutschen Humanismus*. Tübingen, 1907.

Herzog, Emil. *Chronik der Kreisstadt Zwickau*. 2 vols. Zwickau, 1839—1845.

Hildebrandt, Ernst. 'Die kurfürstliche Schloss- und Universitätsbibliothek zu Wittenberg, 1512—1547', *Zeitschrift für Buchkunde*, 2 (1925), 34—42, 109—129, 157—188.

Hoess, Irmgard. *Georg Spalatin, 1484—1545*; ein Leben in der Zeit des Humanismus und der Reformation. Weimar, 1956.

Hoess, Irmgard. 'Georg Spalatins Bedeutung für die Reformation und die Organisation der Lutherischen Landeskirche', *Archiv für Reformationsgeschichte*, 42 (1951), 101—135.

Hoess, Irmgard. 'Die Problematik des spaetmittelalterlichen Landeskirchentums am Beispiel Sachsens', *Geschichte in Wissenschaft und Unterricht*, 10 (1959), 352—362.

Hollstein, F.W.H. *German engravings, etchings and woodcuts*, ca. 1400—1700; vol. VI, edited by K.G. Boon and R.W. Scheller. Amsterdam, 1960.

Hoppe, Willy. 'Markgraf Konrad von Meissen, der Reichsfürst und der Gründer des Wettinischen Staates', *Neues Archiv für Sächsische Geschichte*, 40 (1919), 1—52.

Horn, Johann Gottlob. *Lebens- und Helden-Geschichte Friedrichs des Streitbaren*. Leipzig, 1733.

Hyma, Albert. *The Christian Renaissance*; a history of the 'Devotio Moderna', New York, 1924.

Israel, Friedrich. *Das Wittenberger Universitätsarchiv, seine Geschichte und seine Bestände*. Halle, 1913 (Forschungen zur Thüringisch-Sächsischen Geschichte, 4).

Joachim, Erich. *Die Politik des letzten Hochmeisters in Preussen*. 2 vols. Leipzig, 1892—1895.

Joachim, Harold. 'A rare illustrated book by Cranach', *Bulletin of the Art Institute of Chicago*, 43 (1949), 8—11.

Joachim, Johannes. 'Die Drucker Johannes Grunenberg und Georg Rhau in Wittenberg', *Centralblatt für Bibliothekswesen*, 21 (1904), 433—439.

Joachimsen, Paul. *Gesammelte Aufsätze*; Beiträge zur Renaissance, Humanismus und Reformation; zur Historiographie und zum deutschen Staatsgedanken. Ausgewählt und eingeleitet von Notker Hammerstein. Aalen, 1970.

Joachimsen, Paul. *Geschichtsauffassung und Geschichtsschreibung in Deutschland unter dem Einfluss des Humanismus*. 1. Teil. Leipzig, 1910. (Beiträge zur Kulturgeschichte, 6).

Joachimsen, Paul. 'Der Humanismus und die Entwicklung des deutschen Geistes', *Deutsche Vierteljahrsschrift für Literaturwissenschaft und Geistesgeschichte*, 8 (1930), 419—480.

Joachimsen, Paul. *Die Reformation als Epoche der Deutschen Geschichte*. In vollständiger Fassung erstmals aus dem Nachlass herausgegeben von Otto Schottenloher. Munich, 1951.

Joachimsen, Paul. 'Renaissance, Humanismus und Reformation', *Zeitwende*, 1 (1925), 402—425.

Junghans, Helmar. 'Der Einfluss des Humanismus auf Luthers Entwicklung bis 1518', *Luther-Jahrbuch*, 37 (1970), 37–101.

Justi, Ludwig. 'Vischerstudien', *Repertorium für Kunstwissenschaft*, 24 (1901), 36–53.

Kaegi, Werner. 'Nationale und universale Denkformen im deutschen Humanismus des 16. Jahrhunderts', *Die Erziehung*, 10 (1935), 145–159.

Kalkoff, Paul. *Ablass und Reliquienverehrung an der Schlosskirche zu Wittenberg unter Friedrich dem Weisen.* Gotha, 1907.

Kalkoff, Paul. 'Der Briefwechsel zwischen dem Kurfürsten Friedrich und Cajetan, [1519]', *Zeitschrift für Kirchengeschichte*, 27 (1906), 323–332.

Kalkoff, Paul. *Die Depeschen des Nuntius Aleander vom Wormser Reichstag, 1521.* 2nd ed. Halle, 1897.

Kalkoff, Paul. *Erasmus, Luther und Friedrich der Weise*; eine reformationsgeschichtliche Studie. Leipzig, 1919 (Schriften des Vereins für Reformationsgeschichte, 37).

Kalkoff, Paul. 'Friedrich der Weise, dennoch Beschützer Luthers und des Reformationswerkes', *Zeitschrift für Kirchengeschichte*, 43 (1924), 179–208.

Kalkoff, Paul. 'Friedrich der Weise und Luther', *Historische Zeitschrift*, 132 (1925), 29–42.

Kalkoff, Paul. *Humanismus und Reformation in Erfurt, 1500–1530.* Halle, 1926.

Kalkoff, Paul. 'Der Humanist Hermann von dem Busche und die lutherfreundliche Kundgebung auf dem Wormser Reichstage vom 20. April, 1521', *Archiv für Reformationsgeschichte*, 8 (1910–11), 341–370.

Kalkoff, Paul. *Die Kaiserwahl Friedrichs IV. und Karls V. (am 27. u. 28. Juni, 1519).* Weimar, 1925.

Kalkoff, Paul. 'Die Kaiserwahl Friedrichs des Weisen', *Archiv für Reformationsgeschichte*, 21 (1924), 133–140.

Kalkoff, Paul. 'Die Stellung der deutschen Humanisten zur Reformation', *Zeitschrift für Kirchengeschichte*, 46 (1927), 161–231.

Kalkoff, Paul. *Ulrich von Huttens Vagantenzeit und Untergang.* Weimar, 1925.

Kampschulte, Franz Wilhelm. *Die Universität Erfurt in ihrem Verhältnis zu dem Humanismus und der Reformation.* 2 vols. Trier, 1858.

Kantzow, Thomas. *Pommerania.* Ed. H.G.L. Kosegarten. 2 vols. Greifswald, 1817.

Kaufmann, Georg. *Die Geschichte der deutschen Universitäten.* 2 vols., Stuttgart, 1888–1896.

Kaufmann, Georg. 'Zur Gründung der Wittenberger Universität', *Deutsche Zeitschrift für Geschichtswissenschaft*, 11 (1894), 114–143.

Kaufmann, Hans, 'Albrecht Dürers Dreikönigs-Altar', *Westdeutsches Jahrbuch für Kunstgeschichte, Wallraf-Richartz-Jahrbuch*, 10 (1938), 166–178.

Kautzsch, Rudolf. 'Des Chr. Scheurl *Libellus de laudibus Germaniae*', *Repertorium für Kunstwissenschaft*, 21 (1898), 286–287.

Kirn, Paul. *Friedrich der Weise und die Kirche.* Leipzig, 1926. (Beiträge zur Kulturgeschichte des Mittelalters und der Renaissance, 30).

Kirn, Paul. 'Friedrich der Weise und Jacopo de' Barbari', *Jahrbuch der Königlich-Preusischen Kunstsammlungen*, 46 (1925), 130–134.

Kleineidam, Erich. *Universitas Studii Erffordensis*; Überblick über die Geschichte der Universität Erfurt im Mittelalter, 1392–1521. 2 vols. Leipzig, 1964, 1969. (Erfurter Theologische Studien, 14, 22).

Kleineidam, Erich. 'Die Universität Erfurt in den Jahren 1501–1505', In: *Reformata Reformanda*; Festgabe für Hubert Jedin, ed. F. Iserloh and Konrad Repgen. 2 vols. Munich, 1965 (Reformationsgeschichtliche Studien und Texte, Supplementband 1), I, pp. 142–195.

Kluge, Otto. 'Die griechischen Studien in Renaissance und Humanismus', *Zeitschrift für Geschichte der Erziehung und des Unterrichts*, 24 (1934), 1–54.

Kluge, Otto. 'Die Hebraeische Sprachwissenschaft in Deutschland im Zeitalter des Humanismus', *Zeitschrift für die Geschichte der Juden in Deutschland*, 3 (1931), 81–97, 180–193.

Kluge, Otto. 'Der Humanismus des 16. Jahrhunderts in seinen Beziehungen zu Kirche und Schule, zu den theologischen und philosophischen Studien', *Zeitschrift für Geschichte der Erziehung und des Unterrichts*, 17 (1929), 1–60.

Koepplin, Dieter, and Tilman Falk. *Lukas Cranach, Gemälde, Zeichnungen, Druckgraphik.* Vol. I: Ausstellung im Kunstmuseum Basel 15. Juni bis 8. September 1974. 2nd ed. Basel, 1974.

Köstlin, Julius. *Friedrich der Weise und die Schlosskirche zu Wittenberg.* Wittenberg, 1892.

Kötzschke, Rudolf and Hermann Kretzschmar. *Sächsische Geschichte;* Werden und Wandlungen eines deutschen Stammes und seiner Heimat im Rahmen der deutschen Geschichte. 2 vols. Dresden, 1935.

Kolde, Theodor. *Die deutsche Augustinerkongregation und Johann Staupitz;* ein Beitrag zur Ordens- und Reformationsgeschichte nach meistens ungedruckten Quellen. Gotha, 1879.

Kolde, Theodor. *Friedrich der Weise und die Anfänge der Reformation.* Erlangen, 1881.

Kolde, Theodor. 'Wittenberger Disputationsthesen aus den Jahren 1516 bis 1522', *Zeitschrift für Kirchengeschichte,* 11 (1890), 448–471.

Krencker, Adolf. *Friedrich der Weise von Sachsen beim Beginn der Reformation;* eine Charakterstudie. Heidelberg, 1906.

Krogmann, W. 'Zwei Grabschriften auf Ulenspegel aus dem Jahre 1513', *Jahrbuch des Vereins für niederdeutsche Sprachforschung,* 69/70 (1943/1947), 164–175.

Kropatschek, Friedrich. *Johannes Dölsch aus Feldkirch.* Greifswald, 1898.

Krüger, Gottfried. 'Wie sah die Stadt Wittenberg zu Luthers Lebzeiten aus', *Luther,* 15 (1933), 13–32.

Kueczynski, Arnold. *Thesaurus libellorum historiam reformationis illustrantium.* 1 vol. and supplement. Leipzig, 1870–1874.

Landfester, Rüdiger. *Historia Magistra Vitae;* Untersuchungen zur humanistischen Geschichtstheorie des 14. bis 16. Jahrhunderts. Geneva, 1972 (Travaux d'Humanisme et Renaissance, 123)

Lange, Werner. *Stadt- und Schlosskirche zu Wittenberg.* Berlin, 1954 (Das Christliche Denkmal, 10).

Langerbeck, Hermann. 'Deutschland und der Humanismus', *Deutsche Beiträge,* 2 (1948), 60–76.

Laubach, Ernst. 'Wahlpropaganda im Wahlkampf um die deutsche Königswürde 1519', *Archiv für Kulturgeschichte,* 53 (1971), 207–248.

Lehmann, Paul. 'Grundzüge des Humanismus Deutscher Lande, zumal im Spiegel deutscher Bibliotheken des 15. und 16. Jahrhunderts', *Aevum,* 31 (1957), 253–268.

Liessem, Hermann Joseph. *De Hermanni Buschii vita et scriptis commentatio historica.* Bonn, 1866.

Liessem, Hermann Joseph. *Hermann von dem Busche;* sein Leben und seine Schriften. Nieuwkoop, 1965 (reprint of Cologne edition), Jahresbericht des Königlichen Kaiser Wilhelm-Gymnasiums in Köln, 1884–1908. Includes his *Bibliographisches Verzeichnis der Schriften Hermanns von dem Busche.*

Lippert, Woldemar. 'Die ältesten wettinischen Archive im 14. und 15. Jahrhundert', *Neues Archiv für Sächsische Geschichte,* 44 (1923), 71–99.

Lippert, Woldemar. *Das sächsische Hauptstaatsarchiv;* sein Werden und Wesen. 2nd ed. Dresden, 1930.

Lippert, Woldemar. 'Studien über die wettinische Kanzlei und ihre ältesten Register im 14. Jahrhundert', *Neues Archiv für Sächsische Geschichte,* 24 (1903), 1–42; 25 (1904), 209–230.

Lippmann, Fr. *Lucas Cranach;* Sammlung von Nachbildungen seiner vorzüglichsten Holzschnitte und seiner Stiche. Berlin, 1895.

Lisch, G.C.F. *Geschichte der Buchdruckerkunst in Mecklenburg bis zum Jahre 1540.* Aus den Jahrbüchern des Vereins für Mecklenburgische Geschichte und Alterthumskunde besonders abgedruckt. Schwerin, Rostock, 1839.

Lorenz, C. G. *Die Stadt Grimma im Königreich Sachsen.* Leipzig, 1865.

Lossnitzer, Max. 'Die frühen Bildnisse Kurfürst Friedrichs des Weisen', *Mitteilungen aus den Sächsischen Kunstsammlungen,* 4 (1913), 8–18.

Lotz, Walther. *Die drei Flugschriften über den Münzstreit der sächsischen Albertiner und Ernestiner um 1530.* Leipzig, 1893.

Lucas Cranach der Aeltere, der Künstler seine Zeit. Ed. Heinz Lüdecke. Berlin, 1953 (Veröffentlichung der Deutschen Akademie der Künste)

Lucas Cranach der Aeltere im Spiegel seiner Zeit. Ed. Heinz Lüdecke. Berlin, 1953 (Veröffentlichung der Deutschen Akademie der Künste)

Lucke, Wilhelm. 'Deutsche Studenten in Bologna. Ein Beitrag zur Geschichte der Aufnahme des Humanismus in Deutschland', *Das Gymnasium*, 53 (1942), 43–61.

Lüer, Hermann, and Max Creutz. *Geschichte der Metallkunst.* 2 vols. Stuttgart, 1904–1909.

Lülfing, Hans. *Leipziger Frühdrucker.* Leipzig, 1959.

Luther, Johannes. 'Drucker und Verlegernöte in Wittenberg zur Zeit des Schmalkaldischen Krieges', In: *Aufätze Fritz Milkau gewidmet.* Leipzig, 1921, pp. 229–243.

Luther, Johannes. *Die Entwicklung der landständischen Verfassung in den wettinischen Landen bis 1485.* Leipzig, 1895.

Luther, Johannes. 'Die Schnellarbeit der Wittenberger Buchdruckerpressen in der Reformationszeit', *Zentralblatt für Bibliothekswesen*, 31 (1914), 244–264.

Luther, Johannes. 'Studien zur Bibliographie der Kirchenpostille Martin Luthers', *Zentralblatt für Bibliothekswesen*, 32 (1914), 144–161, 203–219.

Luther, Johannes. 'Der Wittenberger Buchdruck in seinem Uebergang zur Reformationspresse', *Lutherstudien zur 4. Jahrhundertfeier der Reformation*, veröffentlicht von den Mitarbeitern der Weimarer Lutherausgabe. Weimar, 1917, pp. 261–282.

Lutz, Heinrich, 'Albrecht Dürer in der Geschichte der Reformation', *Historische Zeitschrift*, 206 (1968), 22–44.

Lutz, Heinrich. 'Humanismus und Reformation; alte Antworten auf neue Fragen', *Wort und Wahrheit*, 27 (1972), 65–77.

Malsch, Rudolf. *Heinrich Raspe, Landgraf von Thüringen und Deutscher König.* Halle, 1911 (Forschungen zur Thüringischen-Sächsischen Geschichte, 1).

Mann, M. 'Erasme et les débuts de la Réforme française (1517–1536)' *Bibliothèque littéraire de la Renaissance*, 22 (1934), 14ff.

Mannewitz, Paul. *Das Wittenberger und Torgauer Bürgerhaus vor dem Dreissigjährigen Krieg.* Borna-Leipzig, 1914.

Maushake, Walter. *Frankfurt an der Oder als Druckerstadt.* Frankfurt a.d. Oder, 1936.

Meier, Fr. Ludger. 'On the Ockhamism of Martin Luther at Erfurt', *Archivum Franciscanum Historicum*, 43 (1950), 56–67.

Meisner, Johannes. *Descriptio ecclesiae collegiatae omnium sanctorum Wittenbergensis.* Wittenberg, 1668.

Meissinger, Karl August. *Luthers Exegese in der Frühzeit.* 1. Teil. Leipzig, 1910.

Meissnisch-Sächsische Forschungen. Zur Jahrtausendfeier der Mark Meissen und des Sächsischen Staates. Ed. Woldemar Lippert. Dresden, 1929. (Sonderheft to Neues Archiv für Sächsische Geschichte).

Mestwerdt, Paul. *Die Anfänge des Erasmus*; Humanismus und 'Devotio Moderna'. Leipzig, 1917 (Studien zur Kultur und Geschichte der Reformation, 2)

Meyer, Carl S., ed. *Luther for an ecumenical age*; essays in commemoration of the 450th anniversary of the Reformation. St. Louis, 1967.

Meyner, A.M. *Geschichte der Stadt Wittenberg.* Dessau, 1845.

Michaelson, H. 'Cranach des Älteren Beziehungen zur Plastik', *Jahrbuch der Königlich-Preussischen Kunstsammlungen*, 21 (1900), 271–284.

Moeller, Bernd. 'Die deutschen Humanisten und die Anfänge der Reformation', *Zeitschrift für Kirchengeschichte*, 70 (1959), 46–61.

Moeller, Bernd. *Imperial cities and the Reformation*; three essays; ed. and transl. H.C.Erik Midelfort and Mark U.Edwards, Jr. Philadelphia, 1972.

Müller, Ernst. 'Die Ernestinischen Landtage in der Zeit von 1485 bis 1572 unter besonderer Berücksichtigung des Steuerwesens', *In: Forschungen zur Thüringischen Landesgeschichte* (Festschrift Friedrich Schneider), Weimar, 1958 (Veröffentlichungen des Thüringischen Landeshauptarchivs, Weimar, I), pp. 188–228.

Müller, Georg. 'Kurfürst Friedrich von Sachsen und das Leipziger St. Johannis-Hospital', *Neues Archiv für Sächsische Geschichte*, 54 (1933), 1–15.

Müller, Georg. 'Reformation und Visitation sächsischer Klöster gegen Ende des 15. Jahrhunderts', *Neues Archiv für Sächsische Geschichte*, 38 (1917), 46–74.

Müller, Georg. *Verfassungs- und Verwaltungsgeschichte der sächsischen Landeskirche.* 2 vols. Leipzig, 1894–1895. (Beiträge zur sächsischen Kirchengeschichte, 9, 10).

Müller, K.E. Hermann. 'Das *Onomasticum mundi generale* des Dominikanermönches Johannes Lindner zu Pirna und seine Quellen. Ein Beitrag zur Historiographie des Reformationszeitalters', *Neues Archiv für Sächsische Geschichte*, 24 (1903), 217–247.

Müller, Nikolaus. *Die Wittenberger Bewegung 1521 und 1522*; die Vorgänge in und um Wittenberg während Luthers Wartburgaufenthalt. 2nd ed. Leipzig, 1911.

Muther, Richard. *Die deutsche Bücherillustration der Gotik und der Frührenaissance*, (1460–1530). 2 vols. Munich, 1884.

Muther, Richard. 'Sachsens Kunstleben im sechzehnten Jahrhundert', *Die Grenzboten*, 43 (1884), part 1, 21–30, 79–89.

Muther, Theodor. *Aus dem Universitäts- und Gelehrtenleben im Zeitalter der Reformation*. Erlangen, 1866.

Muther, Theodor. 'Die ersten Statuten der Wittenberger Artistenfakultät', *Neue Mittheilungen aus dem Gebiet historisch-antiquarischer Forschungen*, 13 (1874), 177–208.

Naef, Werner. 'Aus der Forschung zur Geschichte des deutschen Humanismus', *Schweizer Beiträge zur allgemeinen Geschichte*, 2 (1944), 211–226.

Nasemann, Otto. *Friedrich der Weise, Kurfürst von Sachsen*. Halle, 1889 (Schriften für das deutsche Volk, 5)

Nauert, Charles G. 'Petrus of Ravenna and the 'Obscure Men' of Cologne; a case of pre-Reformation controversy.' In: *Renaissance: Studies in honor of Hans Baron*. Ed. A. Molho and J.A. Tedeschi. DeKalb, Ill., Florence (Italy), 1971, pp. 607–640.

Naumann, Martin. 'Die Wettinische Landesteilung von 1445', *Neues Archiv für Sächsische Geschichte*, 60 (1939), 171–213.

Neumann, Carl. 'Ende des Mittelalters? Legende der Ablösung des Mittelalters durch die Renaissance', *Deutsche Vierteljahrsschrift für Literaturwissenschaft und Geistesgeschichte*, 12 (1934), 124–171.

Newald, Richard. *Probleme und Gestalten des deutschen Humanismus*. Berlin, 1963.

Pallas, K. 'Die Entstehung des landesherrlichen Kirchenregiments in Kursachsen vor der Reformation', *Neue Mitteilungen aus dem Gebiet historisch-antiquarischer Forschungen*, 24 (1909), 129–171.

Panofsky, Erwin. *Albrecht Dürer*. 3rd ed. 2 vols. Princeton, 1948.

Panofsky, Erwin. 'Conrad Celtes and Kunz von der Rosen: two problems in portrait identification', *Art Bulletin*, 24 (1942), 39–54.

Panzer, Georg Wolfgang. *Annales typographici ab artis inventae origine ad anno [MDXXXVI]...* 11 vols. Nürnberg, 1793–1803.

Patze, Hans, and Walter Schlesinger, eds. *Geschichte Thüringens*. vol. III: Das Zeitalter des Humanismus und der Reformation. Köln, 1967 (Mitteldeutsche Forschungen 48, III)

Paul, Ulrich. *Studien zur Geschichte des deutschen Nationalbewusstseins im Zeitalter des Humanismus und der Reformation*. Berlin, 1936 (Historische Studien, 298)

Petz, H. 'Urkundliche Nachrichten über den literarischen Nachlass Regiomontans und B. Walters, 1478 bis 1522', *Mitteilungen des Vereins für Geschichte der Stadt Nürnberg*, 7 (1888), 237–262.

Plitt, Gustav. *Friedrich der Weise als Schirmherr der Reformation*. Erlangen, 1863.

Plitt, Gustav. *Jodocus Trutfetter von Eisenach*. Erlangen, 1876.

Posse, Hans. *Lucas Cranach d. Ä*. Vienna, 1942.

Prantl, Carl von. *Geschichte der Logik im Abendlande*. 4 vols. Leipzig, 1855–1870.

Preuss, Hans. *Martin Luther der Künstler*. Gütersloh, 1931.

Proctor, Robert. *An index of German books, 1501–1520, in the British Museum*. 2nd ed. London, 1954.

Raeder, Siegfried. *Das Hebräische bei Luther untersucht bis zum Ende der ersten Psalmenvorlesung*. Tübingen, 1961. (Beiträge zur historischen Theologie, 31).

Ranke, Leopold von. *History of the Reformation in Germany*. Transl. from the last edition of the German by Sarah Austin. Philadelphia, 1844.

Reformation 1517–1967. Wittenberger Vorträge. Im Auftrage des vorbereitenden Ausschusses für die zentralen kirchlichen Veranstaltungen herausgegeben von Ernst Kähler. Berlin, 1968.

Reitzenstein, Karl von. 'Unvollständiges Tagebuch auf der Reise Kurfürst Friedrichs des Weisen von Sachsen in die Niederlande zum Römischen König Maximilian I, 1494', *Zeitschrift des Vereins für Thüringische Geschichte*, 4 (1861), 127–137.

Richter, Gregor. *Die Ernestinischen Landesordnungen und ihre Vorläufer, von 1446 und 1482*. Cologne, 1964. (Mitteldeutsche Forschungen, 34).

Ritter, Gerhard. 'Die geschichtliche Bedeutung des deutschen Humanismus', *Historische Zeitschrift*, 127 (1922–1923), 393–453.

Ritter, Gerhard. *Studien zur Spätscholastik, II: via antiqua* und *via moderna* auf den deutschen Universitäten des XV. Jahrhunderts. Heidelberg, 1922 (Sitzungsberichte der Heidelberger Akademie der Wissenschaften, philosophisch-historische Klasse, 1922, 7. Abhandlung).

Röhricht, Reinhold. *Deutsche Pilgerreisen nach dem Heiligen Lande.* Neue Ausgabe. Innsbruck, 1900.

Röhricht, Reinhold, and Heinrich Meisner. 'Hans Hundts Rechnungsbuch, (1493–1494)', *Neues Archiv für Sächsische Geschichte*, 4 (1883), 37–100.

Roemer, Hermann. 'Hans Grueninger und die Buchdruckerfamilie Reinhard aus Markgroeningen', In: *Markgroeningen im Rahmen der Landesgeschichte*, vol. 1, Markgroeningen, 1933, pp. 277–331.

Rommel, Herbert. *Ueber Luthers Randbemerkungen von 1509/10.* Kiel, 1930.

Rückert, H. *Die Stellung der Reformation zur mittelalterlichen Universität.* Stuttgart, 1933.

Rupprich, Hans. *Die deutsche Literatur vom späten Mittelalter bis zum Barock.* part 1: das ausgehende Mittelalter, Humanismus und Renaissance, 1370–1520. Munich, 1970. (Geschichte der deutschen Literatur, von den Anfängen bis zur Gegenwart, vol. IV, part 1).

Sachse, Friedrich. 'Der Streit um die sächsische Kurwürde bis zur Entscheidung durch Kaiser Karl IV', *Archiv für Sächsische Geschichte*, 5 (1867), 202–229.

Sander, Hjalmar, 'Zur Identifizierung zweier Bildnisse von Lucas Cranach, d.Ä.', *Zeitschrift für Kunstwissenschaft*, 4 (1950), 35–48.

Schadow, Johann Gottfried. *Wittenbergs Denkmäler der Bildnerei, Baukunst und Malerei.* Wittenberg, 1825.

Scheel, Otto. *Martin Luther.* Vom Katholizismus zur Reformation. 2 vols. Tübingen, 1917.

Schenke, Friedrich. 'Luther und der Humanismus', *Luther*, 33 (1962), 77–85.

Scheurl, Adolf von. 'Christoph Scheurl', *Mitteilungen des Vereins für die Geschichte der Stadt Nürnberg*, 5 (1884), 13–46.

Schmalenberg, Erich. 'Kirchengeschichte im Gespräch, XI. Der Ungekrönte [Friedrich der Weise]', *Pastoralblätter*, 104 (1964), 204–214.

Schmarsow, A. 'Zur Beurtheilung der sogenannten Spätgothik', *Repertorium für Kunstwissenschaft*, 23 (1900), 290–298.

Schmidt, Julius. 'Beiträge zur Kunstgeschichte Sachsens im 16. Jahrhundert', *Archiv für Sächsische Geschichte*, 11 (1873), 81–114, 121–169.

Schmidt, K. *Wittenberg unter Kurfürst Friedrich dem Weisen.* Erlangen, 1867.

Schmidt, Oswald Gottlob. *Luthers Bekanntschaft mit den alten Classikern*; ein Beitrag zur Lutherforschung. Leipzig, 1883.

Schmidt-Ewald, Walter. 'Die drei kursächsischen Archive zu Wittenberg', *Archivstudien zum siebzigsten Geburtstage von Woldemar Lippert*; ed. Hans Beschorner. Dresden, 1931, pp. 210–224.

Schmidt-Ewald, Walter. 'Der gegenwärtige Stand der sächsisch-thüringischen Archivgeschichtsforschung', *Archivalische Zeitschrift*, 41 (1932), 290–293.

Schneider, Christian W., ed. 'Zehn Briefe Burkhards Schenks von Simau . . . an d. Kurf. zu Sa., Friedrich III und an G. Spalatin', *Bibliothek der Kirchengeschichte*, ed. C.W. Schneider, vol. 2, part 1, Weimar, 1781, pp. 1–90.

Schöffler, Herbert. *Wirkungen der Reformation*; Religionssoziologische Folgerungen für England und Deutschland. Frankfurt, 1960.

Schöttgen, Christian, and Georg Christoph Kreysig. *Diplomatische und curieuse Nachlese der Historie von Ober-Sachsen und angrentzenden Ländern . . .* 3 vols., Dresden, 1730–1733.

Schottenloher, Karl. *Die Widmungsvorrede im Buch des 16. Jahrhunderts.* Münster, 1953 (Reformationsgeschichtliche Studien und Texte, 76/7)

Schubert, Friedrich Hermann. *Die deutschen Reichstage in der Staatslehre der frühen Neuzeit.* Göttingen, 1966 (Schriftenreihe der historischen Kommission bei der Bayerischen Akademie der Wissenschaften, 7).

Schubert, Hans von. *Luthers Vorlesung über den Galaterbrief 1516/17.* Zum ersten Mal herausgegeben von Hans von Schubert. Abhandlungen der Heidelberger Akademie der Wissenschaften, philos.-hist. Kl., V. Heidelberg, 1918.

150

Schubert, Hans von. 'Reformation und Humanismus', *Lutherjahrbuch*, 8 (1926), 1–26.
Schuchardt, Christian. *Lucas Cranach des Älteren Leben und Werke*. 3 vols. Leipzig, 1851–1871.
Schück, Julius. *Aldus Manutius und seine Zeitgenossen in Italien und Deutschland*. Berlin, 1862.
Schulte-Strathaus, Ernst. 'Die Wittenberger Heiligtumsbücher vom Jahre 1509 mit Holzschnitten von Lucas Cranach', *Gutenberg Jahrbuch*, 1930, pp. 175–186.
Schultze, Walther. *Die Geschichtsquellen der Provinz Sachsen im Mittelalter und in der Reformationszeit*. Halle, 1893 (Historische Kommission der Provinz Sachsen).
Schwarz, W. *Principles and Problems of Biblical Translation*; some Reformation controversies and their background. Cambridge, 1955.
Schwarzer, Otfried. 'Gustav Bauch; ein Lebensbild', *Zeitschrift des Vereins für Geschichte Schlesiens*, 59 (1925), 180–187.
Schwiebert, Ernest G. 'The electoral town of Wittenberg', *Medievalia et Humanistica*, 3 (1945), 99–116.
Schwiebert, Ernest G. *Luther and his times*; the Reformation from a new perspective. St. Louis, Mo., 1950.
Schwiebert, Ernest G. 'New groups and ideas at the University of Wittenberg', *Archiv für Reformationsgeschichte*, 49 (1958), 60–79.
Schwiebert, Ernest G. 'The Reformation and theological education at Wittenberg', *The Springfielder*, 28, no. 3, Autumn 1964, pp. 9–43.
Schwiebert, Ernest G. *Reformation Lectures*. Valparaiso, Ind. 1937.
Schwiebert, Ernest G. 'Remnants of a Reformation library', *Library Quarterly*, 10 (1940), 494–531.
Seeger, Georg. *Peter Vischer der Jüngere*; ein Beitrag zur Geschichte der Erzgiesserfamilie Vischer. Leipzig, 1897 (Beiträge zur Kunstgeschichte, 23)
Seelheim, Adolf. *Georg Spalatin als sächsischer Historiograph*; ein Beitrag zur Geschichtsschreibung des Reformationszeitalters. Halle, 1876 (Hallesche Abhandlungen zur neueren Geschichte, 5).
The Social History of the Reformation. Ed. L.P. Buck and J.W. Zophy. Columbus, Ohio, 1972.
Soden, Franz Freiherr von. *Beiträge zur Geschichte der Reformation und der Sitten jener Zeit*; mit besonderem Hinblick auf Christoph Scheurl II. Nürnberg, 1855.
Soden, Franz Freiherr von. *Christoph Scheurl II und sein Wohnhaus in Nürnberg*. Nürnberg, 1837.
Spitz, Lewis W. *Conrad Celtis, the German Arch-Humanist*. Cambridge, Mass., 1957.
Spitz, Lewis W. *The Religious Renaissance of the German Humanists*. Cambridge, Mass., 1963.
Stange, Carl. 'Luther und der Geist der Renaissance', *Zeitschrift für systematische Theologie*, 18 (1941), 3–27.
Steinlein, Hermann. *Luthers Doktorat*. Leipzig, 1912.
Stier, G. *Die Schlosskirche zu Wittenberg*; Uebersicht ihrer Geschichte bis auf die Gegenwart. 2nd ed. Wittenberg, 1873.
Stier, G. *Wittenberg im Mittelalter*; Uebersicht der Geschichte der Stadt von ihrem Ursprunge bis zum Tode Friedrichs des Weisen. Wittenberg, 1855.
Strauss, David Friedrich. *Ulrich von Hutten*. Bonn, 1895.
Streit, Felix Edmund. *Christoph Scheurl, der Ratskonsulent von Nürnberg und seine Stellung zur Reformation*. Plauen, 1908. (Wissenschaftliche Beilage zu dem Jahresbericht des Realgymnasiums mit Realschule zu Plauen, I, 5).
Sturmhoefel, Konrad. *Illustrierte Geschichte der Sächsischen Lande und ihrer Herrscher*. 2 vols. Leipzig, 1897–1909.
Tentzel, Wilhelm Ernst. *Historischer Bericht vom Anfang und ersten Fortgang der Reformation Lutheri*. Leipzig, 1718.
Thieme, Ulrich, and Becker, Felix. *Allgemeines Lexikon der bildenden Künstler von der Antike bis zur Gegenwart*. 37 vols. Leipzig, 1907–1950.
Thode, Henry. *Die Malerschule von Nürnberg im XIV, und XV. Jahrhundert in ihrer Entwicklung bis auf Dürer*. Frankfurt, 1891.

151

Thompson, Lawrence S. 'German translations of the Classics between 1450 and 1550', *Journal of English and Germanic Philology*, 42 (1943), 343–363.

Thulin, Oskar. *Cranach-Altäre der Reformation*. Berlin, 1955.

Thulin, Oskar. *Die Lutherstadt Wittenberg und Torgau*. Berlin, 1932.

Timm, Albrecht. *Die Universität Halle-Wittenberg*; Herrschaft und Wissenschaft im Spiegel ihrer Geschichte. Frankfurt, 1960 (Mitteldeutsche Hochschulen, 5)

Tutzschmann, Max Moritz. *Friedrich der Weise, Kurfürst von Sachsen*; ein Lebensbild aus dem Zeitalter der Reformation, nach den Quellen für alle Stände dargestellt. Grimma, 1848.

Ulmann, Heinrich. *Kaiser Maximilian I*. 2 vols. Stuttgart, 1884–1891.

Ulmann, Heinrich. 'Der Traum des Hans von Hermannsgrün; eine politische Denkschrift aus d. J. 1495', *Forschungen zur deutschen Geschichte*, 20 (1880), 67–92.

Velke, Wilhelm. 'Der erste Lutherdrucker stammt aus Gruenberg in Oberhessen', *Mitteilungen des Oberhessischen Geschichtsvereins*, new series, 24 (1922), 19–27.

Vierhundert Jahre Reformation. Ed. Leo Stern and Max Steinmetz. Berlin, 1967.

450 Jahre Martin-Luther Universität Halle-Wittenberg. 3 vols. Halle-Wittenberg, 1945–1952.

Virck, H. 'Die Ernestiner und Herzog Georg von 1500 bis 1508', *Neues Archiv für Sächsische Geschichte*, 30 (1909), 1–75.

Volz, Hans. 'Die Bibeleinzeichnungen der Wittenberger Reformatoren', *Gutenberg Jahrbuch*, 1971, 122–137.

Volz, Hans. 'Bibliographie der im 16. Jahrhundert erschienen Schriften Georg Spalatins', *Zeitschrift für Bibliothekswesen und Bibliographie*, 5 (1958), 83–119.

Volz, Hans. 'Der Humanist Tileman Conradi aus Göttingen; ein Beitrag zum Thema: Humanismus und Reformation', *Jahrbuch der Gesellschaft für Niedersächsische Kirchengeschichte*, 64 (1966), 76–116.

Volz, Hans. 'Der Traum des Kurfürsten Friedrichs des Weisen vom 30/31 Oktober, 1517', *Gutenberg Jahrbuch*, 1970, 174–211.

Waetzold, Wilhelm. *Dürer und seine Zeit*. Vienna, 1935.

Wagner, Elisabeth. 'Luther und Friedrich der Weise auf dem Wormser Reichstag von 1521', *Zeitschrift für Kirchengeschichte*, 42 (1923), 371–390.

Wartburg-Wittenberg; Beiträge zum Jahr der Jubiläen 1967. Hamburg, 1967 (Die Mitte: Jahrbuch für Geschichte, Kunst- und Kulturgeschichte des mitteldeutschen Raumes, 3)

Weber, Karl von. 'Das Haupt-Staatsarchiv zu Dresden', *Archiv für Sächsische Geschichte*, 2 (1864), 1–26.

Weizsäcker, Heinrich. 'Peter Vischer, Vater und Sohn', *Repertorium für Kunstwissenschaft*, 23 (1900), 299–312.

Weller, Emil. *Repertorium typographicum*. Nördlingen, 1864–74 (Supplement).

Werdermann, Hermann. *Luthers Wittenberger Gemeinde wiederherstellt aus seinen Predigten*. Guetersloh, 1929.

Wernicke, E. 'Sächsische Künstler in Görlitzer Geschichtsquellen', *Neues Archiv für Sächsische Geschichte*, 6 (1885), 251–263.

Wiesflecker, Hermann. 'Der Traum des Hans von Hermannsgrün; eine Reformschrift aus dem Lager des Königs Maximilian', *Festschrift für Karl Eder zum siebzigsten Geburtstag*, Ed. Helmut J. Mezler-Andelberg. Innsbruck, 1959, pp. 13–32.

Winkler, Eberhard, 'Melanchthons lateinische Leichenrede auf Kurfürst Friedrich den Weisen', *Zeitschrift für Religions- und Geistesgeschichte*, 18 (1966), 33–42.

Wintruff, Wilhelm. *Landesherrliche Kirchenpolitik in Thüringen am Ausgang des Mittelalters*. Halle, 1914 (Forschungen zur thüringisch-sächsischen Geschichte, 5).

Wölfflin, Heinrich. *Die Kunst Albrecht Dürers*. Munich, 1905.

Zagel, Milton. "Martin Luther and the embryonic stage of the cultural Reformation." Unpublished M.A. thesis, University of Iowa, 1936.

Zeumer, Karl. *Die Goldene Bulle Kaiser Karls IV*. Weimar, 1908 (Quellen und Studien zur Verfassungsgeschichte des Deutschen Reiches im Mittelalter und Neuzeit, 2).

Zieschang, Rudolf. *Die Anfänge eines landesherrlichen Kirchenregiments in Sachsen am Ausgange des Mittelalters*. Leipzig, 1909 (Beiträge zur Sächsischen Kirchengeschichte, 23).

Zimmermann, Hildegard. *Lucas Cranach d. Ä. Folgen der Wittenberger Heiligtümer und die Illustrationen des Rhau'schen Hortulus animae*. Halle, 1929.

Zimmermann, Hildegard. 'Die Titeleinfassungen des Symphorian Reinhart in Wittenberg', *Zentralblatt für Bibliothekswesen*, 45 (1928), 70–71.
Zweynert, Emil. *Luthers Stellung zur humanistischen Schule und Wissenschaft.* Chemnitz, 1895.

INDEX OF PERSONAL NAMES